Reading Architecture and Culture

Architecture displays the values involved in its inhabitation, construction, procurement and design. It traces the thinking of the individuals who have participated in it, their relationships and their involvement in the cultures where they lived and worked. In this way, buildings, their details and the documents used to make them can be read closely for cultural insights.

Introducing the idea of reading buildings as cultural artefacts, this book presents perceptive readings by eminent writers which demonstrate the power of this approach.

The chapters show that close readings of architecture and its materials can test commonplace assumptions, help architects to appreciate the contexts in which they work and indicate ways to think more astutely about design. The readings collected in this innovative and accessible book address buildings, documents and photographs. They range in time from the fifteenth century – examining the only surviving drawing made by Leon Battista Alberti – to the recent past - projects completed by Norman Foster in 2006 and Herzog and De Meuron in 2008. They range geographically from France to Puerto Rico to Kazakhstan. And they range in fame from buildings celebrated by critics to house extensions and motorway service areas.

Taken together, these essays demonstrate important research methods which yield powerful insights for designers, critics and historians, and lessons for students.

Adam Sharr is Professor of Architecture at Newcastle University, Principal of Adam Sharr Architects, Co-Editor of *Architectural Research Quarterly* (Cambridge University Press) and Series Editor of *Thinkers for Architects* (Routledge).

READING ARCHITECTURE AND CULTURE

RESEARCHING BUILDINGS, SPACES AND DOCUMENTS

EDITED BY
ADAM SHARR

Routledge
Taylor & Francis Group

LONDON AND NEW YORK

Diane M. Halle Library
ENDICOTT COLLEGE
Beverly, MA 01915

First published 2012
by Routledge
2 Park Square, Milton Park, Abingdon, Oxon OX14 4RN

Simultaneously published in the USA and Canada
by Routledge
711 Third Avenue, New York, NY 10017

Routledge is an imprint of the Taylor & Francis Group, an informa business

© 2012 selection and editorial material, Adam Sharr; individual chapters, the contributors

The right of the editor to be identified as the author of the editorial material, and of the authors for their individual chapters, has been asserted in accordance with sections 77 and 78 of the Copyright, Designs and Patents Act 1988.

All rights reserved. No part of this book may be reprinted or reproduced or utilised in any form or by any electronic, mechanical, or other means, now known or hereafter invented, including photocopying and recording, or in any information storage or retrieval system, without permission in writing from the publishers.

Trademark notice: Product or corporate names may be trademarks or registered trademarks, and are used only for identification and explanation without intent to infringe.

British Library Cataloguing in Publication Data
A catalogue record for this book is available from the British Library

Library of Congress Cataloging in Publication Data
Reading architecture & culture : researching buildings, spaces, and documents / edited by Adam Sharr.
p. cm.
Includes bibliographical references and index.
1. Architecture. 2. Architecture--Research. I. Sharr, Adam. II. Title: Reading architecture and culture : researching buildings, spaces, and documents.
NA2560.R38 2012
720--dc23
2011037307

ISBN: 978-0-415-60142-9 (hbk)
ISBN: 978-0-415-60143-6 (pbk)

Typeset in Galliard
by Saxon Graphics Ltd, Derby

Printed and bound in the United States of America
by Edwards Brothers, Inc.

Contents

List of illustrations

Illustration credits

Samuel Austin: Figures 7.1, 7.3, 7.5
Biblioteca Medicea Laurentiana: Figure 13.1
Bundesarchiv: Figure 12.1
Courtesy of the Courtauld Institute Galleries: Figure 5.2
Courtesy of Viscount Coke and the Trustees of the Holkham Estate:
    Figures 5.3, 5.4
Paul Emmons and Jonathan Foote: Figures 13.2–13.5
Suzanne Ewing: Figures 4.2, 4.3
Sverre Fehn: Figure 4.1
Marco Frascari: Figure 15.1
Candida Höfer: Cover and Figure 14.1
Holabird & Root and OMA: Figure 11.4
David Leatherbarrow: Figures 1.1–1.8
Samuel Ludwig: Figures 10.1–10.5
Mhairi McVicar: Figures 11.1–11.3, 11.5
Walter Niedermayr: Figure 14.2
Courtesy of Peter Prideaux-Brune: Figure 5.1
Flora Samuel: Figure 6.1
Christopher Schulte: Figures 8.4, 8.6
Adam Sharr: Figures 2.1–2.7
SIAF / Cité de l'architecture et du patrimoine / Archives d'architecture
    du XXe siècle: Figures 8.1-8.3, 8.5, 8.7
Pilkington United Kingdom Limited: Figures 12.3–12.5
Linus Tan: Figure 12.2
Edward Wainwright: Figures 3.1–3.6
www.motorwayservicesonline.co.uk: Figures: 7.2, 7.4

Every effort has been made to contact the copyright holders of original images.

Notes on contributors

Samuel Austin is a doctoral researcher and tutor in architecture at Cardiff University. He is part of the editorial team of *arq: Architectural Research Quarterly* and has architectural practice experience in the UK and Netherlands. His interests intersect architecture and cultural theory and his current work reads the place of motorway service areas in contemporary culture.

Michael Cadwell is a practising architect and Professor at the Austin E. Knowlton School of Architecture at the Ohio State University. A former Fellow of the American Academy in Rome and the MacDowell Colony, he is the author of *Small Buildings* (Pamphlet Architecture, Princeton, 1996) and *Strange Details* (MIT Press, 2007).

Hugh Campbell is Professor of Architecture at the UCD School of Architecture in Dublin. Alongside his research interests in consciousness, space and photography, he is also joint editor of the major volume *Irish Architecture 1600–2000*, to be published by Yale University Press in 2014.

Paul Emmons is a registered architect and an Associate Professor at the Washington-Alexandria Architecture Center of Virginia Tech, where he coordinates the PhD program in Architecture and Design. He earned a Master of Architecture from the University of Minnesota in 1986 and a PhD from the University of Pennsylvania in 2003.

Suzanne Ewing is an architect and academic who teaches architectural design at the University of Edinburgh. She is a partner at ZONE architects and contributes to public discourse on design in the UK and Europe through workshops, exhibitions and publications.

Marco Frascari is an Italian architect and architectural theorist born under the shadow of the dome of St Andrea in Mantova in 1945. He studied with Carlo Scarpa and Arrigo Rudi at IUAV and received his PhD in architecture from the University of Pennsylvania. He taught for several years at the University of Pennsylvania, then as Visiting Professor at Columbia and Harvard, and is currently director of the David Azrieli School of Architecture and Urbanism in Ottawa, Canada.

Jonathan Foote is a PhD candidate and Lecturer at Virginia Tech's Washington-Alexandria Architecture Center, located in Alexandria, Virginia, USA. His research and teaching focus on the process of translation between the architectural idea and its realised construction. He also maintains a small architectural practice which investigates the in-between realm of sculpture and architecture.

Jonathan Hill is Professor of Architecture and Visual Theory at the Bartlett School of Architecture, UCL, where he is Director of the MPhil/PhD Architectural Design programme. Jonathan is author of *The Illegal Architect* (1998), *Actions of Architecture: Architects and Creative Users* (2003), *Immaterial Architecture* (2006) and *Weather Architecture* (2012).

David Leatherbarrow is Professor of Architecture and Chair of the Graduate Group in Architecture at the University of Pennsylvania. His books include *Topographical Stories*, *Surface Architecture* (with Mohsen Mostafavi), *Uncommon Ground*, *On Weathering: The Life of Buildings in Time* and *Architecture Oriented Otherwise*.

Katie Lloyd Thomas trained as an architect and is Lecturer in Architecture at Newcastle University and the editor of *Material Matters: Architecture and Material Practice* (Routledge, 2007). She researches and publishes on materials, specifications, philosophy of technology, and feminist theory and practice, and is a founder member of the feminist art/architecture practice taking place (www.takingplace.org.uk).

Mhairi McVicar is a Lecturer at the Welsh School of Architecture, Cardiff University, and previously practised as an architect in Chicago. Her publications researching architectural precision include 'Contested Fields: Perfection and Compromise at Caruso St John's Museum of Childhood' in *Architecture and Field/Work* and 'Memory and Progress: Confessions in a Flagstone Wall' in *arq: Architectural Research Quarterly*.

Diana Periton is an architectural historian. She has taught at various UK schools of architecture, including the Architectural Association, London and the Mackintosh School of Architecture, Glasgow. Her current research is on the development of the discipline of urbanism in France in the 1920s.

Jane Rendell is an architectural designer, historian and writer. She is author of *Site-Writing* (2010), *Art and Architecture* (2006) and *The Pursuit of Pleasure* (2002). Her talks/texts have been commissioned by artists/curators/galleries such as Bik van der Pol, Ralph Rugoff and Galerie Perrotin. She is Professor of Architecture and Art, and Vice Dean of Research, at the Bartlett, UCL.

Flora Samuel is an architect and teacher of architecture. She is Professor of Architecture and Head of School at the University of Sheffield School of Architecture. She has published extensively on the subject of Le Corbusier and has a keen interest in conveying the value of architecture to people outside the profession.

Adam Sharr is Professor of Architecture at Newcastle University, Principal of Adam Sharr Architects, Co-Editor of *arq: Architectural Research Quarterly* (Cambridge University Press) and Series Editor of *Thinkers for Architects* (Routledge). Adam's books include *Heidegger's Hut* (MIT Press, 2006).

Edward Wainwright is a freelance consultant, researcher, designer and tutor. Following the award of his doctoral degree from Cardiff University in 2010, he established the consultancy *publish{architecture}* which is currently working on projects about urban design and cultural economics. He teaches at the University of Bath, Cardiff University and Newcastle University.

Acknowledgements

It is rare to be able to locate the idea for a book to a specific moment in time. It is rarer still that that moment might have occurred during an academic committee meeting.

The idea for this volume came from a meeting of the Graduate Student Progress Review Committee held at Cardiff University, where I worked until 2010. One of my doctoral students was being grilled on his project. Why had he not arranged interviews with the architects of the buildings he was studying? What did those architects have in mind? How was he going to get to grips with their intentions? It was only at that meeting that it struck me how my own research methods, and the methods of my graduate students, remained unusual. I was confused that established architectural scholars, indeed close friends and colleagues, could not see why it might be more important to think about what a building *says*, about what it *does*, about *how it works*, rather than try to post-rationalise what its designers might or might not have intended.

After that meeting, trying to work out my bemusement at the proceedings, I drafted the first version of the text that has become this book's introduction. Surprised by my colleagues' surprise, I began to appreciate that research methods which seemed familiar to me were more radical than I had assumed. I realised that consolidation and celebration of these methods were overdue, and that a book like this one was needed.

I'm grateful to the protagonists at that meeting for their provocations. I'm indebted to my PhD students – Ed Wainwright, Sam Austin, Mhairi McVicar, Marga Munar Bauza and Tom Brigden – for their critical engagement with the approaches outlined here and for illuminating conversations that have helped to crystallise this book. Thanks too to my numerous MArch dissertation students who have pursued similar approaches and whose incisive questions have tested my ability to articulate key ideas, particularly to Aisling Shannon and Rachel Witham.

New colleagues, former colleagues and friends have (wittingly or unwittingly) contributed suggestions, questions, support and references. I would like to acknowledge: Andrew Ballantyne, Nathaniel Coleman, Patrick Devlin, Mark Dorrian, Allison Dutoit, Graham Farmer, Adrian Forty, Jonathan Hale, Adam Hardy, Andrew Higgott, Jacob Hotz, Peter Kellett, Andrew Law, Katie Lloyd Thomas, Rhiannon Mason, Neveen Hamza, Stephen Kite, Hentie Louw, Juliet Odgers, John Pendlebury, Tim Pitman, Martyn Dade-Robertson,

Simon Sadler, Flora Samuel, Simon Unwin, Geoff Vigar, Chris Wilkins and Richard Weston. David Leatherbarrow was extremely generous with his time and wisdom on the occasion of his visit to Cardiff. Zeynep Kezer made perceptive suggestions. Joanne Sayner remains, as ever, a huge source of support – and my toughest reader.

I'm indebted to the authors of the essays collected here for participating in this book. Having drawn up a list including many of my favourite architectural writers, I was delighted when everyone I approached agreed to contribute. It's been a pleasure to work with them in shaping this volume. I hope you enjoy the chapters that follow as much as I have done.

Introduction

Man has been a hunter for thousands of years. In the course of countless chases he learned to reconstruct the shapes and movements of his invisible prey from tracks on the ground, broken branches, excrement, tufts of hair, entangled feathers, stagnating odours. He learned to sniff out, record, interpret, and classify such infinitesimal traces as trails of spittle [...] Perhaps the actual idea of narration may have originated in a hunting society, relating the experience of deciphering tracks. This obviously undemonstrable hypothesis nevertheless seems to be reinforced by the fact that the rhetorical figures on which the language of venatic deduction seems to rest today – the part in relation to the whole, the effect in relation to the cause – are traceable to the narrative axis of metonymy [...] The hunter would have been the first 'to tell a story' because he alone was able to read, in the silent, nearly imperceptible tracks left by his pray, a coherent sequence of events.

Carlo Ginzburg, 'Clues: Roots of an Evidential Paradigm' in *Myths, Emblems, Clues*, trans. by John and Anne C. Tedeschi (London: Hutchinson, 1990), pp. 96–125 (pp. 102–103)

Introduction: a case for close reading

Adam Sharr

In the 1950s, Leslie Martin established the parameters of contemporary architectural research in the UK by reforming first the Cambridge School of Architecture and then the pattern of British architectural education.[1] He set out to affirm two research methods in architecture, with the intention of establishing a third. Research in applied science and in history were emphasised initially, securing credibility for architectural researchers among other university academics. Martin's longer-term aim was, however, that these two methods would be overtaken by a third approach to research which would be distinctively architectural. For Martin, coming to academic work from the design studio of the London County Council, this new research involved developing a science of architectural form that, he hoped, could optimise the functional performance of particular building types.[2] By the 1970s, the limitations of this reductive science of form grew increasingly apparent, as phenomenology and cultural theory suggested other – more situated, more committed – ways of appreciating architecture, and indicated problems with the idea of the all-knowing professional architect.[3] With these criticisms, Martin's particular 'third way' withered. However, it left behind his question about what distinctively architectural research might be like. Martin asked what it is that architects – with their particular skills and methods – can contribute to the intellectual commonwealth.

One important opportunity is developed by this book: the close reading of buildings as cultural artefacts.[4] Architects have a distinctive capacity to read the anatomy of buildings and the nuances of their details, and to appreciate the influence of professional conventions over the world. They are well placed to put their abilities to forensic use, deducing cultural insights from architectural fabric and from the documents employed to anticipate architecture.

Reading architecture

Collected in this book are a series of essays which show how the close reading of architecture and its materials can test commonplace assumptions, help architects to appreciate the contexts in which they operate when they design, and suggest ways to think about design more incisively. They help to articulate and consolidate research methods which can yield powerful insights for critics and historians, and lessons for students. These methods are linked by three attitudes to architecture:

1. Buildings are evidence of the cultures that made them. They are artefacts which demonstrate the values informing their construction and their life in use. A building's organisation, atmospheres and details embody the ideologies involved in its inhabitation, construction, procurement and design. It offers clues to the thinking of the individuals who participated in it, their relationships, and their involvement in the cultures where they lived and worked. A building thus records the forces at work in the societies where it was procured and inhabited over time. This suggestion that buildings can be read is not to say that architecture is text – the presence of built fabric is too material for that analogy to stretch meaningfully[5] – but rather that the architect-authors of buildings, and critics awed by authorship, seldom offer the most reliable accounts of them. Instead, a building is the best indicator of its own intellectual position.

2. Buildings have multiple authors. The activity of architecture is conducted more widely than is commonly assumed. Architecture involves the organisation of human relationships with each other, and with the world. Those relationships are delineated by the physical spaces in which they prosper. And physical spaces are, at least in part, set out by social and political configurations. This is a mutually defining process – between the organisation of human relationships and the physical organisation of architecture – which takes place over time. The role of inhabitants in configuring and reconfiguring spaces is just as valid as the role of any professional. The traces of their work embodied in a building are just as present as those of any engineer, contractor or registered architect. Indeed, expert professionals can learn much from the architecture of non-experts. This appreciation that authorship is not decisive, and that all buildings have multiple authors, serves to undermine the hero myth of the genius-designer still promoted by many architects, journalists and critics.

3. Architecture is anticipated through drawings and contract documents. The customs of those anticipations, and the media in which they are made, frequently influence the built fabric that results. They always contain tensions between the technological, Cartesian conventions used to describe future building and the sensuous atmospheres hoped-for in rooms and spaces. Mathematical scales, CAD software packages, the often-absurd precision of specifications, and the abstractions of plan, section and elevation are tools for rational quantification which remain remarkably effective in getting buildings built. But the gaps between their abstract conventions and people's sensuous appreciation of the material world can yield important insights into the professionalised cultures of architects and others in the construction industry. It is important to appreciate the ideologies contained in, and around, the professional habits of building description, and the traces that they leave to be read in built form.

These three attitudes to architecture are informed by particular values. They allow constructed reality to diverge from the designers' intentions. They allow everyone who engages with architecture, and who alters it, to be a designer. They suggest that the architect is only one of many involved in built form; that buildings are never finished, especially on opening day. They imply that insights offered by contemporary buildings are as potent as those to be found in historical structures, and that non-expert architecture can be as meaningful as the products of expert endeavour. Following Roland Barthes' declaration, famous in literary circles, that 'the author is dead', the architect-author here – if not stone dead – is at least out cold; which is to say that close readings of building fabric can provide more enlightening outcomes than research fixated on architects' intentions.[6] The architect-author is only one possible site of meaning among many others.

This position is not new in architectural research, but it remains more radical than it should be. It is more familiar in other disciplines such as sociology, anthropology and history, in practices sometimes referred to as 'material culture'.[7] By collecting together a diverse set of close readings whose methods are nonetheless related, this book aims to consolidate a distinctive approach to architectural research. This research is informed by the challenges of cultural theory and phenomenology in the context of architectural practice, combining diachronic and synchronic approaches. It has practical and theoretical dimensions, involving the exercise of design imagination and the activities of writing and drawing. While those immersed in conventional research practices may be troubled by these still unconventional methods, they are by no means without pedigree. The work of David Leatherbarrow, Marco Frascari, Jane Rendell, Michael Cadwell, Paul Emmons, Katie Lloyd Thomas, Jonathan Hill and others have shown its possibilities.

Culture

It has been argued here that buildings, spaces and documents can be read for their insights into the values of the cultures and individuals that made them. It is important, therefore, to review existing accounts of culture and to outline why it is important to seek cultural insights.

The word 'culture' has multiple, intersecting connotations. Perhaps the most widespread idea of culture is that found expressed in high-brow Sunday newspapers, where it describes art and sculpture shown in galleries, literature of the kind that wins literary prizes, opera, plays and classical music as performed in theatres, *couture* fashion, 'art-house' cinema and novel architecture of the sort that interests journalists. This widespread notion of 'high culture' co-exists with another conception of culture as it is understood in the academic discipline of cultural studies, where culture is something that surrounds us all the time, which influences us – which 'constructs' or 'produces' our habits and values – at least as much as we influence it.[8] This version of culture includes forms of cultural production that wouldn't interest the Sunday broadsheets (such as TV soap operas, 'b-movies', predictable romantic novels and 'cheesy' pop music).

More significantly, it also includes the modes of behaviour which we learn so that we can co-exist in – and appear 'normal' in – society, for example: how to dress appropriately for particular occasions; the boundaries of acceptable humour; what constitutes friendship; what are suitably 'male' or 'female' things to do; what traits allow us to cultivate an identity as 'cool' or quirky or 'emo' or intellectual.[9] Defined in this way, the nuances of different cultures are incredibly subtle and take time to learn. For previous generations, they were described in terms of social decorum, the values necessary for an individual to participate in civilised gentility. Significantly, these subtle and shifting cultural values are not 'kept' by any government or individual. They are imposed, policed, tested and amended in society at large (which is to say – to use the term preferred by the philosopher Antonio Gramsci – that they are 'hegemonic').

These two intersecting connotations are addressed by Raymond Williams in his well-known definition of culture. Williams, one of the founders of British cultural studies, may have been overtaken in importance in the sociology of culture by other thinkers such as Pierre Bourdieu, but his definition remains widely accepted.[10] He emphasised that the word's contemporary resonances have their origins in an agricultural metaphor (only in the seventeenth century was the prefix 'agri-' added to the word 'culture' to describe farming):[11]

> in more general usage, there was a strong development of the sense of 'culture' as the active cultivation of the mind. We can distinguish a range of meanings from (i) *a developed state of mind* – as in a 'person of culture', 'a cultured person' to (ii) *the process of this development* – as in 'cultural interests', 'cultural activities' to (iii) *the means of these processes* – as in culture as 'the arts' and 'humane intellectual works'. In our own time (iii) is the most common general meaning, although all are current. It co-exists, often uneasily, with the anthropological and extended sociological use to indicate the 'whole way of life' of a distinct people or other social group.
>
> The difficulty of the term is then obvious, but can be most usefully seen as the result of earlier kinds of convergence of interests. We can distinguish two main kinds: (a) an emphasis on the *'informing spirit'* of a whole way of life, which is manifest over the whole range of cultural activities but is most evident in 'specifically cultural' activities – a language, styles of art, kinds of intellectual work; and (b) an emphasis on *'a whole social order'* within which a specifiable culture, in styles of art and kinds of intellectual work, is seen as the direct or indirect product of an order primarily constituted by other activities.[12]

Williams thus identified 'cultural production' – art, literature, music, film and architecture *of all kinds* – as a source of insight into the values of culture more broadly. To appreciate the dimensions of a particular culture at a particular moment in time, to appreciate its 'social order', he suggested, evidence should be sought in its intellectual work, whether that work belongs to so-called high culture or popular culture. In his later writing, Williams added to this definition to remind us that:

cultural practice and cultural production are not simply derived from an otherwise constituted social order but are themselves major elements in its constitution [...] instead of the 'informing spirit' which was held to constitute all other activities, it sees culture as the *signifying system* through which necessarily a social order is communicated, reproduced, experienced and explored.[13]

Culture, here, is not just a reflection of a particular 'social order'. It also shapes the values, habits and behaviours which constitute that 'social order'. Particularly for this reason – to Williams and to later sociologists of culture and cultural theorists – cultural values are important because they exert power over us through our learnt, repeated behaviour. To operate effectively and imaginatively as a member of society, and to operate as an architect in society, it is necessary to study these dimensions of cultural politics.[14]

If culture is more than 'high' culture – if it also comprises the values by which we relate to the world and to the people around us – then architecture is more than a rarefied intellectual pursuit or the subject of merely aesthetic interest. When Louis Kahn wrote that 'the plan is a society of rooms' he implied that architecture – appreciated as hierarchies of spaces – inscribes social relations, mirroring culture and also constituting it physically.[15] Architecture, and architectural details, are organised by their designers and inhabitants; but, in turn, they organise people's lives, consolidating power relations. And the documents used to anticipate and describe architecture – drawings, specifications, photographs – are wholly implicated in the cultural and political specificities of the time and place where they were made, and of the people who made them.

People have deep-seated expectations of what is 'normal' in architecture, and what they find acceptable or unacceptable, in relation to their cultural background. Maybe this is why architects – whose education often encourages them to prize novelty – frequently have different values to non-architect clients. People read into architecture – and read architecture through – the familiar 'signifying system' of their culture.[16] As Dalibor Vesely puts it, architecture is:

grasped through a preunderstanding that is based on our familiarity with what is being studied and with the segment of the world to which it belongs. Preunderstanding in this case is a layered experience of the world, acquired through our involvement in the events of everyday life [...][17]

Just as we learn, gradually, how to behave 'appropriately', we learn how to appreciate the nuances of architecture through our cultural values. The organisation, appearance and atmospheres of buildings always have redolent connotations – whether or not they are anticipated by their designers – which are appreciated in relation to the connotations of other buildings which people remember, and in relation to other cultural forms like film, art, literature or music (although those connotations inevitably shift across different people at different times). Architecture's societies of rooms, its atmospheres and appearances, and its material qualities thus can never be value-free.[18]

This notion that people's cultural values are deeply embedded in architecture runs counter to the rhetoric of those who prefer to present buildings as worlds-unto-themselves. In much architectural journalism, for example, it is not just the professional photographs which omit people and crop out a building's surroundings to present an image of 'pure space', so too does the text. Vesely claims that this conception of buildings as autonomous and isolated is symptomatic of relatively recent history:

> Inwardness is the main feature [...] of the twentieth century as a whole. It has resulted from a long-term transformation of European culture, tied to a belief that our life can be entirely represented in terms of scientific, technical rationality, leaving behind all that cannot be subordinated to this vision – mainly the domain of personal experience, praxis and the natural world [...] In the field of architecture, this mode of culture is typically embodied in the Romantic notion of genius, which reduces the traditional complexity of culture to a single, creative gesture [...][19]

He links the idea that buildings are autonomous art-objects to the idea of the architect as a genius who finds inspiration alone. These notions seem to be widespread, building-as-artwork and architect-as-hero-author both working alone in service of some high ideal, supposedly outside culture. Yet this is very rarely the case. Very rarely are buildings and spaces so singular that they are radically disconnected from their social and physical circumstances. And only very rarely does this seem desirable.

If architecture is to make a positive contribution to cultural politics, if architects are to make projects which are critically acute and socially aware, then it can only come about through a deliberate appreciation of the cultural dimensions of architecture: by studying *how* architecture works and *what* it does. Similarly, it remains important for architects and architectural historians to appreciate buildings as the material embodiments of culture (or multiple cultures), and to read the stories that they contain.

Evidence

There are different ways to study what architecture does. J. Mordaunt-Crook posed a threefold distinction. First, he suggested that a building can be studied according to what is written about it 'vicariously, on the basis of external evidence'.[20] Or, second, it can be studied 'conceptually, as a work of art, as a design, in relation to aesthetic theory'. Or, third, it can be read 'as a monument, as a structure, as a tectonic equation, on internal evidence'. The chapters collected here emphasise Mordaunt-Crook's last approach – recognising that buildings themselves, and documents themselves, are the best evidence of their own intellectual position.[21] As he suggests, archaeological parallels are relevant here (although it is important not to take them too far: it is tempting, but overly melodramatic, to suggest that a cultural reading of architecture somehow 'uncovers' realities, that it 'reveals' what was previously hidden). Like archaeology, close reading involves the painstaking study of evidence. As Andrew Ballantyne suggests:

> What people say they care about, in their conversation or in their books, is one kind of evidence for the system of values in a society, but a better guide to what they really believe is to look at how they act. Buildings that are actually built tell us a good deal about the value system of the society that produced them. This is because buildings are always expensive. Their cost is nearly always significant for the person who commissions them, so they are only very rarely frivolous [...] It is this that makes buildings especially valuable for archaeologists. They are evidence of the will of a society, and point to that society's ethos and where the real power lies.[22]

Ballantyne's essay is titled 'Architecture as evidence' and it makes a case for reading architecture responsibly, for the meticulous examination of clues evident in built fabric.

Carlo Ginzburg argued that an interest in the systematic analysis of clues – in what he calls the 'evidential paradigm' of the clue – first emerged in late-nineteenth-century Europe. He associated Arthur Conan Doyle's stories about his super-sleuth Sherlock Holmes with the methods of art-historian Giovanni Morelli (who investigated the attribution of paintings through forensic observation) and the psychoanalytical methods developed by Sigmund Freud.[23] Ginzburg traced the history of the idea of the clue, recognising that it continues to pose problems for contemporary scholarship – about the extent to which the analysis of clues should be scientific (or should pretend to be), and about the relative importance of evidence itself in relation to the subsequent interpretation of that evidence.

In any cultural reading of architecture, there is a balance to be struck between interpretation and evidence. There is no single 'correct' reading to be systematically extracted from a building, space or document.[24] There will be at least as many readings as there are readers, and multiple readings will 'contaminate' each other.[25] That said, any interpretation should not over-reach itself. It is important to tell an insightful story, to appreciate architecture in its cultural contexts, to go beyond a straightforward accounting of the evidence in order to read the values at work in it.[26] A compelling reading will have animatory force. But, equally, it is important not to over-interpret evidence, to concoct fictions out of opportunistic interpretation.

By no means can any reading establish the incontrovertible facts of a subject – even if that were possible – but it does require of the reader the duty of responsible judgement. There are parallels here with Aristotle's notion of *phronesis*, summarised admirably by Marco Frascari:

> According to Aristotle, *phronesis* is the most important kind of knowledge because it deals with how you use the other kinds of knowledge, that is whether you use them 'well' from an ethical point of view. Phronesis is

knowledge that helps man [and woman] to act wisely and make good determinations. Phronesis concerns values and goes beyond analytical, scientific knowledge (*episteme*) and technical sapience (*techne*). Phronesis is focused on particulars and is also context-dependent and has priority over universal rules. Phronesis is lucid, competent and ethical, and deals with things that are good or bad for humanity.[27]

The exercise of reading architecture closely – and reading closely the documents which anticipate and describe architecture – is related to conceptions of history (the formulation of grand narratives about shifts in human culture), historiography (the cultural politics of history-writing),[28] architectural criticism (the exercise of expert opinion)[29] and interpretation (articulating material so that it speaks differently).[30] However, it owes perhaps its greatest debt to the legacy of Aristotle's *phronesis*, as articulated here by Frascari: a debt to the wise exercise of careful judgement on the basis of evidence; and a debt to engaged ethical determination which can reach beyond the supposed moral neutrality of science and technology. It requires the reader to articulate responsibly the distinctions between the evidence embodied in the building or document being studied and the rhetoric that people have tried to frame it with.

The shape of this book

The fourteen chapters which follow offer fourteen readings of buildings, spaces and documents. They are not intended to provide any systematic history or theory. They are offered instead as case studies in the practices of close reading, in the hope that their methods might yield productive examples to be emulated or challenged. The readings range in time from the fifteenth century – a reading of the only surviving drawing made by Leon Battista Alberti – to the recent past – projects completed by Norman Foster in 2006 and Herzog and De Meuron in 2008. They range geographically from France to Puerto Rico to Kazakhstan. They range in fame from buildings celebrated by critics to house extensions and motorway service areas. They address buildings, specifications and photographs. These readings are bound together by their research methods – as outlined in this introduction – and their collective aim is to be interesting, insightful and readable. When taken together as a collection, the essays make a case – a compelling case, I hope – for conducting close readings of buildings in pursuit of their cultural insights.

The chapters which follow are organised in three parts. The first part – 'Extraordinary buildings, divergent readings' – examines buildings and spaces that were designed by architects whose names are familiar from books, articles and Sunday newspaper architecture columns; historical or contemporary names admitted to the 'canon' of high culture. The second part – 'Familiar buildings, unfamiliar readings' – deals with architecture and architects whose designers are nameless in the terms of high culture, or whose names have been effectively forgotten. This part aims to show that readings of these buildings can be at least as interesting and insightful as readings of more famous buildings. The third part zooms in, examining 'Redolent details, insightful documents'. The chapters examine junctions between materials, a drawing, specifications and architectural photographs.[31] They show that scale is no impediment to insightful reading; that even the smallest, the most superficially negligible, detail or document can yield cultural insights when closely read.

The essays collected here, and their methods, are relevant to writers. They are also important to designers. I have argued above that architecture is always imagined, built, inhabited and read by people through their culture or cultures; that no project is an island, isolated from its cultural context in time or place. As architects, we cannot predict precisely how the projects we design will be read by others. This is not necessarily a reason for anxiety, but nor is it a reason to leave potential readings entirely to chance. If we want to design powerfully and perceptively – if we want to engage with the cultural politics with which we work – then we must equip ourselves to read buildings that have already been built and inhabited. We need to become as adept at reading as we are at designing. Reading and designing are not the same skill, but they reinforce one another. And we should remember that reading architecture can be a source of pleasure for us as designers; that good readings can be as imaginative as good designs.

NOTES

1   Leslie Martin was appointed head of the Cambridge School in 1956 and his work is outlined in: Peter Carolin and Trevor Dannatt (eds), *Architecture, Education, Research: The Work of Leslie Martin* (London: Academy Editions, 1996); and Dean Hawkes, 'The Centre and the Periphery: Reflections on the Nature and Conduct of Architectural Research', *arq: Architectural Research Quarterly*, 1, 1 (1995): 8–11. Martin was also instrumental in both organising the RIBA's famous Oxford Conference in 1958 and documenting its outcomes – an event which effectively consolidated architectural education in British universities, established the current pattern of professional training and promoted the formalising of doctoral research. See Mark Crinson and Jules Lubbock, *Architecture: Art or Profession?* (Manchester: Manchester University Press, 1994).

2   Adam Sharr, 'Leslie Martin and the Science of Architectural Form' in Allison Dutoit, Juliet Odgers and Adam Sharr (eds), *Quality Out of Control: Standards for Measuring Architecture* (London: Routledge, 2010), pp. 67–78.

3   There are echoes here with current debates around parametric design.

4   For reasons explained later in this introduction, I deliberately make no distinction here between 'architecture' and 'building' and will treat the terms as synonymous.

5   Barbara Tversky, 'Remembering Spaces' in Endel Tulving and Fergus I. M. Craik (eds), *Handbook of Memory* (Oxford: Oxford University Press, 2000), pp. 363–378.

6   Roland Barthes, 'The Death of the Author' in *Image, Music, Text* (London: Fontana, 1993), pp. 142–148.

7   For an overview of material culture, see: Daniel Miller (ed.), *Material Cultures: Why Some Things Matter* (London: Routledge, 1997). Practices in material culture relate to those of the *Annales* school of history: Peter Burke (ed.), *The French Historical Revolution: Annales School, 1929–1989* (London: Polity, 1990). The Winterthur Museum and its journal *Winterthur Portfolio* have become a centre for material culture studies. See, for example, Jules David Prown, 'Mind in Matter: An Introduction to Material Culture Theory and Method',

Winterthur Portfolio, 17, 1, Spring (1982): 1–19. Material culture has been particularly important in the academic discipline of American Studies, for example: James Deetz, *In Small Things Forgotten: The Archaeology of Early American Life* (New York: Doubleday, 1977). There is a significant crossover here with architecture, including, for example, the work of John Vlach such as *Back of the Big House: The Architecture of Plantation Slavery* (Chapel Hill: University of North Carolina Press, 1993); Bernard Herman, for example, *Town House: Architecture and Material Life in the Early American City, 1760–1830* (Chapel Hill: University of North Carolina Press, 2005); Dell Upton, *Another City: Urban Life and Urban Spaces in the New American Republic* (New Haven: Yale University Press, 2008). See also the Vernacular Architecture Forum and its journal now known as *Buildings and Landscapes*.

8   Stuart Hall, *Representation: Cultural Representations and Signifying Practices* (London: Sage, 1997), p. 7.

9   Hall, *Representation*, p. 2.

10 David Inglis, 'Review of *Raymond Williams's Sociology of Culture* by Paul Jones' in *Theory, Culture and Society*, 24, 3 (2007): 166–169. See also Jones' book which is concerned to show the contemporary relevance of Williams' work: Paul Jones, *Raymond Williams' Sociology of Culture: A Critical Reconstruction* (Basingstoke: Palgrave Macmillan, 2006).

11 Harry Levin, 'Semantics of Culture', *Daedalus*, 94, 1 (1965): 1–13.

12 Raymond Williams, *Culture* (London: Fontana, 1981), pp. 11–12.

13 Ibid., pp. 12–13. Williams added this to his summary of his previous position.

14 Glenn Jordan and Chris Weedon, *Cultural Politics* (Oxford: Wiley-Blackwell, 1994). On the possibility of a 'critical architecture' see: K. Michael Hays, 'Critical Architecture: Between Culture and Form', *Perspecta*, 21 (1981): 14–29 and, for a more recent survey: Jane Rendell, Jonathan Hill, Murray Fraser and Mark Dorrian (eds), *Critical Architecture* (London: Routledge, 2007).

15 John Lobell, *Between Silence and Light: Spirit in the Architecture of Louis I. Kahn* (Boulder: Shambhala, 1979), p. 36.

16 Andrew Ballantyne, 'Architecture as Evidence' in D. Arnold, E. A. Ergut and B. T. Özkaya (eds), *Rethinking Architectural Historiography* (London: Routledge, 2006), pp. 36–49, p. 36.

17 Dalibor Vesely, *Architecture in the Age of Divided Representation: The Question of Creativity in the Shadow of Production* (Cambridge MA: MIT Press, 2004), p. 77. Some scholars have found Vesely's work somewhat in opposition to the work of Raymond Williams, Stuart Hall and other cultural theorists who advocate multiple, intersecting cultures. Arguably, his 'layered experience of the world' is more 'vertical' – preferring to see long historical trajectories – while many cultural theorists prefer to emphasise 'horizontal' layers – multiple layers co-existing in the present and the recent past. This is not to say that these approaches are necessarily incompatible. Thanks to Diana Periton for helping to articulate this distinction.

18 For these reasons, it is hard to think of situations in which architecture can be 'post-critical', as some have attempted to claim. See: Robert Somol and Sarah Whiting, 'Notes around the Doppler Effect and Other Moods of Modernism', *Perspecta*, 33 (2002): 7; Michael Speaks, 'After Theory: Debate in Architecture Schools Rages About the Value of Theory and Its Effect on Innovation in Design', *Architectural Record*, 193, 6, June (2005): 72–75. On the so-called 'post-critical debate', see also: George Baird, 'Criticality and Its Discontents', *Harvard Design Magazine*, 21, Fall/Winter (2004/2005): 16–21; Reinhold Martin, 'On Theory: Critical of What? Toward a Utopian Realism', *Harvard Design Magazine*, 22, Spring/Summer (2005): 1–5.

19 Vesely, *Architecture in the Age of Divided Representation*, p. 29.

20 J. Mordaunt Crook, 'Architecture and History' in *Architectural History*, Design and Practice in British Architecture: Studies in Architectural History Presented to Howard Colvin, 27 (1984): 571. Cited by Nathaniel Coleman in: 'Elusive Interpretations', *Cloud-Cuckoo-Land: International Journal of Architectural Theory*, 12, 2 (2008).

21 Lorraine Daston (ed.), *Things That Talk: Object Lessons from Art and Science* (New York: Zone Books, 2008).

22 Ballantyne, 'Architecture as Evidence' in *Rethinking Architectural Historiography*, p. 37.

23   Carlo Ginzburg, 'Clues: Roots of an Evidential Paradigm' in *Myths, Emblems, Clues*, trans. by
     John and Anne C. Tedeschi (London: Hutchinson, 1990), pp. 96–125.
24   Hall, *Representation*, p. 2.
25   Jane Rendell, 'Critical Architecture' in Rendell *et al.* (eds), *Critical Architecture*, pp. 1–7
     (p. 7).
26   Alberto Pérez-Gómez, in interview, has made a radical claim for the merits of interpretation:
     'Histories are stories after all. Histories that try to be objective and factual could be useful but
     I always miss the dimension of interpretation. I don't know if I would call this "non-negotiable",
     but my preference is to frame architectural history in terms of hermeneutics. [...] Why?
     Because in this kind of framework, the issue is to foreground interpretation [...] And
     interpretation means that we valorise the questions. We first find the questions that are
     important to each one of us and then we understand their importance in terms of their cultural
     significance. Then we look at the material and interpret it through these questions so it can
     speak to us [...] Of course, this is very much at odds with the idea of a historian who thinks of
     the discipline as a scientific endeavour that is going to find the objective facts about one thing
     or another. That is a futile waste of time (even though I use many of these books because
     people do some very serious work and spend all of their lives working in archives and this is
     very, very useful). But in the end [...] what matters is this interpretative framing of the
     historical material that connects in a dialogue with present questions'. Saundra Weddle and
     Marc J. Neveu, 'Interview with Alberto Pérez-Gómez', *Journal of Architectural Education*,
     64, 2, March (2011): 76–81, pp.78–79. Pérez-Gómez echoes the idea of 'emplotment' put
     forward in 1973 by Hayden White in: *Metahistory: The Historical Imagination in Nineteenth
     Century Europe* (Baltimore: Johns Hopkins University Press, 1973).
27   Marco Frascari, *Eleven Exercises in the Art of Architectural Drawing: Slow Food for the
     Architect's Imagination* (London: Routledge, 2011), p. 7.
28   Michael Bentley, *Modern Historiography* (London: Routledge, 1999).
29   See the issue of the *Journal of Architectural Education* which collects twelve 'op-ed' texts
     where various architectural critics – including George Baird, Thomas Fisher, Joan Ockman,
     David Leatherbarrow and R. E. Somol – set out, and question, the terms of architectural
     criticism as they perceive them. Introduced by George Dodds, 'On Criticism in Architecture:
     An Invitation to Practice', *Journal of Architectural Education*, 62, 3, February (2009): 3ff.
30   See Alberto Pérez-Gómez' account of interpretation as a hermeneutical term in the interview
     above. Saundra Weddle and Marc J. Neveu, 'Interview with Alberto Pérez-Gómez', *Journal of
     Architectural Education*: 79.
31   In his well-known essay, Marco Frascari argues that, in architecture, the detail is the 'minimal
     unit in the process of signifcation'. Marco Frascari, 'Tell-the-tale Detail' in Kate Nesbitt (ed.),
     Theorizing a New Agenda for Architecture: An Anthology of Architecture Theory 1965–1995
     (New York: Princeton Architectural Press, 1996), pp. 498–515, p. 498.

Opening

David Leatherbarrow's essay 'Breathing walls' opens this book. It offers a close reading of a 'breathing wall' constructed at the Church of San Martin de Porres in San Juan, Puerto Rico, designed by Henry Klumb and completed in 1950.[1]

To Leatherbarrow, this wall is not just an environmental control device, a technical instrument for cooling space in a hot climate. Rather, the wall is read as a microcosm of the building as a whole, accounting for the ideas at work there. It describes a powerful challenge to the commonplace assumption in architecture whereby the cultural appreciation of buildings is separated from ideas about their functional performance. The wall's performance is 'latent', Leatherbarrow argues, imagined out of the specificities of the place, the community and its culture. The shifting shadows cast by the breathing wall, and its refreshing airflow, are wholly integral with the site and inhabitants; not calculated as a remote, technical mechanism for air handling. Function is not grafted-on to form but is instead fused with it, embedded in a particular way of life in a particular situation at a particular time.[2] The breathing wall thus has the capacity to operate metaphorically as well as functionally.

Leatherbarrow's essay opens this book not just because it is a consummate close reading, but also because of its productive metaphors. He reminds us that walls can *breathe*. They contrive architectural atmospheres. Importantly, they can be imagined as living, animate entities with communicative potential; never complete because they are always open to creative re-imagination. These vivid metaphors provide a colourful re-statement of the aims of the book.

This opening chapter raises important questions. Why is a cultural appreciation of architecture commonly assumed to be only artistic, and commonly set-up in opposition to an idea of performance which is considered technically? How can the idea of performance in architecture be rethought culturally? How might architecture and its details have metaphorical power?

Notes

1 This essay is reprinted, by kind permission of Princeton Architectural Press, from: David Leatherbarrow, *Architecture Oriented Otherwise* (New York: Princeton Architectural Press, 2010), pp. 19–40.

2 These are ideas which Leatherbarrow has developed through his writings, including: *Uncommon Ground: Architecture, Technology and Topography* (Cambridge MA: MIT Press, 2000); *Topographical Stories: Studies in Landscape and Architecture* (Philadelphia: University of Pennsylvania Press, 2004); *Surface Architecture* (Cambridge MA: MIT Press, 2005); and, with Mohsen Mostafavi, *On Weathering: The Life of Buildings in Time* (Cambridge MA: MIT Press, 1993).

Chapter 1

Breathing walls

David Leatherbarrow

The American painter Robert Rauschenberg once explained that throughout his career he had worked on a single problem: bridging the separation between art and life. 'Painting', he said, 'relates to both art and life. Neither can be made. I try to act in that gap between the two'.[1] He was not the first – nor, I suspect, will he be the last – to undertake this task. Friedrich Nietzsche's thought was once described as an effort to overcome the 'raging discord' between art and truth.[2] The problem is especially acute in architecture, where the distinction between art and building is taken for granted in most discussions of a project's functionality. In extreme form, the assumption runs as follows: architectural design leads to artistic *works*, building construction results in shelters that actually *work*. Just as Rauschenberg sought to act in the gap between art and life, I would like to describe the connections between life's bare necessities (shelter) and its expression (art). To do this I will discuss a single wall in a single building.

Atmosphere

When the Dominican fathers of San Juan Puerto Rico first offered Henry Klumb the commission for the Church of San Martin de Porres (1950), he turned them down.[3] In explanation of his refusal, he gave two reasons: as a Protestant he felt he could not design a conventional Roman Catholic church; and as a modern architect he could not build in the Spanish colonial style that everyone on the island had become used to. Eventually he overcame both obstacles and designed a fascinating little sanctuary. My concern, however, is not with the building as a whole, but just one of its parts, an element I will call the *breathing wall* (Figure 1.1). Obviously, the term is metaphorical. So far as I know, this particular formulation was not used by Klumb, who employed a number of other terms to describe the elements that allow buildings to admit fresh and exhaust stale air. Le Corbusier developed an equivalent vocabulary in his proposals for *respiration exacte* in modern buildings.[4] In what follows, I will study this single element in order to use it as a foundation for more basic arguments about architecture and life. The breathing wall is a useful topic because it operates in three ways simultaneously: *technically*, as a device for modifying the climate; *practically*, as a way of structuring the events that define a (religious) institution; and *symbolically*, as their representation. With respect

Figure 1.1 Henry Klumb, San Martín de Porres, Cantaño, Puerto Rico, 1949–66; interior view

to this last aspect, a single quotation from the architect should be sufficient to indicate the amplitude of meanings sustained by the breathing wall: 'one of the human necessities of prayer [Klumb said] is the ability to breathe, therefore the circulation of air is something that has to be considered by the architect [in the design of a church].'[5] That more is involved than getting oxygen into the blood is clear: both religious and prosaic breathing supply the lungs with what they need, but something else is involved in the former. One does not need to be a Catholic to know that the Genesis account of human beginnings hinges on this 'something else', for nothing less than mankind resulted from the *inspiration* of soil: 'the Lord God formed man of the dust of the ground, and breathed into his nostrils the breath of life; and man became a living soul.'[6] Nor is a confession of faith required to see evidences of the extra-respiratory consequences of breathing in the parallel account of origins in the Pentecost myth: communication and community resulted from an inrush of air. The report in *Acts* 2 is as follows: 'suddenly there came a sound from heaven as of a rushing mighty wind, and it filled all the house where they were sitting [...] and every man heard [all the others] speaking in his own language.'[7] In both stories, breath was simultaneously an instrument and sign of new life. The Greek word for breath or vapour, *atmos*, clarifies why the mood or quality of an architectural setting, such as the nave of San Martin de Porres, is often named its *atmosphere*.

When entering this little church, a crucifix designed by the client, a Dominican Father named Marcolino Maas, attracts one's attention, not the building itself. Maas confirmed the tacit presence of the building by describing an unaffected sort of architecture: 'the building', he observed, 'breathes [an] air of freshness and originality [...] There is nothing that could have been copied from somewhere else; yet there is true, honest, and simple building pleasure in and around it without snobbism or any aim for sensationalism'. Father Maas also affirmed the building's suitability for religious practice, for its simplicity, he thought, did not prevent it from expressing 'a deep religious and quite Catholic and liturgical atmosphere'. Nor did the absence of graphic ornament prevent it from revealing the atmosphere of its bayside location. The Dominican Father observed that the floor-to-ceiling piers or fins on either side of the nave isolate the interior from external distractions when one enters the space or faces the altar. Seclusion, he suggested, 'concentrate[d] the attention'. Others saw that they provided for an intimacy that allowed for withdrawn introspection (*recogimiento*). The piers help focus the parishioner's attention during a service because they confine his or her perspective: rotated on plan 45 degrees from the axis of the nave they block lateral views. Despite this, the space is far from being introverted because the fragrance from what Maas called 'the lavish tropical landscape', together with the sea air passing from the bay to the town, enters the building through the same fins that give the interior its seclusion. In addition, when one leaves the building 'these pillars visually open up', Maas observed, allowing the shrine and baptistery, together with the landscape beyond, to come into sight.[8]

All that I want to argue in this study concerns the operational and metaphorical substance of these fins, for they are the means by which the building '*breathes* an air of freshness and originality', also for its religious,

Catholic, and liturgical 'atmosphere'. With them, or this atmosphere, as my example I would like to show that a building's performances are the means by which it simultaneously accomplishes practical purposes and gives them legible articulation. Put differently, the appearance and meaning of an architectural work are essentially tied to the operations performed by its several elements. Representational content is not something *added to* the shaping of settings in response to life's 'bare necessities', as suggested by arguments within the functionalist tradition, but is something internal to the response to those necessities. My claim is that metaphors such as 'breathing' name an essential dimension of a building's operations.

The *quiebra sol*: operation and representation

There are well-known precedents for Klumb's use of elements that regulate the flow of air and light into a building (Figure 1.2). Perhaps the most well-known are those developed by Le Corbusier, particularly his devices for blocking or breaking the heat of the sun: the famous *brise-soleil*. Klumb also made use of the sun-breaker, or *quiebra sol*, throughout his career. It appears prominently in his early work, across the face of his New York Department Store in Santurce, San Juan, for example. A number of his buildings on the campus of the University of Puerto Rico in Rio Piedras are also fitted with this device: the Lazaro Library and the Law School (Figure 1.3), for example. Another elegant example is the central auditorium and library building at the Colegio San Ignacio. There is great variation in the articulation of these sun-shades, however. Only the earliest, the New York Department Store, could be adequately described with Reyner Banham's uncharitable phrase 'external egg-crate of vertical and horizontal shades'.[9]

Banham suggested that the *brise-soleil* emerged historically as a form of compensation. The development of the load-bearing frame created the possibility of replacing the entire wall with a window. Le Corbusier took this possibility as something of a requirement (see, for example, the Salvation Army Building, or the Clarté Apartments). When large expanses of glass faced directions other than the south few environmental problems arose. For walls exposed to the sun throughout the day, the *mur neutralisant* was supposed to handle unwanted heat gain.[10] The idea was that hot or cold air circulating in the cavity of double-glazing would mediate temperature differences between the inside and outside. When this proved to be unworkable, sometimes for non-technical reasons, another device was necessary – assuming that a return to thick-wall construction and 'punched windows' was not an option. That other device was the external sun-screen, which was to compensate for the window wall's miserable thermal performance.

Two decades after Le Corbusier first struggled with this device, Marcel Breuer confidently asserted that the external screening device was the only sensible solution to the heat gain problem of window walls, for the sun had to be 'reflected before it [was] trapped behind the glass and fill[ed] the inside with

Figure 1.2 Henry Klumb, Museum of Anthropology, History and Art, UPR, Río Piedras, Puerto Rico, 1953; courtyard

Figure 1.3 Henry Klumb, College of Law, UPR, Río Piedras, Puerto Rico, 1969–81; entry court and stairway

radiant heat'.[11] Curtains, blinds, shades and moveable panels in the interior were sufficient for altering the amount of light entering the building, but sun control devices on the exterior were the only instruments that could be effective against the heat that resulted from solar gain. Breuer's argument was furthered by Olgyay and Olgyay in their comprehensive study of solar control and sun shading devices. Le Corbusier's solution in the Marseilles Block was, they thought, 'fundamentally sound'. Because it was opaque, the sun breaker intercepted both the direct and diffused types of solar radiation. Correct sizing allowed heat to be excluded in the summer and admitted in the winter. Le Corbusier's design was also praised because it expressed 'a strong spatial character', adding 'new elements to the architectural vocabulary.'[12] This suggests that thermal or environmental performance was not all the sun-breaker allowed. Equally significant was its expressive or aesthetic performance.

This point can be extended. Clearly, in Le Corbusier's post-war projects the *brise-soleil* was as much an instrument of expression as of climate control. In the Maison Curutchet in Argentina (1952), the Millowners' Building in Ahmadabad (1954), the Secretariat at Chandigarh (1958), or the Carpenter Center in Cambridge, Massachusetts (1964), thermal control is achieved by devices that also have aesthetic, even monumental, expression. Alan Colquhoun observed that the sun breaker 'was more than a technical device; it introduced a new architectural element in the form of a thick, permeable wall, whose depth and subdivisions gave the façade the modeling and aedicular expression that had been lost with the suppression of the window and the pilaster'.[13] Expression, however, is not the same as representation – let alone symbolisation. I will return to this distinction below.

Continuity through resistance

Le Corbusier, Breuer and the Olgyay brothers concentrated on the ways that screening devices combat the harmful effects of sunshine (Figures 1.4, 1.5). Resistance is only half the work of these elements, however. The same devices that restrict heat penetration allow the free entry of fresh air – in fact, they do more than allow it, they work to accelerate it. One of the façades of Klumb's IBM building exemplifies this yielding type of external screen: the full-height louvre. A similar device can also be seen on the side wings of his Medical Services building, where it encloses hallways that connect examination and treatment rooms. These elements also exist at the side of the University Museum entry portico and on other Klumb buildings; the Student Center on the Mayaguez campus is a very good example. In some instances, the louvres were fixed in position, standing ready to admit fresh air while counteracting the sun's familiar lines of attack. In other places, they could be moved manually, and in still others they were rotated electrically, as on the IBM building. Not only operation but vantage was key, as is clear from a sketch for the louvres on an apartment building, also in Santurce. This was important to Le Corbusier too, as can bescreen, Le Corbusier's buildings provided ample precedent for the louvre

Figure 1.4 Le Corbusier, Lucio Costa, *et al.*, Ministry of Education and Health, Rio de Janiero, 1937–42; sun-screen from outside

Figure 1.5 Le Corbusier, Lucio Costa, *et al.*, Ministry of Education and Health, Rio de Janiero, 1937–42; sun-screen from inside

Figure 1.6 Oscar Niemeyer, Hall of Industry, Parque Ibirapuéra, São Paolo, 1953; façade

wall: La Tourette and Carpenter Center, for example. Other architects were equally inventive: Neutra in the US; Villanueva in Venezuela; Niemeyer, Costa, Reidy, and the Roberto brothers in Brazil (Figure 1.6).[14]

Klumb's Church of San Martin de Porres presents a subtle variation on the theme, however, for in that building there is not a single but a double row of filters: the fixed vertical louvres that line the parts of outer walls, allowing air, light, and views to pass through the building; and the much larger fins (in plan) that limit the lateral extent of the nave, providing it with enclosure and defining its atmosphere. Depending on one's position and vantage, the louvred walls approximate the continuous planarity of solid partitions. One's view is, indeed, obstructed along such a wall's entire length, but not uniformly so, for darks contrast with lights at each panel's edge, leaving the mid-sections to mediate the opposition. As this rhythmic play of bright against dark spreads its effects laterally, a parallel space at the wall's edges is created – basically a walkway on either side. A precedent for this solution is the famous ABI building (1938) in Rio by the Roberto brothers, with its passageway between the outer enclosure of the offices and the inner face of the sun breaker (Figure 1.7). Another elegant example in Rio is to be found in the apartment buildings in Guinle Park by Lucio Costa (1947–1953) (Figure 1.8).

Because of the church's plan geometry, the wall in San Martin de Porres adds to the room's orthogonality an oblique orientation toward settings outside or beyond. Both effects increase the depth of the building; in the first instance by layering, in the second by opening. As Father Maas observed, depending on

Figure 1.7 Marcelo, Milton and Mauricio Roberto, Brazilian Press Association Building (ABI), Rio de Janiero, 1938; façade

Figure 1.8 Lucio Costa, Parque Guinle, Rio de Janiero, 1947–53; façade

one's standing in the room, the margins of the setting become more or less marginal, more interconnected with the interior they surround, or less a part of it. Thus, they introduce both frontality and obliquity into the building; the latter by angling the openings of their continuous planarity, which concentrates attention at one end of the hall or room (the altar of a church, for example) and releases it at the other (into the building's surrounds or adjoining rooms). The louver wall is partition-like but wider than the typical 'space dividing element' and it is directional: it is more ample because it projects a shadow space and is directional because it alternately concentrates and expands space, like a lens at one end and a manifold at the other.

Here I would like to make a general observation: architecture such as this can be called *productive* because its settings supply what the given location is unable to give on its own. Ambient light, for instance, is made more intense when reflected off the surfaces of the *quiebra sol* – brights are brightened. Shadows are cast and cooled by these same devices. One should not say architecture is the sole source of these conditions, for its real accomplishment is the alteration or adjustment of phenomena that are already there. Its work could be described as a crystallising or cultivating sort of productivity: this is what makes architectural elements metaphorical. Speaking broadly of fiction, Paul Ricœur used the term 'iconic augmentation' to describe artistic productivity.[15] A key to this 'augmentation' in architecture is the relationship between the building and the pre-given milieu. Klumb called prevailing conditions *latent*. He took great pains to understand what was *given* in each location that his buildings were to occupy. Evidence of this concern appears in his attempt to diagram the movement of air across the sites on which he built (percentages and line weights on plan drawings show the intensity of breezes coming from different directions).

Perhaps the building's productivity should be described as adjunctive or adjectival, since its chief role is to modify what it inherits. But this is acceptable only if the modification that is envisaged is understood to include taking a stand against what the natural world offers, discovering in what is not given what might be. Put differently, there would be no continuity if there were no resistance. Modern architecture did not eliminate the separation between inside and outside so that the space of the one could flow into the other; it made that separation much more subtle than it had been in previous architectures. Boundaries between spatial interiors and exteriors are not overcome with the adoption of the structural frame, but thickened. Certainly the elements set up within the edge thickness of a structural frame are less weighty and visible than their load-bearing antecedents, but this is because they approximate themselves so closely to the potentials (not the results) of the world that surrounds them – its latencies. Klumb's buildings work with manifestations of climate and culture by variously resisting and admitting their forces, with no less insistence than intelligence. Although a modest solution, Klumb's Serra Office Building in Santurce shows very clearly how resisting and admitting both climate and culture can be accomplished on the streets of a modern city. The case is helpful because much of the modern architecture that was designed to be 'environmentally responsive' was also anti-urban, which is to say culturally inadequate.

Anterior indivision

The idea of the building as an ensemble of devices that perform movements counter to the actions of the environment is not completely satisfactory because it preserves a dichotomy that is a result of analysis not experience. When one is drawn into some event inside the nave of Klumb's San Martin de Porres it is hardly necessary – barely sensible – to differentiate which aspects of its 'atmosphere' result from the building and which from its climate and culture, neither of which the architect designed. Only designers and theorists puzzle over these distinctions, in ill-considered attempts to grant primary causality to one or another. Children reading in a classroom, friends telling stories in the afternoon shadows of a plaza, or believers with heads down before an altar do not discriminate between the 'natural and artificial elements' of their surroundings. Outside of professional interests, or prior to disciplinary deliberation and reflection, there is no uncertainty about what exists and unfolds in these settings, nor does participation require an intellectual summation of their constitutive conditions. In the church, the light is less bright, the temperature cooler, and the hum of activities quieter than outside. Moreover, the setting has been prepared for particular performances that could not occur outdoors: the altar ahead, the *ambo* pulpit at the front left, the baptistery and shrine to the sides, confessionals front and back, the organ behind, and so on

– each thing at the right distance and in the right position for the enactment of the institution's several services, as a church, sanctuary, and pilgrimage chapel. While the separation between built and un-built conditions seems so obvious, it is in fact a product of analysis, an outcome of reflection that narrows a fuller and more basic grasp of the situation. If we try to catch a building's events as they actually unfold – reading, talking, or praying – there is no separation of the aspects of the setting's *mood* that result from the architect's provisions from those that are the gift of its un-built surround and everyday affairs, together with the historical grounds on which both are established.

When pointing to the relationship between the interior and exterior Klumb spoke of their 'fusion': 'architecture', he wrote, 'fuses man with his environment'.[16] One way to think of this condition is to imagine a connection that is so tight that separation is impossible, like an amalgamation that results from intense heat and melting. Yet, this image, too, is misleading because it preserves traces of each element's 'original' separateness. The concept of 'fusion' must be interpreted differently if the actuality and metaphorical substance of the building are to be adequately described – in this instance, its *respiration*.

Father Maas observed that the interior of San Martin de Porres 'has a deep religious and quite Catholic atmosphere'. This was apparent, he said, in the 'air of freshness and originality' it breathed. How is this atmosphere to be understood? From what does it arise, and what puts it at risk? We are presented, it seems to me, with a condition or quality that unmistakably imposes itself on experience but arises from a source that cannot be clearly identified. An atmosphere, like a mood, impresses itself on experience because it is global or oceanic: it envelops, surrounds, and entirely encloses the events and institutions of our lives. The meanings that Martin Heidegger attached to the word *Stimmung* express this very well. While a room's atmosphere is unmistakable and overpowering, all attempts to explain its several sources or causes are defeated by the unity or *indivision* of the total circumstance. Describing the church's Catholic atmosphere Father Maas did not individuate its several components, he treated the distinctions between architectural, social, or natural conditions as if they really did not matter, as if attending to them would have distracted him from what he was trying to express. Likewise, Klumb's notion of 'fusion' referred not to the blending together, cross-over, or integration of previously separate elements but to *a prior state of indistinctness*, a state that was not only energetic and creative, as he said, but too comprehensive to be seen or treated objectively.

If not as an object, or composition of several distinct things, how can architecture contribute to such an 'atmosphere'? How can a building '*discover and disclose similarities*' in the elements that make up a given situation? An answer to this question will, I think, help us see the connections between a building's practical and metaphorical dimensions. In a book called *Rhetoric as Philosophy*, the philosopher Ernesto Grassi described the logic of metaphor as 'a capacity to see the similar'.[17] In explanation of what is involved in the 'vision of the common', he cited Aristotle: 'Transferal [*metapherein*] must be completed on the basis of similarity'.

In Klumb's architecture, the breathing wall led to certain effects: it *produced* cool shadows, together with a measured supply of fresh air – donations for which all who use his buildings remain grateful. Certainly the building's elements are passive – they do not move or change position – but they can also be seen to be active if their 'behaviour' is seen to result in the creation of qualities the world lacks. This is to say, architectural elements are *passively active*. Seemingly at rest, they are secretly at work. The key is this: in their labour, architectural elements fuse themselves into the latencies of the ambient environment, adopting as their own its capacity for change or *movement*. Obviously, this fusion is fictional; but in the events that define the setting it is entirely believable.

To work or be active in this way the building must accept the fact that its effects are co-dependent on the potentialities of the given situation. When the building operates as it should, the environment is not external but internal to it. If we insist on saying it is part of the landscape, we must also admit that it is also the terrain's *counterpart*, that the two are sides of one coin. Brighter light and cooler shadow depend on the sun screen. Similarly, the animation of the sanctuary depends on the breathing wall. More particularly, prayer on Klumb's account depends on breathing. The measured supply of its source was granted by the louvre walls. Yet when the building produces light and life, it demonstrates qualities it does not possess on its own, qualities it was not given *by design*, for it acts as if it were all-of-a-piece with its *milieu*, disposing itself into an inter-environmental system of correspondences. Father Maas praised Klumb's church for being 'perfectly matched to the surrounding neighbourhood.'[18] But this 'matching' is precisely what is difficult to understand, despite the fact that it is exceedingly obvious.

In unreflective experience neither the building, nor the *milieu*, obtrude themselves into one's awareness. During the liturgy, the service not the setting occupies one's attention, the latter is the material and durable aspect of the former. Focus on the service in its setting does not eliminate the presence of the architecture and landscape, but only treats them as topics of marginal awareness. The decisive characteristic of these margins is their indistinctness or seamlessness. This unity is a condition that *seems* to exist, for architecture can only act *as if* it were part of the natural world. As noted above, the vertical fins are means by which this is accomplished. While the building is not part of the environment – no one can sensibly deny that it was added to it – it presents itself as though it were coextensive with it. What Ricœur described as the 'paradox of fiction' (a productive reference to a world that does not in fact exist) has its parallel in this paradox of productive fusion, *an antecedent indivision disclosed by the building*. In its workings, the building is what it was designed to be, but it acts as if it were part of a world that was never designed. This is how architecture creates the 'atmosphere' of a situation, through its enactments, operations, or performances. Already in its mere functionality, then, the building finds itself taking on a role, acting a part that is not its own. This theatrical role is as much a metaphorical as a practical performance.

Legible operations

The building is thus already a symbolism, already a system of references beyond itself. This is by virtue of the metaphorical nature of some of its elements: in this instance, the breathing wall, in which both measure and rhythm are key. Imagine, one more time, a parishioner at prayer inside this building. The bench on which he or she sits is one of many that are spaced parallel to the regular intervals of the room's floor pattern. Its intervals, in turn, are based on the repetitive spacing and geometry of the vertical fins. Their configuration regulates the infiltration of light and air, which obviously have their source outside the building, even beyond the surrounding gardens, in the open expanse of the Bay of San Juan, at least the line of its shore. The sound of the surf is too distant to be heard inside the building, but the force of its breeze is strong enough to be felt. Just as trees and dust give shape to the wind, the building's louvered walls measure its flow. And they give it scale: what wind is for the world, breath is for the person. Breathing, in most religions, is the foundation of prayer because it is the cradle of rhythm or discipline. Klumb said as much when he observed that prayer depends on measured in- and exhalation.

Despite all its provisions, no building is sufficient for our expectations. Every architectural work suffers a constitutive and intolerable weakness at its core – no natural light, no fresh air, no views, and no real basis for renewal of its cultural heritage. Because of what it lacks, the building cannot escape behaving as if it were something other than it is, behaving as though it were part of the world around it, joined to what sustains and surpasses it. Klumb knew this, for he saw that care for the latent and inherited conditions of building would be necessary for architecture to 'express a way of life'. He once observed that beauty can be found in common things. He referred to this as an 'aesthetics of what there is'.[19]

Klumb worked in collaboration with local artists: a painter, sculptor, and Maas himself. Relief sculpture can be seen behind the altar and above the choir, and a statue of San Martin de Porres stands in the shrine, mediating the nave and the landscape or the church and the world. In post-war architectural debates, in the US and Europe, monumental expression was thought to result from the combination of artistic and functional elements; representational works were to be added to functional solutions as a supplementary form of compensation. Klumb's works cannot be identified with this notion of representation because they are inherently metaphorical, because they express not themselves but 'a way of life' – the latencies and cultural inheritance, the content of which always exceeds every showing, hence their inadequacy. Insofar as the building's performances call for it to act as if it were something it is not, part of the natural world and social *milieu*, the functional solution inaugurates representation. Metaphorical articulation is not supplementary to the enclosure of events; it is their visible face, an outward demonstrating or shining of the ways the building conditions, limits, or resists the energies of those events. The problem with twentieth-century functionalism is that it neglected the potential for metaphorical and symbolic meaning within the subject matter that is proper to architectural articulation. Representation in Klumb's work is not grafted onto the accommodation of pedestrian necessities, it is their legible aspect. Speaking more broadly, in architecture metaphor is neither optional nor conventional. It is a way of showing – articulating – what the building does, how it behaves in contrast to itself, as if it were part of the world it finds itself within but was added to. The building's investment in the unseen fullness of what 'there is' sets the stage for its settings to live and breathe as if they had arisen by virtue of nature itself.

Notes

1   Robert Rauschenberg, in *Sixteen Americans*, ed. by Dorothy C. Miller (New York: Museum of Modern Art, 1959), p. 58.
2   As characterised by Heidegger in his *Nietzsche*, vol. 1. Quoted in David Farrell Krell, 'Art and Truth in Raging Discord: Heidegger and Nietzsche on the Will to Power', *boundary 2*, 4, 2, Winter (1976): 378–92.
3   Recent scholarship is beginning to give Henry Klumb his due. The most thorough study to date is edited by Enrique Vivone, who also directs the archive at the University of Puerto Rico (AACUPR) where the Klumb materials are preserved. See Enrique Vivone (ed.), *Henry Klumb and the Poetic Exuberance of Architecture* (San Juan, Puerto Rico: AACUPR, 2006). See also the recent doctoral dissertation: Rosa Otero, *Permeable Walls and Place Recognition in Henry Klumb's Architecture of Social Concern* (University of Pennsylvania, 2005).
4   Le Corbusier, *Précisions* (Paris: Crès et Cie, 1930), p. 64.
5   Henry Klumb, cited in 'Iglesia Moderna: Arquitectura Funcional Avanca in PR', *Vision*, 3, August 22 (1952): 30. Translation by Juan Manuel Heredia.
6   Gen. 2:7.
7   Acts 2:2–6.
8   Marcolino Maas, 'The Sanctuary of Blessed Martin de Porres at Bayview, Puerto Rico', *Liturgical Arts*, November (1952): 5.
9   Reyner Banham, *The Architecture of the Well-tempered Environment* (Chicago: University of Chicago Press, 1969), p. 158.
10 Le Corbusier, *Précisions*, p. 66.
11 Marcel Breuer, *Sun and Shadow* (New York: Dodd, Mead & Company, 1955), p. 117.
12 Aladar and Victor Olgyay, *Solar Control and Shading Devices* (Princeton: Princeton University Press, 1957), p. 7.
13 Alan Colquhoun, 'The Significance of Le Corbusier', in *Modernity and the Classical Tradition* (Cambridge MA: MIT Press, 1989), p. 187.
14 That early modern architects in Brazil were key in the development of this solution has been persuasively demonstrated by Carlos Eduard Comas in 'Modern Architecture: Brazilian Corollary', *AA Files*, 36, Summer (1998): 3–13. Another Brazilian scholar, Margareth Campos da Silva Pereira, has shown how important a brief communication from Lucio Costa to Le Corbusier was in the very early history of the sun breaker. When advising Le Corbusier on the subject matter of his conferences for Brazilian architects, Costa suggested he not spend too much time discussing light, for the Brazilians had quite enough of that, and were wondering what to do with it – which is to say, how to reduce it, and its negative effects: 'Não falar muito de *Sol*! Temos sol até demais, e não sabemos o que fazer com ele.' Cited in *Le Corbusier e o Brasil* (São Paulo: Tessela, Projeto Editora, 1987), p. 146.
15 Paul Ricœur, 'The Function of Fiction in Shaping Reality', in *A Ricœur Reader* (Toronto: University of Toronto Press, 1991), p. 130.
16 Henry Klumb, 'My Architectural Design Philosophy'. Talk presented at the 65th annual FAIA convention, 2 October 1979. Quoted in Otero, *Permeable Walls*, p. 322.
17 Ernesto Grassi, *Rhetoric as Philosophy* (University Park, Pennsylvania State University Press, 1980), pp. 94ff.
18 Maas, 'The Sanctuary of Blessed Martin de Porres at Bayview', *ibid*.
19 Henry Klumb, 'My Architectural Design Philosophy' in Otero, *Permeable Walls*, p. 322.

Part one

Extraordinary buildings,
divergent readings

The first part of this book contains four close readings. They are readings of buildings and spaces designed by architects whose names are familiar from history books, practice monographs and journal articles; architects whose names have been admitted to the 'canon' of high culture because of their extraordinary projects. Where conventional architectural journalism can be over-generous to these famous architects and their 'landmark' projects – a phenomenon which Martin Pawley described as 'the strange death of architectural criticism'[1] – these essays show that close readings of architectural artefacts can yield interpretations which diverge from conventional wisdom, or from the rhetoric that architects use in relation to their own work.

The first chapter reads the CaixaForum art gallery in Madrid, reworked from a derelict power station by architects Herzog and De Meuron in a project celebrated by the global architectural media. It examines how the reworking embodies, simultaneously, the two key tactics used by post-war Western architects to make memorial architecture: the archaeological layering of building fabric; and the construction of 'other worlds' which aim to transport visitors into spaces of reflection. Reading the CaixaForum as a memorial, the chapter questions precisely what the gallery commemorates, and how its commemorative meaning might have shifted in the light of recent global events.

The subsequent chapter, by Edward Wainwright, concerns the Palace of Peace and Concord in Astana, Kazakhstan, a pyramid designed by architects Foster + Partners for President Nursultan Nazarbayev. The work of Foster + Partners is also fêted by the global architectural press, celebrated for consistently legible, transparent architecture across different building types and across the world. The pyramid – designed to house a triennial Congress of World Religions inaugurated by Nazarbayev in Astana – is clearly recognisable as a product of the Foster office. Wainwright examines how the pyramid is produced by, and produces, the rhetoric of transparency; and how it functions in projecting a post-Soviet national identity for Kazakhstan.

In Chapter 4, Suzanne Ewing reads a building by an architect who is, perhaps, a less 'famous name' than Herzog and De Meuron or Norman Foster, but whose work remains highly respected among professionals. She studies Sverre Fehn's Hamar Museum, exploring how the building reinvented its site. She examines how the architecture emphasises the ground and the horizon, encouraging the situation to be re-imagined as somehow more primal, the building somehow in immediate confrontation with the earth and sky. The site, Ewing argues, is never just found but is always invented in new ways by the architect. Indeed, she implies that the architect's cultural reading of the situation is a vital part of that process of invention.

Developing Ewing's interpretation of site, moving from the scale of the architectural object to the scale of landscape and climate – and echoing David Leatherbarrow's discussion of air and atmosphere – Jonathan Hill takes a journey from the 'presumptuous smoake' of seventeenth century London to the 'very clear air' of Houghton Hall and Holkham Hall in Norfolk.[2] Houghton was the subject of the first architectural book dedicated to a single British house and, like its near neighbour, embodied the dialogue between nature and culture that became 'one of the principal themes of the early eighteenth century'. One interior, the other exterior, Houghton and Holkham attest to the number of architectural authors at work. Seen in this light, authorship is multiplied and juxtaposed. Multiplied because, rather than a sole author, a number of authors are identified, including various designers, clients, builders and the weather. Juxtaposed because – sometimes competing, sometimes affirming – each authorial influence may appear to have informed or denied the others, in a conversation of various voices and unexpected conclusions.

These chapters raise important questions. To what extent can designers ever anticipate how their architecture will be read? Through a cultural reading of the situation, how can architecture come to re-invent its site? To what extent are canonical buildings produced out of their architect's rhetoric, and do they reproduce that rhetoric? Can architects who are immersed in one culture design successfully in another and, if so, how can they do it? Do architects inevitably reproduce their familiar cultural politics when they design, particularly when they are working in less familiar cultures? How do buildings attest to the multiple authors at work?

Notes

1   Martin Pawley, *The Strange Death of Architectural Criticism and Other Essays: Martin Pawley Collected Writings*, ed. by David Jenkins (London: Black Dog, 2007).
2   See also: Jonathan Hill, *Weather Architecture* (London: Routledge, 2012).

Chapter 2

An augury of collapse: Herzog and De Meuron's CaixaForum in Madrid

Adam Sharr

This chapter is about the CaixaForum art gallery in Madrid, a product of one of the world's most famous architecture brands: Herzog and De Meuron. Celebrated by the architectural media, the project was funded by – and bears the name of – Spain's largest savings bank. It opened in February 2008, at a time when the so-called 'credit crunch' was causing chaos in global financial markets. The CaixaForum was arguably the last major 'signature' project from the boom times to be completed before the recession hit in 2008, which many economists believe to have been the worst since the Great Depression of the 1930s.[1] I will argue that the CaixaForum can be read, in retrospect, as an augury of collapse, as a curiously prescient anticipation of disaster.[2]

La Caixa buys a Herzog and De Meuron

La Caixa Group is Spain's largest savings bank and its third largest financial institution, with more than 5,500 branches. In 2008, it had a turnover of €411,522 million.[3] Despite (or perhaps because of) its size, the organisation remains quick to highlight its corporate social responsibility, keen to point out its mid-nineteenth-century origins offering credit and savings facilities to poor families.[4] In memory of these origins – La Caixa claims – it funds and controls the Caixa Foundation, Spain's biggest private foundation. According to the European Foundation, this is the fifth largest in the world in terms of budgetary volume.[5] The Caixa Foundation runs a social welfare programme with four stated aims: 'attending the main social problems [sic]; training for all kinds of groups; care and preservation of the environment; and, dissemination of culture'.[6] Following this last commitment, it manages a large private art collection on behalf of the bank. This is exhibited free to the public at the CaixaForum gallery in Barcelona, the bank's home city, and also, from 2008, at the CaixaForum in Madrid.

  The sociologist Pierre Bourdieu has argued that, in Western societies, the dominant realm of financial services – what he refers to as the economic field[7] – is approached in power and influence only by the fields of art and high culture.[8] Power relations in all these fields operate similarly, he has claimed, crystallising around the competing consumption of goods, resources and values.[9] Those immersed in the fields of art and high culture have tended to see banks as vulgar. But by trading in art – especially in contemporary art which can be portrayed as *avant-garde* – financial institutions have an opportunity to accrue a different sort of capital, distinguishing their cultural credentials.[10] Banks can demonstrate good taste and perspicacious judgement with their art collections, which allow them to cultivate an image as magnanimous patrons. Moreover, art, as traded on the markets, has asset value and can be understood readily by bankers as a commodity like any other. Thus, just as some wealthy individuals acquire art works for their speculative commercial value and their potential to display cultural capital, so too do large organisations like banks.[11] La Caixa seems to have been aware for some time of the potential for art and artists to embellish its self-proclaimed social mission and to broaden its reputation from fiscal expertise into high culture: it commissioned its logo from the artist Joan Miró in 1980, partly in a demonstration of Catalan patriotism but also as a display of cultural patronage.[12].

At this intersection of high finance and high culture, buying architecture as art is arguably as important as buying artworks. The architectural canon bulges with projects commissioned by financial institutions, from John Soane's work for the Bank of England in the eighteenth century to numerous twentieth-century examples including Richard Rogers' Lloyd's of London and Norman Foster's HSBC headquarters in Hong Kong. Particularly in the post-war era, banks have bought work from famous architectural brands in order to bolster the cultural credit of their own brand. Herzog and De Meuron, distinguished by a litany of architectural awards including the Pritzker Prize in 2001, was clearly a reliable choice for La Caixa. Its work has had global reach and media appeal, attested by commissions such as the Tate Modern gallery in London, the Prada store in Tokyo's Ometesando Hills (Figure 2.1) and the 'Bird's Nest' Olympic Stadium in Beijing. The decision to buy an H&DeM was predictably

Figure 2.1 The H&deM brand alongside the Prada brand at their store in Tokyo's Omotesando Hills

unpredictable; the building would undoubtedly have both popular and expert capital as an edgy contemporary art object but it would also be delivered reliably, more-or-less on time and budget, with assured media attention. For both brand and cultural reasons, it was therefore no risk – or perhaps only the most reliable of risks – for the Caixa Foundation to hire Herzog and de Meuron for their new gallery in Madrid.

Theatrical idiosyncrasies

The CaixaForum is conspicuously branded, displaying the bank's Miró logo in neon. It is set back from the Paseo del Prado – Madrid's famous boulevard of museums and galleries – and reworks the derelict Mediodía power station bought by La Caixa in 2001. The structure dates from 1899, designed by architect Jesús Carrasco-Muñoz Encina and engineer José María Hernández.[13] It primarily comprised one large volume under two parallel pitched roofs, with thick walls in red brick sat on a rusticated stone plinth. By the time of its purchase – although it was disused and its roof was in an advanced state of disrepair – the structure had been listed by the city's civic authorities.

The Herzog and de Meuron project involved hollowing out what remained of the brick shell, excavating beneath the building to deepen its basement and doubling its volume with a substantial rooftop extension (Figure 2.2). Most provocatively, the design removed the power station's rusticated stone plinth in order to open up the 'excavated' space left behind to the air, making a public plaza beneath the building's bulk which extends down to the Paseo del Prado. To achieve this, the thick brick walls were cantilevered out using concrete and steel (Figure 2.3). These cantilevers test the limits of structural possibility because of the mass supported and the distances involved, yet the necessary shear walls, struts, brackets and pins are hidden from view. To achieve these cantilevers whilst simultaneously building above and digging beneath was no small constructional accomplishment, achieved at no small cost. It would have undoubtedly been cheaper – and it would probably have been more appropriate for the artworks displayed – if the power station had been demolished and a new gallery built instead. While the existing building was listed (at a low grade), a persuasive case for replacement could undoubtedly have been made by a rich bank aspiring to build a national cultural institution. Instead, both architect and client seem to have enjoyed the possibility of reworking, conspicuously, a building from the past.

In post-war architectural practice, there have been arguably two primary tactics by which architects have sought conspicuously to deal with the past.[14] The first – seen for example at Carlo Scarpa's reworking of the Castelvecchio in Verona, at Sverre Fehn's Hamar Museum and at Peter Zumthor's Kolumba Diocesan Museum in Cologne– involves articulating new fabric around, and on top of, existing fabric in order to make a series of layers, and tell stories about those layers. This architecture of curated archaeology stands in contrast to the second tactic, used in Berlin by Daniel Libeskind at the Jewish Museum and by

Figure 2.2 The CaixaForum from Paseo del Prado, showing the 'excavated' plinth and rooftop extension in corten steel. The planted gable end to the right encloses a new public space in front of the gallery

Figure 2.3 Brickwork is supported on an almost unbelievable cantilever

Peter Eisenman (initially in collaboration with Richard Serra) at the Memorial to the Murdered Jews of Europe. These projects involve making other worlds which aim to dislocate their inhabitants from the site for a time in the hope of prompting reflection. While first approach – that of Scarpa, Fehn and Zumthor – serves to amplify the traces of the past apparent on site, the second approach – that of Libeskind and Eisenman – aims to subsume visitors' appreciation of the site into another experience; to make another world which is internalised according to its own intellectual system, its own *schema*. The CaixaForum employs simultaneously both of these commemorative tactics. To appreciate how it does so, it is necessary to give quite a detailed account of the reworked building. A description of the gallery follows, moving from bottom to top (Figure 2.4).

The basement of the CaixaForum has two levels containing an auditorium, dressing rooms and storage, its spaces set out by the concrete shear walls that transmit the weight of both new and existing structures to the foundations. The public plaza at ground level – carved out beneath the looming mass of the former power station – is a horizontal slice of space punctured by three stair cores which also bear the structural loads of the building above. Because of the slope of the adjacent streets and the stepping geometry of the power station's obliterated plinth, the undulating ceiling of the plaza becomes so low in places

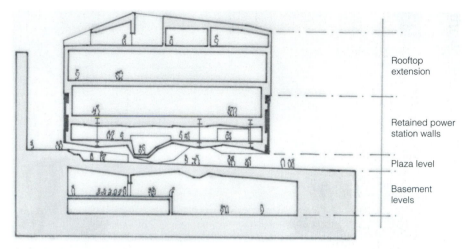

Rooftop
extension

Retained power
station walls

Plaza level

Basement
levels

Figure 2.4 Section through the CaixaForum

that adults cannot stand beneath it. Its soffit is clad in stainless steel plate welded together to form a continuous faceted surface; a treatment which also wraps the main entrance stair, giving the appearance that walls and ceiling together comprise one single folded plane (Figure 2.5). The steel surface extends to the edge of the cantilevered brickwork and wraps up around it by one course, a device which, crucially, seems to dematerialise the walls' mass, effectively rendering the masonry as another inscrutable surface like the folded soffit (Figure 2.6). This impression is compounded by the treatment of the original and new window openings. The originals are infilled flush to the face of the wall with matching bricks, emphasising the continuity of the brick plane. Four new openings are then gouged out, not following the rhythm of the original openings but instead relating to another compositional logic deriving from the new floors inserted behind. These openings cut – almost randomly it would seem – through existing cills and lintels, involving further structural gymnastics.

Two floors are located within the remaining power station shell, set to new floor and ceiling heights. These floors are internalised like the basement levels, lit and ventilated largely by artificial means. The lower of these two floors – reached by a twisting entrance stair almost at the centre of the plan – is the building's foyer. Even in order to enter the basement auditorium, visitors climb up to this foyer before descending back through one of the other cores. Above it is the first gallery level whose plan largely comprises a single 'white box' space, subdivided with temporary partitions to suit each exhibition fit-out.

Working up the building, we reach the rooftop extension. This is a steel framed structure whose top floor appears irregularly eroded, making a complex skyline. Structurally, this extension bears off both the concrete cores and the power station's cantilevered brick walls. It is clad with square corten steel panels

Figure 2.5 The space 'excavated' beneath the gallery, showing the folded stainless soffit which also wraps the stair core housing the main entrance

Figure 2.6 The stainless steel soffit wraps the edge of the brickwork

set out according to a geometry independent of the primary structure below or behind. Around a third of the panels are perforated with a pixellated pattern. These cover window openings, the pattern serving to conceal rather than reveal window locations (Figure 2.7). Again, the external finish is expressed as a continuous enigmatic surface. Curiously perhaps, the plan of the gallery floor in the rooftop structure is almost identical to the one below it in the retained shell. The top floor, meanwhile, contains the only naturally lit spaces in the building – a café, restaurant, offices and a VIP lounge – whose geometries are determined as much by the visual composition of the rooftop mass as by any logic of functional planning.

The reworked building's interiors are strangely unrelated to its façades, and are equally idiosyncratic. There are four interior themes, related to use but largely independent of external expression. The first is found in the foyer – whose shop, reception and cloakroom are expressed as furniture objects in veneered ply beneath a diagrid of fluorescent strip lights. The second theme occurs in the basement, where the auditorium and its foyer are lined in undulating corten mesh – a miniaturised echo of the rooftop cladding – with a polished hardwood floor. The third – gallery – theme is white, with plasterboard linings, painted concrete soffits and polyester powder coated floor panels. Services are concealed and fittings are mostly recessed here, as they are in the basement. The final theme is that of the rooftop rooms, with a timber boarded floor, white ceiling and floor-to-ceiling glass panels behind the fretted corten cladding. Some connection with the outside is permitted here, although it is hard to make out much of the view through the pixellated pattern.

Figure 2.7 The pixellated cladding of the rooftop extension seen from outside (left) and inside (right)

Not only are the interiors are almost wholly independent of the exterior, there are remarkably few opportunities for visitors to orientate one with respect to the other. The only possible views out are through the pixellated cladding on the top floor and from the four large openings cut through the brick shell. Importantly, the brickwork walls, which are so striking outside, can never be seen from inside: the corten rooftop extension begins from the outermost extent of the corbelled brick mouldings, and the splayed reveals of the four punched openings are lined with a metal pressing that covers the brickwork.

This necessarily detailed account of the CaixaForum demonstrates the project's rejection of key modernist doctrines: the idea of truth to materials; and the concern with the honest visual expression of function. Instead, the building seems concerned with surprise and excess. It is highly theatrical, conspicuously performing – and performed by – its visitors. Indeed, it has all the hallmarks of a would-be blockbuster, a lavish production showing off all the latest special effects.

Is the CaixaForum a memorial?

Predictably, this big-budget production attracted the attention of the global media when it first opened to the public.[15] Published images mostly showed the principal elevation of the CaixaForum, celebrating the homogenising corten cladding of the rooftop extension and the shadow gap of the plaza, emphasising the retained shell. Photographs focused on the brickwork's infilled openings and the new cuts in its surface, highlighting the building's apparent self-consciousness about its own past. Journalists' texts also concentrated on the building's exteriors and the conspicuous reworking of the power station shell. Thus, in words and pictures, the media initiated the CaixaForum into the canon of post-war buildings which seek to make the past apparent, aligning its fabric with the architectural archaeology of Scarpa's and Fehn's work where new fabric is built onto old in order to display layers of history, one on top of the next.

But the CaixaForum has an uneasy relationship with this particular canon. At Scarpa's Castelvecchio and Fehn's Hamar Museum, for example, at least as much archaeological storytelling occurs internally as externally.[16] Historic fabric is celebrated and expressed, and new work is clearly differentiated from old. In the Herzog and De Meuron project, while the brick shell is obviously reworked to make the alterations apparent externally – while it has clearly been accorded value – the interior of the shell is covered up and is accorded no value at all. This curiosity is compounded by other architectural decisions. The decision to retain the shell was expensive, especially considering the structural gymnastics necessary to make the plaza and rooftop extension. To pay it so much reverence, and then to punch through new openings ignoring the rhythm of the old, appears incongruously irreverent. Likewise, paying so much attention to the brickwork and then obliterating the rusticated stone plinth seems odd. If this is archaeology, then its values are selective and inscrutable.

The CaixaForum's hermetic interiors also recall the other familiar memorial tactic of post-war architectural practice: the introspective world-making of Daniel Libeskind's Jewish Museum and Peter Eisenman's Memorial to the Murdered Jews of Europe – projects which aim to dislocate people from the city for a time, transporting them into the vicarious experience of trauma.[17] Partly because of the atrocity of the Holocaust that both projects memorialise in different ways, their intellectual reasoning serves to un-site the architectural fabric as much as to site it. But they are not so much fragments of apocalyptic worlds (as they are sometimes described) as experiences which diminish the forces of location, wrenching visitors away from the specifics of the site to inspire reflection.[18] It is uncomfortable to compare the CaixaForum with these projects; commemorating a power station in Madrid and commemorating the deportations and mass murder of the Holocaust are hardly equal tasks. Yet the gallery appears to pursue the same architectural tactic with its internalised, introvert interiors. This almost hermetic world obeys its own logic, or multiple logics, independent of the exterior and almost wholly detached from the site and the city. Like the Libeskind and Eisenman projects, the gallery's interiors transport visitors somewhere else – into the display of art capital, here, rather than into the vicarious experience of trauma.

Thus, the CaixaForum employs – at great structural expense – not just one but *both* of the key post-war architectural commemorative strategies, attempting to exploit them simultaneously. But, while the building appears to have been conceived as a memorial, its commemorations don't seem much related to the locality. The Mediodía power station was certainly stitched into the social history of the city, its fabric describing nineteenth-century aspirations to civic social improvement in Madrid. However, the structure itself was relatively anonymous. Hidden away a block behind the Paseo del Prado, it was by no means an urban landmark like the Bankside power station in London which Herzog and De Meuron had previously transformed into a gallery for the Tate. And the structure would have been so much cheaper to demolish than rework, and the regeneration argument for a new art gallery so strong, that the effort involved in its retention and manipulation seems disproportionate. The project's disconnections of interior from exterior, and its literal and metaphorical undermining of the power station shell, are intellectual games that seem to owe more to the global market of branded novelty architecture – to the power of the economic field and the field of high culture – than to the specifics of the Mediodía power station and its surrounding streets.

So to summarise, when the CaixaForum is first encountered, it appears to express the past in the spirit of Scarpa, Fehn and Zumthor, its pattern of new and infilled openings displaying an architectural archaeology. But the project's archaeology has a surprisingly modest story to tell about the 'found' artefact and its site. Simultaneously, its largely hermetic interiors deploy Libeskind's and Eisenman's other-worlding tactic, although this other world does not have the commemorative impact of its more loaded siblings. While the project goes to great lengths to dramatise commemoration, its reasons for doing so are ambiguous. As a memorial, the CaixaForum is curiously reticent about what it actually commemorates.

Memorial capacities

James E. Young has reviewed the status of memorials in the late twentieth century. Drawing from examples which include the work of Libeskind and Eisenman in Berlin, he suggests why the figurative memorials of the nineteenth and early twentieth century – the stereotypical men on plinths in bronze – have more recently been rejected in favour of other, more complex, signifiers:

> The status of monuments in the twentieth century remains double-edged and is fraught with an essential tension: outside of those nations with totalitarian pasts, the public and governmental hunger for traditional, self-aggrandising monuments is matched only by the contemporary artists' scepticism of the monument. As a result, even as monuments continue to be commissioned and designed by governments and public agencies eager to assign singular meaning to complicated events and people, artists increasingly plant in them the seeds of self-doubt and impermanence. The state's need for monuments is acknowledged, even as the traditional forms and functions of monuments are increasingly challenged. Monuments at the end of the twentieth century are thus born resisting the very premises of their birth. Thus, the monument has increasingly become the site of contested and competing meanings, more likely the site of cultural conflict than one of shared national values and ideals.[19]

Young argues that historians, artists and critics have sought increasingly to demonstrate the complexities of events, their political difficulties and contradictions. And so the creators of memorials have also become more conscious of the politics surrounding the processes of making memorials, questioning who remembers what, for whom, and why. Contemporary memorials are frequently concerned less with the transmission of intended meaning than contrived as devices which encourage people to read shifting, complex and contingent meanings into them. Young writes:

> The most important 'space of memory' for these artists has not been the space in the ground or above it but the space between the memorial and the viewer, between the viewer and his or her own memory: the place of the memorial in the viewer's mind, heart and conscience.[20]

Recognising their opposition to traditional figurative memorials, Young names these memorials of invitation 'countermemorials'.

It could be argued that the CaixaForum is the definitive countermemorial. Both of the key post-war architectural memorial tactics operate in parallel here while, to some extent, each also undermines the other. The obsessive detachment of interior from exterior serves to hide rather than display much of the archaeological story of the brickwork and its retention, opening up its narrative possibilities to question. The obvious manipulation of the brick shell sets up prior expectations for visitors that something strange is going on and, in doing so, undermines the difference of the interior when it is encountered, again opening up its narrative capacity to question. Moreover, the CaixaForum's conspicuous memorialising only highlights the ambiguity of what it actually serves to commemorate. If countermemorials actively seek to undermine singular attributions of meaning, then what better than one which is so ambiguous that, in the end, it commemorates little more or less than itself? In Young's terms, the space between memorial and viewer is thrown wide open, asking the visitor to puzzle out what the building is, and why it is like it is.

I would argue, however, that any such interpretation is misguided. The suggestion that ambiguity is end enough, in itself, for a memorial seems too glib. Indeed, to elide the CaixaForum with recent countermemorials potentially robs the events that those structures commemorate of their significance. Memorials that remain self-aware of the social and political circumstances of their own birth must be more potent. But taking that self-awareness so far that they become monuments only to the idea of memorialisation – so they become only empty signifiers – is a vain intellectual game.

Most memorials are made because people feel the need to commemorate people or events, because they have a deep sense that some loss or action must be remembered. Thus, memorials are testament to conviction; and the power of that conviction remains the primary impulse of any commemorative act. So a largely empty memorial can only strip conviction of significance. I would argue that, when it was built, the CaixaForum – making a dramatic show out of minimal resonance – was neither memorial nor countermemorial. Instead, it seems to have been a counter-countermemorial, undermining itself – effectively cancelling itself out – with its own double negative.

In the short time since the completion and publication of the CaixaForum in 2008, however, its circumstances have changed. In the context of global financial collapse, it seems to have acquired a newer and more potent significance.

An augury

The wealth of international banks like La Caixa, and confidence in them, plummeted in the global financial crisis.[21] Journalists have accused the financial services markets of causing the catastrophe by their intransigence and hubris, as evidenced by the lavish salaries and bonuses that bank executives agreed to pay themselves.[22] As taxpayers' money continues to be used by Western governments to bail out banks' huge debts while bankers keep their personal wealth, cultural critics and some economists have called for a wholesale rethinking of economic and political priorities.[23] The widely unchallenged dominance of the economic field has been thrown into sharper relief. The idea of a bank as a speculator, rather than just a straightforward provider of savings and mortgages, has been found wanting. Similarly, the idea of a bank intent on using fine art as cultural capital to demonstrate its virility in competition with other banks has grown more distasteful. To savers made redundant, or borrowers whose houses are repossessed, the thought of their bank using art and architecture as trophies to gild its brand and position itself within its own field must seem another sign of financial institutions' remoteness from everyday life. Distant, inaccessible, unsympathetic; games played between banks and bankers involving sums of incomprehensible magnitude have come to stand as testament to excess. Resulting public anger shows little sign of diminishing, demonstrated in Spain by the protest group '*los Indignados*' ('the indignant') who, for example, organised national marches of the unemployed and who occupied Madrid's Puerta del Sol in July 2011.[24]

In more straitened times, the conspicuous lavishness of the CaixaForum is painfully apparent. The unashamed expense of its structural dramatics, the multiple architectural idioms involved, the project's indulgence – to ambiguous ends – in not just one architectural memorial tactic but two, stand as testament to vanity and hubris. They demonstrate the obsession of the gallery's promoters with the competitive fields of financial and cultural capital to the exclusion of more everyday priorities. The distance between bank and customer – between expensively endowed gallery and visitor – has grown in intensity.

But, as Young points out, it is distances like these which afford opportunities for recollection. They open up the mental spaces which prompt individuals to reflect, the spaces in which memorials aquire their authority. In the space revealed by the new nakedness of the financial services industry, Madrid's CaixaForum – which was arguably a memorial empty of commemoration – has acquired a more potent meaning. It has come to stand for its promoters' jostling for position in the economic and cultural fields. Its new circumstances ask us to read it differently: as a memorial to the excesses of high finance at the birth of the new millennium.

The story of the CaixaForum illustrates how fluid a building's interpretation can be, how architectural fabric can accommodate very different readings even in a short history – shifting in this case from the apparent display of corporate magnanimity to the display of vanity and hubris. It also illustrates how widely readings can diverge from the intentions of client and architect.

Any architectural design inevitably anticipates a future. But that future is always bound up with the past: no architect can escape their education and the cultural currents in which they work; and no site is without traces of history, whether physically apparent or constituted in stories that leave no trace. And, while some projects negotiate past and future only implicitly, others – like this one – seek to do so more conspicuously. In 2008, the CaixaForum was a memorial with an ambiguous connection to the past. But our present, occasioned by global financial collapse, has equipped it with a new future as a potent memorial. However, it is perhaps surprising that no one in the recent past – journalist, architect or client – read the project as an augury of imminent collapse. Surely, whenever financial institutions lavish huge resources on gilding their self-image, whenever they indulge so conspicuously in the accumulation of trophy art and architecture, it can only ever be a premonition of disaster?

NOTES

1   Howard Davies, *The Financial Crisis: Who is to Blame?* (London: Polity, 2010); George Soros, *The New Paradigm for Financial Markets: The Credit Crunch of 2008 and What it Means* (New York: PublicAffairs, 2008).

2   By no means does this reading accord with the architects' own reading of their project. Their description of it is couched in terms that mix publicity with art criticism, as characterises much architectural journalism: 'The only material of the old power station that we could use was the classified brick shell. In order to conceive and insert the new architectural components of the CaixaForum Project, we began with a surgical operation, separating and removing the base and the parts of the building no longer needed. This opened a completely novel and spectacular perspective that simultaneously solved a number of problems posed by the site. The removal of the base of the building left a covered plaza under the brick shell, which now appears to float above the street level. This sheltered space under the CaixaForum offers its shade to visitors who want to spend time or meet outside and is at the same time the entrance to the Forum itself. Problems such as the narrowness of the surrounding streets, the placement of the main entrance, and the architectural identity of this contemporary art institution could be addressed and solved in a single urbanistic and sculptural gesture'. Herzog and De Meuron Architects at: http://www.arcspace.com/architects/herzog_meuron/caixa/caixa.html [accessed: 12.08.09].

3   http://www.lacaixa.com/corporate/home_en.html [accessed: 31.07.09].

4   http://www.lacaixa.com/corporate/obrasocial_en.html [accessed: 31.07.09].

5   Ibid.

6   Ibid.

7   Angela McRobbie, *The Uses of Cultural Studies* (London: Sage, 2005), pp. 130–131.

8   Pierre Bourdieu, *Distinction: A Social Critique of the Judgement of Taste*, trans. by Richard Nice (London: Routledge, 1984); Pierre Bourdieu, 'Outline of a Sociological Theory of Art Perception', trans. by Randal Johnson, in *The Field of Cultural Production* (Cambridge: Polity, 2003), pp. 215–237.

9   Writing about Bourdieu's thinking, Lois McNay suggests that: 'The distribution of certain types of capital – economic, social, cultural and symbolic – denotes the different goods, resources and values around which power relations in a particular field crystallise. Any field is marked by a tension or conflict between the interests of different groups who struggle to gain control over a field's capital. In the final instance, all fields are determined by the demands of the capitalist system of accumulation, however, each field is autonomous in that it has a specific internal logic which establishes non-synchronous, uneven relations with other fields and which renders it irreducible to any overarching dynamic.' Cited in: McRobbie, *The Uses of Cultural Studies*, pp. 130–131.

10 For a discussion of Bourdieu's thinking in relation to architecture, see: Helena Webster, *Bourdieu for Architects* (London: Routledge, 2010).

11 Bourdieu deals with these mechanisms at length in his book: *The Rules of Art: Genesis and Structure of the Literary Field*, trans. by Susan Emanuel (Cambridge: Polity, 1996).

12 Miró's cultural politics are traced in a collection of essays by Matthew Gale and Marko Daniel (eds), *Joan Miró: The Ladder of Escape* (London: Tate Publishing, 2011).

13 Roger de Llúria, 'Centro Social y Cultural CaixaForum en Madrid: Herzog & de Meuron Architectos', *On Diseño*, 292, 2007: 152–183.

14 I have developed this idea further in the context of Berlin in: Adam Sharr, 'The Sedimentation of Memory', *Journal of Architecture*, 15, 4 (2010): 499–515.

15 In Britain, for example, reviews appeared in the architecture columns of *The Guardian* and *The Times* newspapers; in Germany in *Die Welt*, *Süddeutsche Zeitung* and *Frankfurter Allgemeine Zeitung*. Articles in the architectural press include: David Cohn, 'CaixaForum, Madrid, Spain', *Architectural Record*, June (2008): 108–120; Michael Webb, 'Cultural Levitation', *Architectural Review*, 1336, June (2008): 46–52; Dominique Boudet, 'CaixaForum, Madrid; Architects: Herzog & de Meuron', *Moniteur Architecture AMC*, 181, September (2008):

146–156; Juan Salgado, 'Madrid; Herzog and de Meuron, *Architecture Today*, 187, April (2008): 12–17.

16 See for example: Richard Murphy, *Carlo Scarpa and the Castelvecchio* (London: Architectural Press, 1991); Christian Norberg-Schulz and Gennaro Postiglione, *Sverre Fehn: Works, Projects, Writings, 1949–1996* (London: The Monacelli Press, 1997).

17 Andreas Huyssen, *Twilight Memories: Marking Time in a Culture of Amnesia* (London: Routledge, 1995).

18 Martin Jay, 'The Apocalyptic Imagination and the Ability to Mourn,' in *Force Fields: Between Intellectual History and Cultural Critique* (London: Routledge, 2003); Saul Friedländer, Gerald Holton, Leo Marx and Eugene Skolnikoff (eds), *Visions of Apocalypse: End or Rebirth* (New York: Holmes and Meier, 1985).

19 James E. Young, *At Memory's Edge: After Images of the Holocaust in Contemporary Art and Architecture* (New Haven: Yale, 2000), p. 118.

20 Ibid.

21 Davies, *The Financial Crisis*.

22 By way of extended example of the huge amount of newsprint produced, see two books by financial journalists: Robert Peston, *Who Runs Britain? And Who's to Blame for the Economic Mess We're In?* (London: Hodder, 2008); Alex Brummer, *The Crunch: How Greed and Incompetence Sparked the Credit Crisis* (London: Random House, 2009).

23 Andrew Gamble, *The Spectre at the Feast: Capitalist Crisis and the Politics of Recession* (London: Palgrave Macmillan, 2009).

24 See the news report in Spain's *El Pais* newspaper: http://www.elpais.com/articulo/madrid/Riadas/indignados/recorren/Madrid/elpepiespmad/20110620elpmad_1/Tes [accessed: 25.07.11].

Chapter 3

Fostering relations in Kazakhstan

Edward Wainwright

Kazakhstan gained its independence from the USSR in 1991. Following ten years of political and economic turmoil, the country experienced a period of dramatic growth. Political stability brought economic development, and a middle class established itself following the emergence of oligarchs and oil barons. The initial free-market rush has now calmed and the nation claims that its financial model is derived from that of Norway, with vast reserves of oil and mineral deposits to secure its economic future. It is also a large country: its total area, at 2.7 million sq km, is approximately the size of Western Europe; and its population in 2008 was 15 million.[1]

Positioned on axis with the Presidential Palace (Figure 3.1) and government offices in Astana – the new capital of Kazakhstan, built largely from scratch – is the Palace of Peace and Concord (Figure 3.2), a project conceived by President Nursultan Nazarbayev and designed by architects Foster + Partners. The Palace

Figure 3.1 The Presidential Palace, Astana, with which the Palace of Peace and Concord is aligned

Figure 3.2 The Palace of Peace and Concord, Foster + Partners, Astana, Kazakhstan

takes the form of a pyramid. Opened in 2006, it was commissioned to provide a permanent home for the Congress of Leaders of World and Traditional Religions.[2] It provides a visual termination to the newly constructed 'mall' which houses much of Kazakhstan's recently relocated government. Standing isolated on a small hill, the pyramid strikes an aggressively isolationist pose. It forms an important part of this new 'city of the Steppe'; the city that is the 'centrepiece of the official nation-building project' of the country.

Like many Foster + Partners projects around the world, the project emphasises material transparency – through the use of glass and other smooth reflective surfaces, and in the visual expression of structure. These materials project an image of technology and global modernity which – in association with interior atrium voids and the views they afford into multiple spaces – becomes equated in Foster buildings with democratic transparency.[3] Rationality, singularity of focus, clarity and homogeneity are central to the pyramid project, which plays out the notion of transparency as rationality and order as discussed by the theorist Henri Lefebvre.[4]

The President's pyramid

Initiated by President Nazarbayev, the Congress was established as a triennial event, designed to function as an international forum for religious leaders to meet and discuss ways of encouraging tolerance and understanding between faiths.[5] It first met in Astana in September 2003. By the time of the Second Congress in September 2006, the event was accommodated in its newly constructed home and attended by delegates representing Islam, Christianity, Buddhism, Judaism, Shintoism, Taoism and Hinduism.[6] Each meeting focuses on producing a united declaration which progresses the Congress's aim of improved stability and security.[7]

The Congress' physical location in the country, and in Astana, was initiated by the President. The pyramid is situated on the eastern side of the Isihm River at what is currently the extremity of the city, although urban development is set to continue eastwards, to engulf a group of small villages as it expands from its current population of 600,000 to approximately 1.2 million. The project's basic form was conceived by Nazarbayev and the design contract was awarded to Foster + Partners following an approach from Sembol Construction.[8] The President's initial premise was to mimic the proportions of the Great Pyramid of Cheops which, at fourteen times the size of the final scheme, would have been capable of accommodating 80,000 people at its base. His ownership of the scheme, and its conception, is inscribed in the mythology of the institution and its home, establishing a relationship between the goals of the Congress, the institution of the President and his nation-building project. As Nazarbayev suggested in an address to the Kazakh nation:

> Consistency is the main rule for our fast development in the modern world for the next ten years.
>
> All prerequisites are available to us.
>
> We possess vast territory, favourable geographic, transport and communications locations, and considerable natural resources.
>
> We have achieved a leading role in the regional economy, constructive relations with international partners, political, social and economic stability.[9]

Leading roles with international partners are only possible, he claimed, with stability. The programme of 'comprehensive accelerated modernisation of Kazakhstan'[10] requires the peaceful acceptance of the ideals of modernisation by the populous, as well as the continued confidence of Western investors in the country. This confidence is established through both policy and projects; implemented projects and built projects.

Initiated in the summer of 2004, the project's design development and construction were rapid, the final stages requiring the mobilisation of the Kazakhstan army to assist with completion.[11]

A diagram of light and transparency

Structurally, the building is supported on a concrete base buried in the artificial hill on which the upper pyramid sits (Figure 3.3). A 1,500-seat concert hall occupies this subterranean space. The hall and congress areas are accessed

Figure 3.3 The Palace of Peace and Concord sits atop an artificial hill, housing an auditorium and lobby spaces

through Mayan-like cuts in this mound.[12] The pyramid has a steel frame structure which is infilled with granite-faced pre-cast concrete cladding panels and low-level glazed diamond windows that admit light into the central atrium. Other than these openings, the sides of the pyramid are uninterrupted from the top of the mound to the apex, where twelve glazed panels light the uppermost congress chamber.

The pyramid is approached from a snow-blown road which appears to be cut into the concrete base. Visitors enter through tinted glass swing doors, where the contrast of dark and brightness is great. The reflective quality of the light grey snow-covered concrete court outside contrasts starkly with the dark-wood and black-granite clad interior. Visitors' eyes take time to adjust. Details swim into focus until the scale and depth of the subterranean lobby is visible. According to the building's guide, the contrast between the dark base and light apex of the pyramid represents the 'shared views that all life and religions have, of darkness being hell, the middle ground being life and the top, the light, heaven.'[13] This narrative echoes Lefebvre's analysis of transparent conditions, which indicate the prevalence of a positivist, redemptive approach to light that equates illumination with virtue.[14]

The main route from the dark undercroft passes through the 'learning' and 'shared experiences of life' which, the guide argues, are evoked in the main atrium, up to the epiphanic space of the Congress Chamber. This is where the representatives of the World Religions meet and, through consensus, issue their declarations of 'peace and concord'. The sequence of spaces is choreographed

Figure 3.4 The apex, with stained glass 'Doves of Peace' by artist Brian Clark

largely through light and contrast. When, eventually, the upper chamber is reached, the stark brilliance of snow-reflected light streaming through stained glass displaying super-sized Doves of Peace – by glass artist Brian Clark – is blinding (Figure 3.4). The apex of the pyramid is the only materially transparent part of the building. By night, it offers a glowing indication of the presence of the pyramid to the city and, by day, it admits some light into the atrium.

Conceptually and programmatically, the pyramid is defined by its central void. Sixty metres above the floor is the oculus, the structure that holds the round table used for religious discussion. The table doubles as a lens for admitting light into the void space: diffuse, pale blue and yellow-white illumination, likened to being underwater by Ellis Woodman of *Building Design* magazine.[15] The oculus is supported at four points by what the guides call the 'hands of peace' (Figure 3.5); structural supports in the frame. The void of the central atrium is echoed by the void of the oculus, framing a view from the

Figure 3.5 The winter garden, directly below the 'hands of peace' that hold the congressional table/oculus

atrium floor to the bright glow of the upper chamber. Light is used here to demarcate the hierarchy established by programme, function and space. Light is tied, symbolically, to the activities of the Congress, to the conceptual demands of the programme and to the implied philosophical ordering of the building. Light defines, through its absence at the basis of the pyramid and its increasing presence as visitors ascend, the significance of the spaces within. This reinforces the diagrammatic hierarchy imposed by the pyramidal form. Woodman writes:

> [David] Nelson's [a senior partner in Foster + Partners] point is a functional one. 'We liked the hierarchical disposition of the pyramid,' he explains. 'The top is clearly the most important part and the base is broader. It is a perfect hierarchical diagram. We could therefore dedicate a space at the top to a focused religious activity and accommodate large gatherings at the base.'[16]

The architecture here renders an organisational diagram into physical form. Just as the city of Astana is itself conceived as a diagram for a 'new' Kazakhstan, the hierarchical quality of the pyramid is conceived as an ideological tool: the president presides over this building, and the culminating position – the apex – is dramatically transparent. This 'perfect hierarchical diagram' is made manifest through light and dark. Through brightness, the pinnacle of both the structure, the purpose of the congress and the superficial equation of religion with light are set into operation. Activity in the atrium becomes focused (both metaphorically and literally) up into the oculus above. From this point of focus, the agenda of the Congress is concretised into its declarations, proclaimed to the world through global media. Symbolically and practically, the messages of unity, peace, stability, security – the outcomes of the Congress – are broadcast from this beacon; signals of a progressive liberalism that originate from the host country: Kazakhstan.

Secondary spaces

The atrium void is surrounded by smaller side halls, where exhibitions and models of future developments in Astana and Kazakhstan are situated (Figure 3.6). Pictures of the President invoke his relationship with the future of Kazakhstan's built infrastructure. Flanking these models and exhibitions are the diamond windows which admit ethereal luminescence into the halls. With the snow-covered mound outside reflecting white light through these windows, the contrast between inside and outside is heightened, the effect enhancing the interiority of the atrium by denying views out. Attention is focused on the weaker light reaching the atrium from the oculus above and the slightly domed centre of the floor that, together with a tiled star motif incorporating inset glazed panels, denotes the auditorium below which is linked, conceptually, to the centrality of the void.

Figure 3.6 The side-halls off the main atrium space

Between the skin of the pyramid and the atrium void at higher level is a suite of ancillary accommodation. Planned, initially, to accommodate a 'University of Civilizations', these spaces now accommodate offices and galleries. Secondary in their conception and design, they emphasise the role of the symbolic over the functional. Narrow, with no exterior glazing, opening onto the void through fretted glass panels, these spaces are designed primarily to establish the primacy of the atrium void to the programme, function and structure of the pyramid. Artificially lit because of the largely blank elevations, the ancillary rooms are on a par with the service spaces hidden in the undercroft. The lack of lighting, here, establishes their lack of significance in the hierarchy of major spaces in the pyramid. Their configuration and construction follow the orthodoxies of speculative office space: low floor-to-ceiling heights, mechanical and electrical services hidden behind suspended ceilings and fluorescent strip lighting. They are the 'low-grade stuffing required to pad out the pyramid form.'[17] But, more than that, they provide a degree of functional thickness to the skin, substantiating the interior emptiness with a peripheral fill.

In somewhat token fashion, these rooms accommodate a sparsely attended commercial gallery of modern Kazakh and Russian art, a museum space showing Kazakh historical artefacts, a mock-up of the 'Golden Man' of Kazakh folklore replete with replica gold armour and an exhibition of archaeological discoveries from the Steppe. Thus, cultural artefacts which speak of a specifically 'Kazakh' identity are packaged around the void space of the atrium. The void comes to operate as metaphor: the conceptual voiding of Kazakh culture by technological, diagrammatic, global modernity; its visual permeability projecting the image of transparency. The symbolic and organisational significance of this transparent identity should not be overlooked. National identity becomes secondary. The pyramid's identity becomes similar to the identity of the city as a whole: an easily appropriable international aesthetic; a weak national identity wrapping a core of conceptual emptiness.

International corporate material

An international aesthetic – combining the corporate material palette regularly deployed by Foster + Partners (glass, steel, stone) with the generic, universal symbol of the pyramid, as the President would see it – is central to the building's operation. Formally, the Palace is radically a-contextual, addressing the city principally through its position on axis with the Presidential Palace. Its materials and construction techniques are, largely, climatically unresponsive, taking almost no account of the microclimate of the Steppe. The climatically controlled internal environment is maintained at a constant temperature with dramatic swings in the weather outside barely registering inside the building.

On the upper levels, prior to reaching the sanctuary of the Congress Chamber, a wintergarden provides the backdrop to a set of intertwined ramps leading to the oculus. Described as a 'hanging garden', it houses generic indoor plants against a plastic-leaf backing of the kind found in shopping malls. Bleached pale by the light of the stained glass windows, this space is effectively empty of symbolic content, ready and waiting for an international event that occurs only triennially.

Clad in sleek white fireproof panels, the pyramid's structure – where expressed in symbolic demonstration of the building's structural frame – projects the image of an international identity. Glass sits next to white painted steel and stands above marble flooring. Details visible externally express almost seamlessly junctions between textureless materials. But open a door to a fire escape, or enter a service void, and this sleek surface perfection becomes clear. The details that orchestrate a smooth, homogenous aesthetic surface belie the pragmatics of construction in a country with a workforce unskilled in the production of technically complex architecture. Rough rendered blockwork walls are a reminder of the on-site wet trades which built them rapidly. Mechanical services are not dimensionally coordinated and modularised in the manner of other Foster + Partners projects like the airports at Stansted or Chek Lap Kok. Service areas and back-stage provisions for the auditorium are finished roughly with cheap materials and equipment. The most technically advanced and structurally challenging elements of the building are deployed to maximum visual effect in the most public areas in order to reinforce the pyramid's hierarchy of space.

From the entrance, the stairs leading from the undercroft to the atrium hall level are structurally self-supporting and aesthetically seamless. They hang from the floor above and have been engineered for maximum structural slenderness. At the apex, the 'hands of peace' that hold the Congress Chamber comprise a four-point support, designed to allow the round-table to hang unobtrusively from the pyramid's structure. Through a connecting ring-beam, they allow the table also to function as the oculus: the conceptual pinnacle of the project. In these two examples, technical and design effort has been applied where it will be most operative and its functional symbolism most evident.

The most tactile material details are reserved for the most highly trafficked areas. The subterranean foyer has a dark veneer panelling surrounding the drum of the auditorium. Dark and richly polished granite is applied to the supporting columns and, at no small expense, a dark marble floor is laid. But step into the office and gallery spaces between the exterior and the void and the materials are evidently much cheaper. So too is the spatial experience. Located in the dark undercroft is a generically corporate bar equipped with dark-leather chairs. It reproduces the familiar look of the business-class airport lounge, bought off-the-shelf from a Foster + Partners style-sheet.

The exterior echoes the attention to aesthetics and structure evident in the interiors. The tessellating panels that form the four sides of the pyramid have a material and formal attention to detail that is immediately readable, and perceived as elegant by some commentators such as Woodman:

> the structure is faced in granite – pre-mounted on large concrete panels – save for a run of small, diamond-shaped windows at low level. With so little glazing, the building presents an enigmatic, not to say forbidding, image. Yet, watching the light calibrate the relationship between the stainless steel and grey granite, I had to admit that it had a beauty, however chilly.[18]

There is a universal, rigid quality to these façades, isolated in their landscaped park; the surface quality of the façades multiplied four times, nearly identical save for a slight change in window positions. Any difference in aspect is eradicated by the dominant form of the pyramid. From whichever direction it is photographed, the iconographic potential of the building remains the same. With this form, there is no back and there are no sides. All is front. All is façade and all sides serve maximum visual impact. And this is sure to remain: a pyramid on a mound cannot easily be built up against; its form necessitates its independence, enforcing and maintaining its visual significance in the city.

Visualising the pyramid

Publicity material from Foster + Partners emphasises the centrality of the visual impression of the project. The key drawing of the project, widely published and included in the practice's 2007 catalogue, shows an inhabited perspective section.[19] Set in a city of generic international appearance, made up of medium-rise blocks under a darkening sky, the interior of the building is shown in this drawing to focus light down into the auditorium through the central atrium void. The section is cut through the centre of this void and it shows what appears to be a glowing, almost gaseous, cloud of light floating in space. The apex glows and extends its luminescence outwards into the dusk sky.

This depiction of the project emphasises its inherent dualities: contrasts between brightness and darkness; below ground and above ground; interior and exterior. It emphasises the centrality of void, where content is evacuated to make way for formal, appropriable emptiness and active functions are pushed to the periphery of the void, defining it and anchoring it in place. The glowing section implies that the void continues up and out of the building, projecting the vacuity of formal, appropriable emptiness out into the city through the transparent apex. This drawing is used to communicate both the technological qualities of this building and its openness to immediate appropriation by an international audience. There is nothing alienating to transnational capital in the presentation of this project, nothing notably Kazakh or distinctly 'other' in its qualities. The pyramidal form is advanced as a supposedly 'universal' signifier.[20] The image actively makes transparent the glowing heart of the project – the atrium – and opens to view the inner workings of the idea – a place for peace, concord, beneficial discourse – to the world's press. The image is the first, and most singularly transparent, aspect of the project.

Aligning the pyramid in the city

The pyramid, positioned on axis with the administrative centre of the capital, extends itself out through the Mayan cuts indicated in plan view. These entry cuts align the pyramid with the axis of development, rooting it physically as well as symbolically in the new Astana. It is suggested that a tunnel will link the Presidential Palace and the pyramid for the President's private access, and an axial bridge is indicated on plan which will link the presidential park to the park surrounding the pyramid.[21] Even though it is currently positioned on the edge of the new city, the pyramid has already become a crucial part of the capital's identity, functioning as a marker for the desired growth of the city. Its image, frequently reproduced on billboards and digital displays, forms a key part of city branding exercises.

Within the context of the city, the pyramid is unique for its formal homogeneity. The dominant mode of building in Astana is a Kazakh variant of post-modernism. Minarets mingle with reflective gold mirror-glass and Western architectural motifs. The Presidential Palace, for example, sited in front of the pyramid, attempts this fusion of Kazakh and Western. Its base, an exaggerated copy of Washington's White House, is topped with a blue-tiled dome and golden spire. The Presidential Palace attempts a statesman-like presentation of Kazakh democracy. Its form, however, is more resonant to a Russian and Central Asian audience than a Western one.

Connected axially, the pyramid and Presidential Palace have some similarities. Both taper to a pinnacle, raised on domed mounds. Both are adorned with cultural references that echo each other. The materially unified base of the two buildings (both in grey stone) is topped by a materially and formally symbolic form. In the case of the Presidential Palace, this is a blue Islamic dome, which is echoed in the pyramid with the blue-tinted stained glass of the congress chamber, inscribed on closer inspection with gaudy representations of doves. On closer inspection still, uncharacteristically ornamented for Foster + Partners, the very top of the pyramid is finished with a golden sunburst: a Kazakh motif and part of the iconography of the Kazakh flag.[22] Finishing the Presidential Palace is a golden spire, topped with a golden Steppe eagle, carrying a golden orb.

Its form supposedly standing as a non-denominational religious structure, the pyramid's construction materials and processes belong to a Western architectural epistemology, rooted in sub-Miesian logic. However, the idea of a traditional, semi-tribal Kazakh identity that Nazarbayev uses as a regulatory device is still enacted in the design – albeit in a reduced, abstracted and symbolically safe way – through the icons of the Golden Man in the gallery space, the sun-burst in the atrium floor and the relics housed in the museum and art gallery. Symbolic content is thus controlled: like the Presidential Palace, Kazakh national icons are incorporated into the architecture, but they are somewhat reticent and do not dominate the structure. From a distance, the icons are not readable as Kazakh symbols but appear as delicate decorative effects. Through these elements of national iconography, both structures are easily linked with an appropriable national identity. They are symbols of a modern nation; national identity evacuated of radical potential, the thinnest and most blandly acceptable of references to their cultural context. They are not symbols which demonstrate power or muster aggressive nationalism but which instead comprise the visual production of a symbolic form of national unity. The literal transparency of the symbols on the apex of the pyramid is matched by a symbolic transparency of appropriable images.

Transparency and decryption

Astana's position in the north-central area of Kazakhstan is crucial at all levels to the consolidation of identity: national, regional, economic, political and social. Within Astana, architecture and infrastructure are understood as crucial devices for changing the identities established under the Soviet system. Architecture is used, following Reinhold Martin's argument, as a regulating device.[23] Through the media of material, structure and space, geopolitical goals and ambitions can be partially realised. The pyramid is at the confluence of these goals and ambitions. Its architecture displays an attempt to communicate symbolic content: content that is effectively transparent to itself: empty, as Jean Baudrillard would suggest; the minimum necessary to establish an image of stability, economic potential, technological modernisation and global accessibility.[24] By largely emptying specific meaning from form, structure and material, the pyramid has the capacity to accept multiple readings. It is effectively a multi-sided, ever-shifting billboard for Kazakhstan; shifting between images of international capital, religious tolerance, peace, stability, openness, safety, security and technological progress.

The media – steel, concrete, stone, glass, light, void – are the message. The use of these materials, and their overt tectonic expression, demonstrates the technical capacity within Kazakhstan to produce the transparent materiality and image of the building. The commissioning of Foster + Partners is as important as the realisation of the project: an international corporation whose appointment demonstrates the progressive late-modernity of the President. But the core of the project is the emptying of content through the void of the atrium.

The pyramid is structured around this atrium which, programmatically, connects the base to the top and enables multiple meanings to be read into the structure. Kazakh identity exists, made transparent. Conveying 'economic openness' requires a weak identity, one that can be appropriated and made 'global'.[25] By seeing through the architecture and planning of Astana, the international investor is made aware of the generic qualities of the city and the desire of the country for inward investment. The architecture of the pyramid achieves this. Through the void at its core and the reductive representation of Kazakh identity, internationally recognisable architecture is achieved.

This is an architecture of surface; one that necessitates a form of openness and focuses on the surface presentation of identities and materiality, with the density of depth emptied.[26] It is architecture in production of the image of itself. The architecture becomes, as Baudrillard suggests, transparent:

> the murder of the image [...] lies in this enforced visibility as source of power and control, beyond even the 'panoptical': it is no longer a question of making things visible to an external eye, but of making them transparent to themselves. The power of control is, as it were, internalised, and human beings are no longer victims of images, but rather transform themselves into images.[27]

The lucidity of the surface becomes central to the production of images of Kazakhstan, specifically intended to signify a dramatic break with Soviet epistemologies and ideologies. Within the city, the use of architecture is intended to allow the 'opening' of a previously closed society. Transparency, here, is rendered in the manner which Lefebvre discusses: the decryption of the hidden and secretive, the transparent becoming aligned with the transformation of the state of Kazakhstan.[28] Through its architecture, the pyramid allows this generic 'enlightenment' to take place. As Lefebvre would suggest, a decrypting through transparency occurs, and the progression from dark spaces to light spaces highlights this 'opening-up' of a supposedly closed and secretive society.[29] It appeals to the supposedly 'universal truth' of world religions united in humanity through the association of light and knowledge.

Transparency and stability

Its generic symbolic appeal directed internationally, the pyramid also has national significance in the promotion of the image of a stable state. As Shonin Anacker argues, writing in *Eurasian Geography and Economics*:

> the focus is [...] on *internal* legitimacy. The capital move [to Astana] represented a unique way of changing the demography of the north and re-territorialising the Kazakh nation without inspiring much immediate resistance from either inside or outside the country.[30]

The construction of the pyramid played an important role, as part of the construction of the capital city, in demonstrating the cultural, social and religious tolerance of the Nazarbayev regime. With this overt display of openness to all forms of religious expression, Nazarbayev is able to absorb potential external influences into his concept of the Kazakh nation. The pyramid, in its programmatic association with the Congress, constitutes an image of this commitment to religious and cultural tolerance. Its iconic centrality to the establishment of the new Astana lodges this attitude firmly in the national consciousness: the image of Astana is tied to this 'high-profile' building and hence tied to the programme of the Congress.

Irrespective of government policy, the impression of a transparent Kazakhstan, communicated internally to potentially dissident groups, suggests the acceptance of difference. By absorbing all differences into a single national identity, radical resistance is thwarted: what is there to rail against when the object of your reaction *is* your culture? Through the non-specific form of the building, the subtle integration of a weak national identity and the universalising tendency of the pronouncements of the Congress, the 're-territorialising' of parts of Kazakhstan is promoted.

Entropic tendencies in recently defined states can be partially regulated through the voided content of buildings like the pyramid. Competing groups are allowed to appropriate it into any religious and cultural identity, its generic formal, material and spatial qualities, and its transparent identity, allowing this to take place. By fostering an image of transparency – constituted as a brand-identity for the country – irredentist drives can be mitigated, national unity preserved and regional stability promoted. Transparency is used to produce a simulation of the conditions of democratic openness and religious tolerance, used as a means by which space is organised and ordered through an active process of decryption. By choosing an architecture which celebrates faith in technology, the condition of modernity and progress becomes attached to the national image of Kazakhstan. The architecture plays a central role in both fostering the idea of a progressive central Asian nation and a progressive President, open to the West and engaged in a supposedly democratic transformation of this previously Soviet republic.

NOTES

1   Central Intelligence Agency, *The World Factbook*, www.cia.gov/library/publications/the-world-factbook/geos/kz.html [accessed: 09.04.08].

2   The members of the Congress are representatives of the world's religious groups. These are not necessarily the appointed leaders of religious organisations. For a full list of attendees, see http://www.religions-congress.org/index.php?lang=English [accessed: 24.05.10].

3   Deborah Ascher Barnstone, *The Transparent State: Architecture and Politics in Postwar Germany* (London: Routledge, 2005); Annette Fierro, *The Glass State: The Technology of the Spectacle, Paris 1981–1998* (Cambridge MA: MIT Press, 2003).

4   Henri Lefebvre, *The Production of Space*, trans. by Donald Nicholson-Smith (Oxford: Blackwell, 1991).

5   Embassy of Kazakhstan in Israel, 'First Congress of World and Traditional Religions', http://www.kazakhemb.org.il [accessed: 22.04.08].

6   Embassy of Kazakhstan in Israel, 'Second Congress of World and Traditional Religions', http://www.kazakhemb.org.il [accessed: 22.04.08].

7   BBCNews.com, 'Kazakh stage for religious event', http://news.bbc.co.uk/1/hi/world/asia-pacific/5341822.stm [accessed: 22.04.08].

8   EllisWoodman, 'Palace of Peace & Accord, Kazakhstan by Foster + Partners', *Building Design Online*, http://www.bdonline.co.uk/story.asp?sectioncode=428&storycode=30738 [accessed: 10.04.08].

9   Embassy of Kazakhstan in Israel, 'Part 1. New Kazakhstan in a New World', http://www.kazakhemb.org.il [accessed: 01.05.08].

10 Ibid.

11 Ibid.

12 Observations and recordings on the Palace of Peace and Concord made in February 2008, during research visit to Astana. From the author's own notes and sketches, February 2008.

13 Comments made by the building's tour guide, 19.02.08, and a similar theme reiterated by the building's security manager on the return visit, 20.02.08.

14 Lefebvre, *The Production of Space*, p. 23.

15 Ibid.

16 Ibid.

17 Ibid.

18 Woodman, 'Palace of Peace & Accord'.

19 Foster + Partners, *Catalogue: Foster + Partners* (Munich: Prestel, 2005), p. 40.

20 Woodman, 'Palace of Peace & Accord'.

21 Ibid.

22 'The flag of Kazakhstan consists of a light blue base. There is a golden sun with 32 rays in the center of the flag, and below the sun there is an eagle. There is also a golden webbed pattern running vertically down the left side of the flag [...] The pattern on the flag represents the artistic and cultural traditions of the old Khanate and Kazakh people. The light blue symbolizes the various Turkic peoples who make up today's population of the country – including the Tatars, Mongols, Uyghurs and others. The blue has a religious significance, representing the Sky God to many of these people. A modern interpretation states the blue background stands for Kazakhstan's broad skies, and for freedom. The steppe eagle and the sun represent freedom and the flight toward greater heights and fulfillment of aspiration.' World Flags 101.com, Country: Republic of Kazakhstan, http://www.worldflags101.com/k/kazakhstan-flag.aspx [accessed: 05.05.08].

23 Martin, Reinhold *The Organizational Complex* (Cambridge, MA: MIT Press, 2003), pp. 101, 117, 159.

24 See Baudrillard on the production of the image as centre and source of power, through the idea of all becoming 'real' made open to view – 'integral reality', as he terms it: Jean Baudrillard, *The Intelligence of Evil, or the Lucidity Pact* (Oxford: Berg, 2005).

25 Ibid.

26   Jean Baudrillard, *Simulacra and Simulation* (Ann Arbor MI: The University of Michigan Press, 1994), p. 6.
27   Baudrillard, *The Intelligence of Evil*, p. 94.
28   Lefebvre, *The Production of Space*, p. 257.
29   Ibid., p. 27.
30   Shonin Anacker, 'Geographies of Power in Nazarbayev's Astana', *Eurasian Geography and Economics*, 45, 7 (2004): 531.

Chapter 4

Reading the site at Sverre Fehn's Hamar Museum

Suzanne Ewing

> At this point I can cut out the mass where the shadow screens the construction. This gives me my place, and time stands still.
>
> Outside, the tree fractures the horizon. Time will allow it to grow and add to its room. The tree mobilises light and casts its shadow on the earth, a realisation of place [...] It is here the story is told.
>
> (Sverre Fehn in 1988)[1]

Following the completion of the Archbishopric Museum at Hamar, Norway in 1979,[2] many references to 'horizon' and 'trees' appeared in the writings of architect Sverre Fehn and in publications of his work by others.[3] The image of the tree fracturing the horizon is important, both in defining conceptual and physical limits in relation to a particular place such as the Hamar Museum, and more broadly as an architectural device which is fundamental to the choreography and ordering of inhabited spaces. It can be seen to relate directly to the conception of architecture as captured space or realised place. Sites are always, to some extent, invented. The invention of site in Fehn's work is a significant element of the process of making architecture – and therefore in the experiencing, understanding and interpretation of those buildings where 'the story is told'.

Sverre Fehn suggests that his work has come of age 'in the shadow of modernism'.[4] His built work, mainly in Scandinavia, recognised by the 1997 award of the Pritzker Prize, has been described as poetic, sculptural, humanistic and inclusive. Following media exposure early in his career, in the 1950s, with the publication of the Nordic Pavilion in Venice, wider acclaim came in the 1980s and 1990s. Peter Cook who, in 1981, included Fehn's work in a series on 'unappreciated architects', noted that in 'Sverre Fehn we have a believing architect, and we ignore his quiet and lyrical approach to modern architecture at our peril.'[5] Fellow Norwegian Christian Norberg-Schulz commented in 1997 that 'the belated recognition of Fehn is due to the fact that his works suddenly appear to "adapt" themselves to the international situation and to offer compelling answers to difficult and complex conditions'.[6]

The invention of site

It has been suggested that the subject of site has been 'systematically ignored by both architectural and urban design discourse'[7] and is subject to the dualisms which, it is claimed, are inherent in modernism:[8] before/after; above/below; new/old; urban/landscape. The writings of Steven Holl are preoccupied with the anchoring of buildings in their sites. He argues that:

> Architecture is bound to situation [...] The site of a building is more than an ingredient in its conception. It is its physical and metaphysical foundation [...] Today the link between site and architecture must be found in new ways, which are part of the constructive transformation of modern life.[9]

Andrea Kahn observes that we are usually 'in the midst of site' rather than 'hovering over' it, as in most modernist conceptions.[10] She unravels the myth of the contained and controllable site – an assumed 'blank canvas' which requires erasure or cleansing – and challenges the assumption that site analysis is merely a scientifically objective, neutral description of data. She suggests instead that interpretation, assumption and invention are critical to how an architect responds to a particular place. Similarly, David Leatherbarrow notes in *The Roots of Architectural Invention* that 'the existence of a defined building site is always taken for granted in contemporary architectural design, yet attempts to understand the reasons underlying its definition are surprisingly rare'.[11] He presents three partial understandings or assumptions which are prevalent: site as a division of space, site as context and site as real estate. Like Kahn, Leatherbarrow argues that site, in relation to the act of building, is always a matter of invention. He cites Alberti and the notion of site platform, which may order and limit vertically, and the mediating, staged sites of Borromini that influenced the external configuration of spaces adjacent to a site, as being different from modernist notions. He cites early modernist experiments with axonometric projection, such as Van Doesberg's, as aimed at removing 'the composition from the horizon of perspectival experience, which confers frontality on whatever (object or person) reciprocates the "frontalism" of one's body'. This abstraction dislocates from real time, with the potential confusion of horizon and perspective, or vista, as 'a view on reality' rather than understood implicit presence.

Two well-known twentieth century images come to mind.[12] The first is Le Corbusier's 'eye of man to see a wide horizon', constructed in the grass floored 'room' on the roof of the de Beistegui apartment in Paris (1932) which – by maximising the sense of being in a room beneath the vast expanse of the sky – effectively obscures the urban landscape of Paris, except for a top slice of the monumental *Arc de Triomphe* in the background. The context is edited to enhance the switch between fireplace and triumphal arch, suggesting that the partially bounded white-walled room is encircled by an imaginary territory marked by the city monument. The second image is the roofscape of the *Unité d'Habitation* in Marseilles (1945–1952), where sculptural forms are set against the clean horizon of the mountains and clear sky in the background, the whole on an elevated plane or platform. There is a heightened sense in these two images of what is near or far, and of the bounding of a room located in relation to a surrounding horizon. The modernist conception of 'hovering over', noted by Louis Kahn, is combined with some sense of Holl's 'expression linked to idea joined to site'.

The philosopher Martin Heidegger's rethinking of the nature of space, place and inhabitation is also relevant. His work from the late 1920s to the 1960s arguably freed the question of space from its previous disciplinary boundaries, breaking from a Cartesian ontology of neutral, flattened space – site as a division of space – reasserting instead an investigation into the spatiality of the world in which we find ourselves; what he called 'the concrete context of actual life'. It has been suggested that Heidegger's concepts of '*horismos*' (horizon) and '*raum*' (space) are preoccupations of Fehn's work.[13] Heidegger observes:

> What the word for space, *raum*, designates is said by its ancient meaning. *Raum* means a place cleared or freed for settlement and lodging. A space is something that has been made room for, something that is cleared and free, namely within a boundary, Greek *peras*. A boundary is not that at which something stops but, as the Greeks recognised, the boundary is that from which something begins its presencing. That is why the concept of *horismos*, that is the horizon, the boundary. Space is in essence that for which room has been made, that which is let into bounds.[14]

Confrontation and control

Confrontation and struggle are recurrent themes in the language used by Fehn. He calls the act of building 'brutal', suggesting that it acts 'violently in order to emphasise [...] latent, secret, hidden qualities'. Fehn says:

> [W]hen I build on a site in nature that is totally unspoiled, it is a fight, an attack by our culture on nature. In this confrontation I strive to make a building in the setting, a hope for a new consciousness to see the beauty there as well.[15]

Analogies with ships and conquest recur in Fehn's writings, as do his diagrams of the line of a boat forging through the sea (Figure 4.1). The implicit analogy of conquest has been read as a male–female interaction, with the site viewed as potentially fertile for building.[16]

There is resonance here with both Norwegian tradition and the Vitruvian identification of sites, as described by Leatherbarrow, where the soil is literally ploughed and cut to mark off a site from its surrounding expanse, and the resulting boundary wall denotes 'not a line but a container symbolically equivalent to the wall of a ceramic jar or vase, a limit that served as a receptacle of civic life, generative and abundant because female'. The horizon 'without'

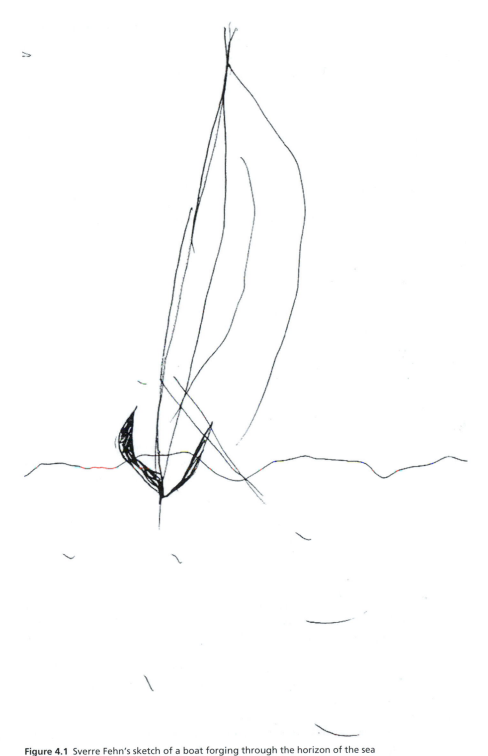

Figure 4.1 Sverre Fehn's sketch of a boat forging through the horizon of the sea

Diane M. Halle Library
ENDICOTT COLLEGE
Beverly, MA 01915

was perceived as an open expanse, an unbounded and formless field, perhaps analogous to the sea. The notion that the boat sailed to 'fight the horizon'[17] reveals, to some extent, a fabricated modernist dualism of nature versus culture – with the implication that the marking vessel is the focus in undifferentiated ground, rather than the balancer of territory enclosed or exposed, within or without.

Fehn refers to 'the dramatic confrontation between earth and sky' which he called 'the point of intersection'. Referring to an old idea of horizon, he noted that:

> [In those days] the horizon was an instrument of architecture determining the large exterior 'room'. The vista then served the practical purpose of defence, extending no further than the eye could see. The sight on the weapon was an extension of the eye and its view was a definition of mortality […] The conversation with nature was not based on aestheticism or sentimentality, for every opening not only admitted light, but also determined survival in relation to topography.[18]

It is not, perhaps, a surprise that this invention of site seems somewhat instrumental, loaded with military overtones and supposedly 'primitive' attitudes to surroundings. 'Survival in relation to topography' recalls the act of building as a primal confrontation with nature.

Fehn claims to understand architecture as 'subject to the layout of the ground'. He observes that 'Sites […] contain in their profundity the sense of the project, to which the architecture must conform'. Closest, perhaps, to Leatherbarrow's category of partial understanding of site as context, Fehn describes site as an archive distanced from the present and future, a source of information and knowledge, perhaps to be plundered, and certainly to be discovered. At Hamar, Fehn is conscious of the paradox of intervention, saying 'the past is suddenly present, the stones come close to you, the ruins look more material and real, because they make up a story at the same time as they are attacked'.[19] In keeping with the myth of the untouched site identified by Andrea Kahn, Fehn – to a certain extent – invents the site at Hamar as untouched prior to the construction of the museum in order to enhance the sense of 'confrontation'.

The building was described in the 1997 Pritzker Prize proceedings as 'A suspended itinerary, […] overhanging [that] reveals the story of the passing of time, the unchanging pursuit of its course, the confrontation between old and new'. John Hedjuk has described the place as:

> A site where the frozen earth grips in its vice the retaining and foundation walls of past acts and occurrences. The present archaeologist reveals the earth-encrusted tombs of past joys and of past sadness. We know we are in the presence of an event and we are strangely enough participating spectators. The lake and the mountain are the proscenium.[20]

Peter Cook describes Hamar as 'a poised machine in its purest form hanging above the archaeology [...] [W]e are unused to a building that collages together devices, as in the tradition of the clockmaker, so that they seem naturally interdependent'. In describing Fehn as a choreographer, Cook further observes that 'the whole has a fascinating violence in its configuration'.[21]

The site at Hamar – an archaeological site that incorporates medieval and nineteenth-century buildings, remains and artefacts – is clearly one that has been touched previously. Fehn's approach of built detachment from the past exaggerates, to some extent, the interpretation of confrontation between old and new, stillness and movement, ground and sky. Movement through new spaces above or below the historic ground, combined with the ramps and gradually sloping floors of interior spaces and bridges, is carefully choreographed. Shifts of movement are articulated within constructed horizons that are fractured by stairs, the main ramp and other elements in order to make interior and exterior rooms for new occupation.

Limits and landscape

Norberg-Schulz outlines a narrative interpretation of the forming of limits and boundaries in relation to building: first, the earth as given territory; second, the marking or making of lines related to cultivation; and, third, enclosure or the containing of inhabited space. In Leatherbarrow's Vitruvian ordering of territory, the line of cut ground primarily separated different presences. In Fehn's rhetoric, ordering moves set up confrontations between nature and man, earth and sky, boat and sea. Architecture is imagined as a charged void contained or bounded in opposition to all that surrounds it in nature. The focus thus moves to the line or the actual boundary itself – on the vessel or architectural space – rather than on the differentiated ground where it is situated.

Despite its usual connotation of visual limit, the term horizon was not, it is claimed, originally connected to seeing and intuition. 'It means, in accordance with the Greek verb *horizein*, what limits, surrounds, encloses'.[22] As the *apparent* 'line that divides the earth and the sky', it is the aspect of imagined or interpreted horizon which is pertinent to site invention.[23] The defined limits of the Hedmark Museum site come from previous inhabitation, from previously defined buildings and edges. Where territory is less clearly defined in the semi-enclosed courtyard excavation area, a new visitors' ramp, of the same plan configuration as the remains of one boundary wall, is introduced in a shifted plan location. The ramp, which contains visitor movement, becomes a line cutting through the invented space bounded by the more solid wings of the museum (Figure 4.2). Imagining movement along this ramp, Fehn argues that:

When the ground becomes history: man's position leaves the horizon as the bridge brings him in a state of looking down at the ornamental walls from the middle ages. All answers are given by his position in relation to the earth and the sky.[24]

Figure 4.2 View of the external courtyard showing the sinuous ramp

The new spaces of the Hamar Museum are positioned in a highly deliberate way within the surrounding landscape of mountains and lake. The external ramp's furthest point from the entrance reveals a view of the wider surroundings. Unlike the Corbusian examples noted earlier, however, this is a position of 'hovering over', more analogous with the theatre of Borromini's staged, mediated sites than with Alberti's concept of bounded platform.[25] If the ramp in the Hamar Museum is interpreted as a container, or as a vessel within a wider territory, it can also be seen as a partial boundary which allows the external courtyard to be understood as a series of overlapping spaces within the wider landscape. Just as the shadow of the tree realises a place on earth, or conversely makes a place real, the impact of the ramp within the building and the courtyard gives the internal and external spaces their presence.

Telling a story

The simple linear buildings of the museum, defined by a timber pitched roof and masonry base, recall the basic form of Norwegian folk buildings. The spatial organisation of the galleries, which house a museum of peasant life, emphasises the linearity of the low-level nineteenth-century barns that run perpendicular to the entrance block. Two levels are joined by a sloping concrete floor which appears to float within the space in which the existing stone walls below, and the new timber post-and-beam frame above, are differentiated. There is an ambiguity between the relative importance of lower and upper levels, one connected with the revealed depth of the earth, the other with the light and rhythm of the sky (Figure 4.3).

Figure 4.3 The sloping floor appears to float in a space with the existing stone below and the new timber post-and-beam frame above

In the entrance area, it can be seen clearly that the fusion of the historic medieval fort walls with the nineteenth-century farm buildings remains unresolved. The new entrance is directly opposite a major opening into the external courtyard, which gives a view of the new ramp that re-bounds the exterior space. The ground is revealed as uncertain. What was assumed to be ground level at the entrance is contradicted by the deepening rough stone trenches that become evident as you move through the building. The smooth concrete bridge linking the gallery areas to the external ramp, and the stair around which it pivots, provides a higher level datum for the insertion of concrete boxes containing especially valued objects and fragments extracted from the rough ground below. Space appears to be compressed at ground level by these monolithic, vertically oriented insertions in the space. The focus is on the cave-like quality of the excavated ground area, recalling the underground feeling of Fehn's earlier Venice Pavilion.

Materials are used to orient human experience in relation to both ground and sky. Throughout the building the fundamental relationship of being 'above' accentuates the experience of being 'below'.[26] Within the stone walls of the museum, the transition between above and below consistently relates to penetrating light and concrete finish as seen in the stairs, the ramp and in places where what seems to be floor is articulated as bridge, allowing interaction between the two overlapping spaces. Although the highest part of the walls in the central entrance block is related to the highest point of the ramp in the courtyard, Fehn's conceptual 'point of intersection' in this building relates to the inserted routes of platform, ramp and stairs rather than the material datum between wall and roof. All below is treated as part of the dark, cave-like, rough terrain. Above is the even rhythm of the articulated timber frame.

Two less apparent spaces above and below are created by the bold introduction of the ramp in the courtyard. The existing ground is read as one area bounded by the wings of the museum and located within the wider context of the lake and mountains beyond. On arrival at the lowest level, a more interior space related to the entrance of the museum is experienced, partially enclosed by the boundary of the turning ramp. In contrast with the medieval walls, this 'space below' is not an enclosed fortress-like space, but one where the wider archaeological site and landscape beyond the museum wings are emphasised. As Norberg-Schulz observes, 'the project culminates in the development of a route that, uncoiling itself in space, seeks to discover a new horizon'.[27] It is only from the highest point of the ramp externally that a sense of the larger space beyond the Hamar buildings is revealed.

The ramp, which carries visitors on a spatial journey around the museum, is also fundamental to the reinvention of the perceived boundaries of the new museum site. Expressed through its plan geometry and form, the ramp shifts fundamentally from being a protective boundary that separates within from without to being an open route, a line cutting through unbounded territory. Its slope, by definition, is about movement and the shifting relationship between suspended route and historic ground. It can therefore also be seen as the line of intersection between the two 'rooms' of the courtyard. Moving through the spaces of the museum, participation in the charged void between above and below, between earth and sky, is accentuated by various moments of fracture. At the place where the ramp penetrates the building at high level, vertical proportions and vertical elements invert the spatial horizontality of the other areas of the building. The ramp's puncture of the building adjacent to the spiral stair can therefore be interpreted as a vertical pivot or fracture, the place of real spatial shift from the end of the linear barn to the outdoor '*raum*'.

Fracture

Returning to the image of the tree breaking the horizon, Fehn claims that it is only in the fracturing of horizon that place can be realised. The line of the horizon implies a story about pure or original nature, where it is inferred that spatial infinity is analogous with timelessness and purity. Interventions – the shade of the tree, the support of a column, the corner or edge of a room, the beginning of a building – serve to transform, conquer, change and fracture both space and time to enable human inhabitation. Fehn claims his architecture attempts to provide 'a horizon for man' so that each project identifies a place between earth and sky which he calls *mellomron,* or the space between, in Norwegian. The 'point of intersection' or 'fracture' of what is understood physically and conceptually as horizon is fundamental to the act of inventing and making the spaces between, and it also allows the opportunity to redefine the horizons of earth and sky. At Hamar, the surface of the earth is revealed as having historic depth and the sky's potential to cast shadows is exploited. An ordering is choreographed in which the new raised ground of the contained ramp is established between the redefined horizontal datum of the roof and uneven stone remains.

The interpretation of horizon at the Museum draws together an elemental understanding of human beings, building and situation. It is primarily spatial and physical. Fehn writes:

> What was especially lost was the horizon, which human beings forgot with the discovery of the roundness of the earth. And with the loss of horizon we also lost known and unknown space. We have lost the earth underneath the sky and what is beyond […] Let the people in their individual homes own the horizon. Let the apartment roof be the large piazza […] for a visual conversation with the elements of the sky.[28]

Horizon and the invention of site

Fehn sees the horizon as being critical to the invention of site. While the site at Hamar is reinvented as untouched, the insertion of new layers of ground, and the roof construction, enables the resulting place to develop a series of new relationships relating to space 'above' and 'below'. The articulation and manipulation of concrete and light within these new vessels, or lines of occupation, creates a charged void between earth and sky, a positioning of experience in relation to the visible horizon bounded by the rebuilt stone and timber structure, and also to the imagined boundary of the horizon.

Within the existing boundary walls of the archaeological remains, the ramp emphasises a new orientation, a line inserted into free terrain. The ramp places the visitor to some extent outside or beyond an interpreted sequence of history. A fracture at the point of pivot of the ramp's junction with the upper level walkway and the spiral stair provides the vertical fixing point of the platforms of the interdependent museum spaces. In the Hedmark Museum, Fehn manipulates the horizon in terms of physical limits and experience and uses horizon as an instrument of orientation, movement and engagement. The literal 'realising of the place' is finally a process of participation on location in the reinvented site.

NOTES

1   Christian Norberg-Schulz and Gennaro Postiglione, *Sverre Fehn: Works, Projects, Writings 1949–1996* (New York: Monacelli, 1997), p. 243.

2   The Archbishopric Museum of Hamar, Norway, 1967–1979, is built over an archaeological site, significant in the late Middle Ages as it lay along the Kaumpung trail which was the route of the Bishop of Hamar's journey to Rome in 1302. The remains of an early nineteenth-century farm structure rest on the top of the ruins of a medieval fortress, demolished in the second half of the sixteenth century. The building has been well documented, see Norberg-Schulz and Postiglione, *Sverre Fehn*, pp. 129–144, with bibliography of articles 1975–1994 on p. 138; also 'Hamar Bispegard Museum', *GA Document*, 11 (1984): 72–81; Richard Weston, 'Nordic Light', *Architects Journal*, 30 September (1987): 25–29.

3   Sverre Fehn, '*L'albero e l'orizzonte*' ('The Tree and the Horizon'), *Spazio & Societa* 10 (1980): 32–55; Peter Cook, 'Trees and Horizons: The Architecture of Sverre Fehn', *Architectural Review*, August (1981): 102–106; Per Olaf Fjeld, 'The Fall of Horizon' in *Sverre Fehn: The Thought of Construction* (New York: Rizzoli, 1983); Richard Weston, 'A Sense of the Horizon', *Architects Journal*, 19 November (1988): 38–46.

4   From award speech by Sverre Fehn '...about Sverre Fehn', *Sverre Fehn Pritzker Architecture Prize Laureate*, Los Angeles: The Hyatt Foundation, 1997, online at www.pritzkerprize.com/svbio.htm [accessed 15.08.11].

5   Cook, 'Trees and Horizons': 102.

6   Norberg-Schulz and Postiglione, *Sverre Fehn*, p. 19.

7   Andrea Kahn, 'Overlooking: A Look at How We Look at Site or ... Site as "Discrete Object" of Desire' in Sarah McCorquodale, Katerina Ruedi, Sarah Wigglesworth, *Desiring Practices* (London: Black Dog, 1996), pp. 174–185.

8   Ananya Roy, 'Traditions of the Modern: A Corrupt View' in *Traditional Dwellings & Settlements Review*, XII, 11 (2001): 7–19.

9   'A building has one site. In this one situation, its intentions are collected. Building and site have been interdependent since the beginning of Architecture. In the past, this connection was manifest without conscious intention through the use of local materials and craft, and by an association of the landscape with events of history and myth [...] Ideas cultivated from the first perception of the site, meditations upon initial thoughts, or a reconsideration of existing topography can become the framework for invention. This mode of invention is focused through a relative space, as distinct from universal space. It is in a bounded domain'. Stephen Holl, Anchoring (New York: Princeton Architectural Press, 1989), p. 11.

10 Kahn, 'Overlooking', pp. 176–178. Kahn develops a model of Site Constructions in architectural education which acknowledge the interpretative reality of engagement with a particular physical location which is also a conceptual construction.

11 'We have largely missed the creative aspect of site definition and the architect's responsibility to "invent" the site of any design project.' David Leatherbarrow, *The Roots of Architectural Invention: Site, Enclosure, Materials* (Cambridge: Cambridge University Press, 1993), p. 7.

12 Illustrations 46 and 47 in *Le Corbusier: Architect of the Century* (London: Hayward Gallery and Arts Council of Great Britain with Balding & Mansell, 1987), pp. 138–139.

13 Kenneth Frampton, 'The Constructive Thought' in Norberg-Schulz and Postiglione, *Sverre Fehn*, pp. 253–255. Frampton links Louis Kahn and Sverre Fehn to Heidegger's distinction between evenly divided and distant space.

14 Heidegger, 1954, quoted in C. McCann (ed.), *Critical Heidegger* (London: Routledge, 1996).

15 Sverre Fehn '...about Sverre Fehn'.

16 Peter Cook describes Fehn's approach to the proposed 1972 National Museum of Fine Arts: 'the city floor is not touched. The new structure "fertilises" the old. The gentle slope of the bridges activate the pedestrian's view [...] a city floor full of life and activities'. Cook, 'Trees and Horizons': 104.

17 Fjeld, 'The Fall of Horizon', p. 256.

18 Per Olaf Fjeld, 'The Precision of Place' in *The Thought of Construction* (New York: Rizzoli, 1983), p. 256.

19 Sverre Fehn 'An Architectural Autobiography' in *The Poetry of the Straight Line: Five Masters of the North* (Helsinki: Museum of Finnish Architecture, 1992), quoted in Norberg-Schulz and Postiglione, *Sverre Fehn*, p. 246.

20 Quoted in Norberg-Schulz and Postiglione, *Sverre Fehn*, p. 257.

21 Cook, 'Trees and Horizons': 106.

22 F. Dastur, 'The Ekstatico-horizonal Constitution of Temporality' in McCann, *Critical Heidegger*, p. 164.

23 'The deeper meaning of horizon has its origin in the experience of the imaginary line where the earth meets the sky. The nature of this imaginary horizontal line is revealed in its power to define the boundary of our visible world as well as in the invitation to transcend this boundary'. Dalibor Vesely, 'Introduction' in Eric Parry, *Eric Parry Architects* (London: Black Dog, 2002).

24 Sverre Fehn, *Signs & Insights* lecture, Urbino, 1979, quoted in Cook, 'Trees and Horizons': 105.

25 Weston, in 'Northern Light', p. 29, links the parti of this building with Corbusian vocabulary and *promenade architecturale*.

26 Kenneth Frampton cites four primary relationships noted by Holl: *under, in, on* and *over* the earth: 'the surface of earth as self-evident but fundamental datum' in Holl, *Anchorings*, p. 7.

27 See Norberg-Schulz and Postiglione, *Sverre Fehn*, p. 58, on Hamar and the Wasa museum competition project.

28 Norberg-Schulz and Postiglione, *Sverre Fehn*, p. 257.

Chapter 5

A hellish cloud and a very clear air: industry, nature and weather in early eighteenth-century England

Jonathan Hill

Composed as a journey from London to the North Sea, this chapter examines Houghton Hall and Holkham Hall in Norfolk, reflecting on the relations between nature and culture in early eighteenth-century England and examining the multiple authors at work. Houghton was built for Sir Robert Walpole, familiarly described as Britain's first Prime Minister, holding the position for over twenty years until his retirement in 1742. But the title was not then official and his contemporaries used it pejoratively to criticise him for acquiring too much power and influence. Even Walpole's nickname – The Great Man – was not necessarily flattering. J. H. Plumb remarks that Walpole 'was frequently regarded as obscene in an age when men and women were not prudes', while William Speck writes that he 'projected the image of a gross Norfolk squire, boasting that he read letters from his gamekeeper before those of his Cabinet ministers, and rarely read books' although he had an extensive library.[1] Even an admirer, Queen Caroline, the wife of King George II, noted 'that gross body, those swollen [sic] legs, and that ugly belly'.[2] But Walpole's demeanour was not unusual. Englishmen relished their cantankerous and contrary behaviour, which they explained by reference to the fickle and variable weather.[3]

A presumptuous smoake

Due to government business as well as social life, Walpole spent much of the year in London. Reports of the city's polluted skies were frequent even in the sixteenth and seventeenth centuries, when coal replaced wood as the principal domestic fuel. Early coals had sulphur levels twice that of coals used centuries later. On combustion, sulphur in coal oxidised to introduce sulphur dioxide into the air and a secondary oxidation created sulphuric acid, which was detrimental to human health and building materials.[4] Fog, coal smoke and industrial fumes combined to turn the air into a darkly odorous smog, making streets and squares at times unbearable. A new building had a shadow of soot even before the end of its construction.[5]

John Evelyn's *Fumifugium: or The Inconvenience of the Aer and Smoak of London Dissipated* (1661) was the first book to consider the city's polluted atmosphere as a whole. Opening with a dedication to King Charles II, Evelyn claims that he conceived *Fumifugium* in response to a 'pernicious Accident' in the royal palace of Whitehall. A 'presumptuous Smoake [...] did so invade the Court: that all the Rooms, Galleries, and Places about it were filled and infested with it; and that to such a degree, as Men could hardly discern one another'.[6] Remarking that a 'Hellish and dismall Cloud of SEA-COALE' blankets the city, Evelyn recalls the ancient Greek principle that the air – the breath – is 'the *Vehicle* of *the Soul*, as well as that of the Earth' and recounts Hippocratic opinion that the character of a people depends upon the character of 'the *Aer* of those *Climates*' they breathe.[7] Convinced that London's air is unhealthy, Evelyn furthers the medical analogy. Offering a 'Remedy' for 'this pernicious *Nuisance*', he proposes a number of practical and poetic measures, including the relocation of coal-burning trades to the east of the city so that the prevailing westerly wind would carry the smoke away from London.[8] The edges of the conurbation are to be forested and planted with fragrant shrubs so that 'the whole City, would be sensible of the sweet and ravishing varieties of the perfumes'.[9] Evelyn's enduring fascination for gardens was influenced by Francis Bacon's advice that the philosopher required a garden as well as a library and laboratory. Evelyn's remedy – a perfumed botanical garden – would have implied good health due to the known medical properties of certain plants and herbs and was also associated with Heaven and the Garden of Eden.[10]

Emphasising the allegorical as well as the practical and poetic significance of Evelyn's treatise, Mark Jenner notes that contemporary imagery equated the monarch with the illuminating sun and the interregnum – between the execution of Charles I in 1649 and accession of Charles II in 1660 – as 'the obscuring cloud'.[11] Recalling ancient Greece and an Old Testament verse, making a clear distinction between pure and polluted air, Evelyn eulogises 'our Illustrious *CHARLES*, who is the very Breath of our Nostrils, in whose health all our happiness resides'.[12] Evelyn also considered the sun to be an appropriate emblem for the intellectual enlightenment of the Royal Society, which was founded in 1660 with the purpose to advance scientific knowledge through empirical investigation and received a royal charter in 1662.

In January that year, at the king's request, Evelyn prepared a parliamentary bill to counter London's pollution but the legislation progressed no further.[13] Evelyn implicitly acknowledged the interdependence of nature and industry in London's climate and weather, but *Fumifugium* had no practical effect and there was no significant demand for a reduction in urban pollution. Property rights and the economic interests of London's industries, as well as popular identification of a fire with a home – a private rather than a public space – made legislation unlikely.

This monstrous city

London's coal consumption continued to increase, doubling from 800,000 tons in 1700 to 1,500,000 tons in 1750. As its population remained nearly the same, the rising fuel consumption was principally due to increasing demand from the city's industries. The high mortality rate in this period, when there were more deaths than births in the city, meant that immigrants from English counties and other countries maintained the population.[14] At all levels of society, many London inhabitants were new to the city. In 1690, three-quarters of the city's apprentices were not born there, as were most members of the elite Whig social club, the Kit-Cat.[15]

In *A Tour through the Whole Island of Great Britain* (1724–1726), Daniel Defoe describes London as 'this monstrous city'.[16] Among its many industries were glue and tallow manufacture, which boiled carcasses from Smithfield market. Breweries, rope-works, shipyards, tanneries and other industries were mostly focused along the south bank of the river. Poorer housing dominated the east and south of the city, while elegant squares were created to the west, away from the port and to suit the prevailing wind. Upon returning from the Grand Tour in 1718, Walpole's relative, Thomas Coke, lived in Great Russell Street, Bloomsbury, one of the new residential districts begun in the late seventeenth century.[17] His Thanet House was then at the edge of London, close to fields, and had a generous garden noted for its honeysuckle.[18] In around 1714, Walpole moved to Orford House in Chelsea, a village to the west of London. In 1732 George II offered him property in the City of Westminster, close to Parliament and to the west of London's principal conurbation. Walpole accepted on the condition that 10 Downing Street became the residence of the First Lord of the Treasury, his principal title, and commissioned William Kent to remodel the house.

The Kit-Cat Club

In 1688, a confrontation between the absolutist Catholic monarch, James II, and the dominant Protestant parliamentary grouping, the Whigs, led to James' daughter, Mary, and son-in law, William of Orange, becoming constitutional monarchs, with the overriding power of Parliament affirmed. Just as political power was increasingly concentrated in Parliament, cultural influence moved away from the royal court to assembly rooms, learned societies, literary journals and dining clubs.[19] In 1703 Walpole became a member of the Kit-Cat, which was named after the mutton pie made by Christopher Cat, or Catling, a Norfolk pastry cook and the proprietor of the *Cat and Fiddle* in Gray's Inn Lane where the Club first met. Ophelia Field remarks: 'As pies and puddings were considered the best of English cookery, the Club's favourite dish would have signified the founders' self-consciously English, as opposed to French, tastes.'[20] Active from around 1696 to 1722, the Kit-Cat's membership was mostly aristocratic but also included writers, dramatists and architects such as Joseph Addison, William Congreve, Richard Steele and John Vanbrugh. Sir Godfrey Kneller's portraits of Kit-Cat members depicted peers and commoners as though they were equals, shocking many of their contemporaries. The sitters were notably rotund and well fed. Alongside the pleasures of food, wine and male company, the Kit-Cat's purpose was political influence and cultural patronage. William Kent was not a member but a number of his clients belonged to the Kit-Cat, including Walpole,

General James Dormer, Richard Boyle, third Earl of Burlington, and Richard Temple, first Viscount Cobham, for whom he respectively designed interiors, buildings and gardens at Houghton, Chiswick, Rousham and Stowe. Born in 1697, twenty-one years after Walpole, Coke was a generation younger than the Kit-Cat members and the Club was in decline by the time that he inherited his estates.

The polluted air affected the Kit-Cat as it did other aspects of London life. In 1702, the Club considered moving their summer meetings to enjoy the better climate of the higher ground to the north of London. Richard Blakemore's *The Kit-Cats, A Poem*, 1708, confirms the attraction of Hampstead's 'airy head'.[21] In 1703 the Kit-Cat's convenor, the publisher Jacob Tonson, acquired the lease of the Club's new summer venue and asked Vanbrugh to remodel the interior. Sited on the south bank of the Thames seven miles west of London, Barn Elms was easily accessible by boat, which was safer than travelling by road. Field concludes that 'The westerly migration from the stink of London into fresher air represented [...] the Club's rising status since the 1690s'.[22] As many of the Kit-Cat's members were wealthy landowners, the westerly location of a London residence was accompanied by the clearer air of a country estate, which Evelyn acknowledged in *Fumifugium*:

> But, it is manifest, that those who repair to *London*, no sooner enter into it, but they find a universal alteration to their Bodies, which are either dryed up or enflamed, the humours being exasperated and made apt to putrifie, their sensories and perspiration so exceedingly stopped, with the loss of Appetite, and a kind of general stupefaction, succeeded with such *Catharrs* and *Dissillations*, as do never, or very rarely quit them, without some further Symptomes of dangerous Inconveniency so long as they abide in the place; which yet are immediately restored to their former habit; so soon as they are retired to their Homes and enjoy fresh *Aer* again.[23]

Four days north

Walpole and Coke were Norfolk neighbours as well as relatives. The Prime Minister resided at Houghton in the northwest of the county while Coke's coastal estate was ten miles to the northeast at Holkham. London was over a hundred miles distant. Even a simple journey could be dangerous as well as uncomfortable, as Horace Walpole observed: 'One is forced to travel, even at noon, as if one was going to battle.'[24] Farm animals followed the same routes as people; in wet weather a road dissolved into mud while a frozen surface made wheels bump and jar. With no street lighting and towns sparsely lit, the countryside was truly dark at night and passage along poorly maintained roads was treacherous.[25] Divided into daytime travel and overnight rest, the journey from London to Norfolk took four days, covering just twenty-five miles a day. Attuned to natural time as well as the mechanical time of the clock, daily life was sensitive to the rhythms of the seasons, the shifts in the weather and the changes from day to night. Arduous travel made time and distance seem long and slow, especially in the bleak depth of winter when draughty carriages and rudimentary medicines offered little protection. John Buxton, a Norfolk gentleman, writes of bad weather more often than good in letters to his son. In November 1729, the weather could postpone even a local visit:

> I fear this has been too bad to let us now think of performing that journey. The season being also so very sickly I'm not for running any hazard of taking colds, having hitherto pretty well escaped the epidemical one, but I think London feels most of it.[26]

Having passed through Cambridge, a carriage bound for Houghton either ventured north to King's Lynn or turned towards Newmarket, following the same route as a carriage travelling to Holkham, which entered Norfolk at Swaffham.[27] In December 1731, a traveller was advised: 'You must by no means stop at Swaffam for the man's sake, but rather take warm at Hillborough if need be. The smallpox rages at Swaffam'.[28]

Georgic England

Outside of the few industrial centres, England remained overwhelmingly rural and sparsely populated. Ninety per cent of the workforce was employed in agriculture or related activities and land ownership was the principal measure of wealth, status and influence. In *Philosophiae Naturalis Principia Mathematica* (Mathematical Principles of Natural Philosophy) (1687), Isaac Newton concludes that material objects possess mass and are dependent on forces of attraction and repulsion as in a mechanical system.[29] As nature was conceived as a machine, mankind could have been its driver and mechanic, making adjustments to improve performance. But in an era that was fortified by descriptions of rural life and yet to face the full force of industrialisation, another analogy was more appropriate. Advocating the farmer as a model for the enlightened management of nature and society, Virgil's first book of the *Georgics* (37 BC) was particularly influential, explaining Walpole's pleasure in presenting himself as a bluff Norfolk squire.[30]

A concern for farming inevitably included a concern for the weather. A scientific approach to the weather was in its infancy and an alternative was widely supported despite the increasing influence of empirical investigation. In classical antiquity there were two distinct attitudes to atmospheric phenomena, one a theory of meteors expressed in Aristotle's *Meteorologica*, c.350 BC, the other a practical guide to the weather exemplified by Virgil. Verse not prose, and interpretation not explanation, the first book of the *Georgics* identifies changes in nature that foretell impending weather, such as the behaviour of insects and birds, plants and skies. Virgil emphasises weather's creative influence on the arts as well as daily life and even acknowledges inclement weather as a stimulus to artistic production. The *Georgics* was a model for pastoral verse in the Renaissance and afterwards. An English translation appeared in 1697, inspiring Alexander

Pope's *Pastorals* (1709).[31] James Thomson's *The Seasons* (1730) was the most influential Georgic poem of the eighteenth century, presenting human activity in dialogue with an evolving natural world to a greater extent that Pope's more restrained poetry.[32] Sharing Thomson's sensitivity to the contrasting seasons, Kent provided illustrations for 'Spring', 'Summer', 'Autumn' and 'Winter', no doubt recognising parallels between the relaxed and evocative flow of Thomson's poetry and his own developing gardening concerns.[33] Thomson combined a Georgic sensibility with a Newtonian conception of the universe. He celebrated weather's variety but recognised a fundamental order in the natural sequence of the seasons, which provided a setting for the primacy of culture. In 'A Poem Sacred to the Memory of Sir Isaac Newton', which was published with *The Seasons*, nature is female, passive and subject to Newton: 'Nature herself / Stood all subdu'd by him, and open laid / Her very latent glory to his view'.[34]

A drawing of Kent's pyramidal monument to Newton immediately precedes Thomson's poem to the scientist, implying that the architect and poet may have had a comparable conception of nature. Carved in white and grey marble and installed in Westminster Abbey in 1731, Newton reclines on a sarcophagus, resting an arm on his most famous volumes.[35] Above, a figure representing astronomy surmounts a celestial globe. The Latin inscription praises 'a strength of mind almost divine, and mathematical principles peculiarly his own'.[36] It is likely that, in common with his age, Kent recognised a practical and spiritual appreciation of nature and a mechanical and secular one. But rather than a discourse on Newtonian thought, his garden designs emphasise an engaged, lyrical and hedonistic appreciation of the natural world.

Following continental Europe, in 1752, Britain and its colonies adopted the Gregorian calendar's uniform system of measurement in place of the Julian calendar, which reflected the seasonal rhythms of farming. The introduction of a standard timescale allowed the climate to be more readily conceived as regular and subject to order. But confidence in the weather guide persisted well into the eighteenth century. First, because it affirmed rural traditions, emphasising the social, practical and spiritual benefits that arose from co-existence with nature, which tied rural customs and celebrations to the seasonal calendar. Second, because it countered the mechanical and secular conception of time and nature that suited the agricultural reforms of the political establishment and provided an early indication of industrialisation.[37] However, the two conceptions of the natural world were not simply opposed in class terms. The tradition of weather signs was communicated to prosperous and poor alike. Attempts to resolve the two traditions were evident in farming guides as well as poems. One of the best-known guides was written by John Claridge in 1670 and republished as *The Shepherd of Banbury's Rules To Judge of the Changes of the Weather, Grounded on Forty Years Experience* in 1744. The subtitle of the 1744 edition describes 'A Rational Account ... on the Principles of *Newtonian* Philosophy'. After an unexplained piece of weather advice, the author remarks:

> This must be allow'd a very extraordinary Aphorism from a Country Shepherd, but at the Same Time it is very agreeable to the Observations of

Dr. *Hooke*, Dr. *Derham*, Dr. *Grew*, and other able Naturalists, who with unwearied Pains and Diligence have calculated the Quality of Rain falling in one Year and compared it with what fell in another.[38]

The park ranger

Beginning in the seventeenth century and increasing after 1724, parliamentary land enclosures transferred over six million acres from public to private use, benefiting wealthy landowners who could afford to invest and profit from the economies of scale, while undermining the rural poor who relied on common land for a part of their livelihood. In Norfolk 75 per cent of land enclosures occurred by 1760.[39] As heaths and pastures were ordered into regular fields, gardens and parks cultivated a natural image.

Norfolk is the driest county in England and summer droughts are a frequent problem. A cold northeast wind blows in from the sea, ensuring that winters can be harsh, causing frost damage to young trees and less hardy species. In 1774 Mrs Delany remarked: 'The country all round here is *entirely bare*, as if there were some *strict law* that *not a tree, not a shrub* should shade the *turnips*'. But due to Walpole and Coke's efforts she recognised 'a great extent of plantations enough to inform the country that trees *will grow in Norfolk*'.[40]

In 1730, Walpole expanded the park at Houghton and relocated the villagers beyond its gates, demolishing the existing village two years later. Walpole's favourite landscape artist was his contemporary John Wootton, the pre-eminent early eighteenth-century painter of hunting and sporting scenes who painted in a style reminiscent of Claude Lorrain and Gaspar Dughet. Together with Jonathan Richardson, Wootton painted *Sir Robert Walpole*, *c.*1726, as a Ranger of Richmond Park, the model of a country squire surrounded by his dogs.[41] Echoing themes expressed in Thomson's *The Seasons*, the autumnal hues of Wootton's *Classical Landscape*, *c.*1740, hung in the dressing room adjacent to Walpole's bedchamber.[42] John Barrell concludes that the English Georgic tradition allowed 'its inhabitants a life of work and play together' and was 'concerned to soften as much as to recommend the hard moral lessons of Virgil's original *Georgics*' in which 'rewards and pleasures are always in the future'.[43] Empiricism's attention to subjective experience and the natural world tempered the Elysian narrative of classical antiquity so that the transitory pleasures of the present were emphasised more often than the eternal joy of the afterlife.[44] Although industriousness was a virtue for rich and poor, the prosperous were more likely to be rewarded with recreation and repose.

The November Congresses

Simpler than a seventeenth-century layout but still formal rather than picturesque, the new garden at Houghton was largely realised by 1720, when Walpole decided to demolish the existing house and commission a new one.

Construction began in 1722, soon after he became Prime Minster. In Edmund Prideaux's depiction a few years later, three sets of elegantly attired figures stroll sequentially along the broadwalk, which is edged by rows of conical topiary to the north and south. Further to each side, the hedges are fully grown and trees are maturing in two 'wilderness' gardens.[45] Houghton Hall's west elevation is partly obscured by a temporary building associated with its construction. One of James Gibbs' corner domes is complete, while another is yet to be started. As the new house was slightly to the east of the old one, the diagonal paths cutting through the wilderness gardens no longer converged at the centre of the west elevation, indicating a discrepancy between house and garden and retaining the memory of the demolished house in the presence of the new one (Figure 5.1).

With his political career in London, Walpole's visits to Houghton followed a fixed pattern from around 1725. He visited in May for two weeks, while later in the year he stayed for a month, entertaining friends and allies at the 'November Congresses' which combined social life, political intrigue and cultural patronage, continuing the tradition and spirit of the Kit-Cat Club. Walpole's expenditure was lavish; £1,500 a year was spent on wine. In the vaulted ground floor arcade where hunting parties would gather, silver taps served 'Hogan', a particularly

Figure 5.1 Edmund Prideaux, *Album of Topographical Views of England c.1716–1727*, open at a view of Houghton Hall from the west, *c.*1725

strong beer. John Hervey, second Baron Hervey, wrote in 1731: 'In public we drank loyal healths, talked of the times and cultivated popularity; in private we drew plans and cultivated the country.'[46]

The Stone Hall

Houghton Hall is not large in comparison to other grand houses but it was designed to be a fitting setting for the Prime Minister and his lavish art collection. The plan and proportions of the first floor rooms were already decided when Kent was given responsibility for their design and decoration in 1725; a wonderful commission from a prestigious client. In 1722, Kent began to transform a number of rooms at Kensington Palace for King George I, which may have alerted Walpole to his skill. After climbing a curving double flight of stairs, visitors arrived at Kent's rusticated Great Door on the first floor of Houghton's east elevation, which was then the main entrance to the house.[47] Entering into the Stone Hall, they passed first under sculptures of Neptune and Britannia and then under figures representing Peace and Plenty, which emphasised Walpole's guardianship of a prosperous sea-trading nation.[48] The Stone Hall was richly carpeted like Houghton's other main reception rooms but it was sparsely furnished with just six timber benches and two side tables, as was then typical of an entrance hall. Especially in mid-winter, the double-height room was difficult to heat. Its volume, hard materials, sparse furniture and low temperature suggested an external room as much as an internal one.[49]

The focus of the room is John Michael Rysbrack's bust of Walpole on the north wall. Combining Roman and British iconography, the bust depicts Walpole in a toga adorned with the Garter Star, celebrating his election as a Knight in 1726. Arguments for a limited monarchy and strong parliament found a model in 'the Roman pattern of consuls (which equated to the Monarch), patricians (equating to the Lords), and *comitiae* (equating to the House of Commons)'.[50] Ancient Rome offered Georgian Britain a semblance of authority and a model to emulate and surpass. Walpole is placed slightly higher than that the ancient busts that line the room, including Roman emperors such as Commodus, Marcus Aurelius and Trajan.

One of the principal themes of the early eighteenth century – the dialogue between nature and culture – developed to such an extent that 'the nation came to be understood *as* nature', writes Anne Janowitz.[51] Farming and cultivated nature dominated the estate but hunting and uncultivated nature were emphasised in the house's internal decoration. Unlike the arduous manual labour associated with arable farming, hunting was a gentlemanly pursuit legally restricted to landowners. Walpole's bust stands before a relief of *The Sacrifice of Diana*, goddess of hunting, while the carved head of a fox appears in the broken pediment above.[52] In Kent's *Preparatory Drawing for an Engraving of the Stone Hall Chimneypiece, Houghton Hall*, 1726, *The Sacrifice to Diana* appears as it was later constructed. Eyeing any visitor, Walpole looks to his left, towards the Great Door and the park beyond (Figure 5.2). However, in the completed chimneypiece, Walpole looks to his right, into the house and towards the doorways leading to the Saloon and Great Staircase. The reason for the change is unknown but it is unlikely to have been error or omission. A very particular patron, Walpole would have given careful attention to his own image in such an important location and it can safely be assumed that the bust faces the direction he wished. The *piano nobile* offered views across the estate and in 1740 Walpole sculpted the land to extend the view to the east. But the gaze of Walpole's bust suggests that his principal focus may have been towards the representations of nature and culture within the house.

Figure 5.2 William Kent, *Preparatory Drawing for an Engraving of the Stone Hall Chimneypiece, Houghton Hall*, 1726

Walpole's bust crowns the Stone Hall's only heat source; a large fireplace. In cooler months, the fire would have drawn visitors closer to the image of their host, the warmth and illumination of the fire alluding to his generosity and patronage. At night, the other principal light source was the gilt chandelier with eighteen candles suspended from the centre of the ceiling. In 1731, the Duke of Lorraine, the future Francis I, Holy Roman Emperor, visited Houghton. Dinner was held in the Stone Hall because the Marble Parlour was incomplete. At a cost of £15 per night, 130 candles illuminated the Hall, while a further 50 lit the Saloon, associating illumination with ostentation as well as enlightenment. But Houghton's open fires and candles affected the climate of the house in another way, creating a smoky haze that obscured rather than illuminated, allowing soot to land on fabrics and paintings.

The Saloon

Beyond the Stone Hall, the double-height Saloon is a somewhat smaller but still substantial room. The goddess of hunting reappears in the decoration. In contrast to the hard off-white Stone Hall or the dark *trompe l'oeil* Great Staircase, the Saloon was vibrant in crimson and gold and populated by paintings and furniture so that it was both physically and perceptually warmer than either of the other rooms. While a visit to the Stone Hall was usually brief, important guests conversed with their host in the Saloon. The Stone Hall emphasised Walpole's political status while the adjacent room focused more on his cultural patronage. Houghton and Holkham were key influences on a new development imported from Italy: the integration of paintings into the design of interiors, which led to the gradual demise of distracting ceiling paintings. Kent's earliest surviving designs of an interior – 1725 elevations of the north and south walls of the Saloon – were then unusual in England because he depicted paintings and furniture alongside doors, windows and fireplaces so that they all formed a coherent architectural ensemble.[53] Horace Walpole suggested that his father restrained Kent, insisting that the ceilings should be painted in muted colours, presumably so that they would not draw attention away from the paintings.[54] But his claim cannot be validated and Houghton's exuberance suggests otherwise. Sharing a passion for art, architecture, landscape and food, Kent and Walpole were compatible characters. Burlington characterised Kent as 'the little rogue'.[55] Pope teasingly encouraged Burlington to 'eat a Mutton Stake in ye manner of that great Master Signor Kent'. Elsewhere, Pope simply described his friend as 'very hot and very fat', concluding that 'he must expect not to imitate Raphael in anything but his untimely end'.[56] Coupling Walpole's character with that of Houghton, Plumb remarks that: 'There was no arid aestheticism about him; his taste glowed with warmth. Vigorous and grand it was an expression of his own rich personality.'[57] Celebrating Walpole's achievement, Isaac Ware and Thomas Ripley's *The Plans, Elevations and Sections; Chimney-pieces and Ceilings of Houghton in Norfolk*, 1735, was the first architectural book dedicated to a single British house.[58]

The Great Staircase

Kent's development as a garden designer was gradual and occurred alongside his career as a painter and architect. Reflecting the diversity of his practice, the interdependence of exterior and interior is evident in his work at Houghton, although he did not contribute to the landscape. Rising the full height of the house, roofed with glass and also difficult to heat, the Great Staircase connects the Stone Hall on the first floor to the Arcade below. Suggesting the courtyard of a Renaissance palazzo, internal windows line its walls, which are decorated with mythological hunting scenes. Creating a further ambiguity between interior and exterior, the Doric temple that fills the 'courtyard' is provocatively large for the space, implying that it should really be outside. Surmounting the temple, Hubert Le Sueur's *Gladiator* – a seventeenth-century copy of a classical original – aggressively mediates between the *trompe l'oeil* decoration of the Great Staircase and the muscular carving of the Stone Hall. The Saloon is very much an internal room but the Stone Hall and Great Staircase refer to a *cortile* as much as a *piano nobile*. The Great Staircase is particularly rich and complex because it is an internal room that mimics an external one, while its painted scenes refer to the woods beyond the garden, implying a wilderness setting for the temple rather than the expected rolling lawn. The temple's status was particularly intriguing at the time of its construction because the garden then contained no buildings, which was unusual in the early eighteenth century.[59] As garden buildings were a means to mediate between culture and nature, their absence drew greater attention to the temple and the representations of uncultivated nature in the house. Together, the Stone Hall, Saloon and Great Staircase offer a vibrant dialogue on representation and reality, power and patronage, the house, the garden and the hunt, which is represented in all three rooms. In the year following his retirement as Prime Minister, Walpole poignantly recognised his isolation and that of his estate as well as Houghton's dual attractions, the park and notably the interior: 'my flatterers here are all mutes, the Oaks the Beeches and the Chestnuts [...] Within doors we come a little nearer to real life and admire upon the almost speaking Canvas'![60]

The South Lawn and the North Sea

The early eighteenth century is associated with a significant transformation in the English landscape, when the picturesque garden came to the fore with Kent as its principal exponent. Houghton has one of his most exuberant interiors but he had no involvement in the nondescript garden and austere park.[61] However, while working at Houghton in the 1720s and 1730s, Kent also contributed designs for Coke, at Holkham, who he had first met in 1714. In that year, Coke remarked to his grandfather and guardian, Sir John Newton: 'I am become since my stay in Rome, a perfect virtuoso, a great lover of pictures'.[62] The virtuoso's love of art identified him as the finest of early eighteenth-century gentlemen; which Coke's knowledgeable and growing collection of antiquities, books, drawings, manuscript, paintings and sculptures seemed to confirm. However, others identified loud and coarse behaviour that was confirmed in Horace Walpole's description of 'a very cunning man but not a deep one. He affected frankness and a noisy kind of buffoonery, both to disguise his art, and his superficial understanding'.[63] Reminiscent of Sir Robert Walpole, the sporting and learned sides of Coke's character were recalled by a Norfolk neighbour:

> I remember, when we were Fox-Hunters, and a long Day's Sport had rather tir'd than satisfied us, we often pass'd the Evening in reading the Ancient Authors: when the Beauty of their Language, the Strength, and Justness of their thoughts for ever glowing with a noble Spirit of Liberty, made us forget not only the Pains, but the Pleasures of the Day.[64]

Houghton Hall was fully complete in 1735. Travelling from Houghton to Holkham, Kent would have arrived at the top of a ridge four miles from the sea, passing the site of the Triumphal Arch which he had drawn in 1732 to mark the estate's formal approach (Figure 5.3).[65] Gently undulating, the north Norfolk landscape offers, conceals and then reveals views to the coast. At 67 metres above sea level, the Triumphal Arch is the highest point of the Holkham estate. Framed within the central archway, Kent's distant Obelisk bisects the horizon of the North Sea. The avenue is straight but the land dips slowly and evenly so that the view of the sea is lost and fields are seen to each side, which Coke lined with *Quercus ilex*, the Holm Oak, a massive Mediterranean evergreen with a round head and low-hanging branches that can withstand coastal locations and cold salt winds. The avenue then rises to the highest point within the park at 36 metres above sea level, where Obelisk Wood was planted by 1730. The avenue bifurcates to encircle the Obelisk before proceeding north to the edge of the Wood, where the sea is visible once again, returning the vista that had been hidden since the Triumphal Arch while expanding it into a panorama.

Figure 5.3 William Kent, *Triumphal Arch with Donkey, Holkham, c.*1732

Figure 5.4 William Kent, *Seat on the Mount with Irregular Basin, Holkham,* c.1739

In the second half of the 1730s, Kent began to influence the design of the garden as well as its buildings. When the Hanoverian court director of buildings and gardens, Friedrich Carl von Hardenberg, visited Holkham in 1744, Coke remarked that the gardens were 'all by Kent'.[66] Beyond Obelisk Wood was the South Lawn. To the west of an irregular basin, an artificial hillock was flanked by a casually planted wood and surmounted by the Seat on the Mount (Figure 5.4). Peter Scheemaker's sculptures of basket-bearing nymphs adorned its four pilasters, each representing a season.[67] To the east, a wilderness garden concealed an orangery. In the centre, trees framed the downward slope from Obelisk Wood, terminating at porches on the basin's edge.[68]

A very clear air

Coke's financial difficulties are assumed to have delayed Holkham Hall – which took nearly thirty years to complete, about three times as long as Houghton.[69] But the initial attention given to the park and garden may have been due to desire as well as necessity. In 1734 Coke recognised the garden buildings as a more immediate priority than the house[70] and in a poem written before 1742 he proclaimed: 'Here kent [sic] and I are planting Clumps/ Not minding whom our Monarch Rumps [...] Contented I enjoy my home/ Design a temple, Build a Dome,/ Or raise an Obelisk [...] In time you'll come to think like me/ And love your Country Seat.'[71] As he journeyed from one commission to the other, Kent may have imagined Houghton's exuberant interior and Holkham's picturesque landscape as one glorious Arcadian estate.

Seen from Obelisk Wood, the sequential arrangement of gardens, plantations and waves recreated the third, second and first natures theorised in the Renaissance and Ancient Rome.[72] Before the late seventeenth century, unfettered nature was usually considered to be brutish and deformed. But, alongside a concern for cultivation, the eighteenth century developed a fascination for seas and mountains. Recuperation in nature was not a new theme but it found new expression as nature and moral virtue were linked for the first time. Sensitivity to one's environment became as necessary as sensitivity to others. In the second volume of *Characteristicks of Men, Manners, Opinions, Times* (1711), Anthony Ashley Cooper, third Earl of Shaftesbury, praises nature and weather: 'enliven'd by the Sun, and temper'd by the fresh AIR of fanning *Breezes*! […] I shall no longer resist the Passion growing in me for Things of a *natural* kind'.[73]

Associated with the second half of the eighteenth century, reaction to the industrial revolution is cited as a catalyst for the romantic appreciation of nature. England was primarily rural in the first half of the century but London's atmosphere was already heavily polluted. Over twenty times more populous than the next largest English city, the capital dominated the nation's political and cultural life, ensuring that all of England's influential citizens experienced London's 'Hellish Cloud'. Eulogising nature as the means of self-revelation, the early eighteenth century heralded an engagement with nature beyond Georgic England and industrial London. In 1721, ten years after Shaftesbury declared his passion for nature, Coke's cousin, Michael Newton, remarked that Holkham 'is as beautiful as other places, it stands in a very clear Air, & no Fenns within Twenty miles of it […] Mr Coke likes this place so well now that I believe if ever he builds it will be here'.[74]

Acknowledgements

I very much appreciate the generous assistance and advice of Christine Hiskey as well as the comments of Dr Suzanne Reynolds, respectively the Holkham Archivist and Manuscript Curator.

NOTES

1   J. H. Plumb, *Sir Robert Walpole: The Making of a Statesman* (London: The Cresset Press, 1956), p. xii; William Speck, 'Britain's First Prime Minister' in Andrew Moore (ed.), *Houghton Hall: The Prime Minister, The Empress and the Heritage* (London: Philip Wilson, 1996), p. 12.
2   Queen Caroline quoted in Speck, p. 12.
3   Roy Porter, *English Society in the Eighteenth Century* (London: Penguin, 1991), p. 10.
4   Peter Brimblecombe, 'Interest in Air Pollution Among the Early Fellows of the Royal Society', *Notes and Records of the Royal Society of London*, 32, 2, March (1978): 66, 123.
5   An idea suggested to me by Adrian Petrenco.
6   John Evelyn, *Fumifugium: Or, The Inconvenience of the Aer, and Smoake of London Dissipated* (London: B. White, 1772), pp. 1–2. The title of this edition is slightly different from the 1661 original.

7   Hippocrates was born in the fifth century BC. *Airs, Waters, Places* and *Breaths* were highly influential but it is uncertain whether the treatises attributed to Hippocrates were actually written by him. Evelyn, *Fumifugium*, pp. 18, 11–13.

8   Evelyn, *Fumifugium*, pp. 3, 34–37.

9   Evelyn, *Fumifugium*, pp. 47, 49.

10   Mark Jenner, 'The Politics of London Air: John Evelyn's *Fumifugium* and the Restoration', *The Historical Journal*, 38, 3 (1995): 544–546.

11   Jenner, 'The Politics of London Air': 542–543.

12   Jenner notes that this 'is a quotation from *Lamentations* 4.20 and refers to the Lord's Annointed'. Evelyn, *Fumifugium*, p. 44; Jenner, 'The Politics of London Air': 543–544.

13   Ibid.: 549; Steven R. Smith, 'John Evelyn and London Air', *History Today*, 23, 3, March (1975): 186.

14   Dorothy M. George, *London Life in the Eighteenth Century* (Chicago: Academy Chicago Publishers, 1984), pp. 37–41. First published in 1925.

15   Ophelia Field, *The Kit-Cat Club* (London: Harper Perennial, 2009), pp. 10, 255.

16   Daniel Defoe, *A Tour through the Whole Island of Great Britain* (London: J. M. Dent, 1974), p. 316. First published in 1724–1726.

17   The second husband of Coke's grandmother, Lady Anne Walpole, was Colonel Horatio Walpole, the uncle of Sir Robert Walpole.

18   Coke's father-in-law, Thomas Tufton, sixth Earl of Thanet, had acquired the lease in 1693. Charles Warburton James, *Chief Justice Coke, His Family & Descendents at Holkham* (London: Country Life, 1929), p. 210.

19   John Brewer, *The Pleasures of the Imagination: English Culture in the Eighteenth Century* (New York: Farrar Straus Giroux, 1997), pp. xxiv–xxviii, 40–49.

20   Field, *The Kit-Cat Club*, p. 35.

21   A purpose-built clubhouse was considered but not constructed and the Club may have instead met in the gardens of the Upper Flask tavern. Ibid., pp. 113–115.

22   Ibid., p. 114.

23   Evelyn, *Fumifugium*, p. 24.

24   Horace Walpole quoted in Porter, p. 17.

25   William Albert, *The Turnpike Road System in England, 1663–1840* (Cambridge: Cambridge University Press, 1972), pp. 44, 55.

26   John Buxton to Robert Buxton, 18 November 1729, quoted in Alan Mackley (ed.), *John Buxton Norfolk Gentleman and Architect: Letters to his son 1717–1729* (Norwich: Norfolk Record Society, vol 69, 2005), p. 164.

27   James, *Chief Justice Coke*, p. 132; Mackley, *John Buxton*, p. 14.

28   Roger North, 17 December 1731, quoted in Jack Lindsay, *The Monster City, Defoe's London, 1688–1730* (London: Granada, 1978), p. 28.

29   Isaac Newton, *Mathematical Principles of Natural Philosophy*, trans. Florian Cajori (Berkeley: University of California Press, 1962).

30   John Barrell, *The Dark Side of the Landscape: The Rural Poor in English Painting 1730–1840* (Cambridge: Cambridge University Press, 1980), pp. 8–9; Vladimir Jankovic, *Reading the Skies: A Cultural History of English Weather, 1650–1820*, (Manchester; Manchester University Press, 2000), pp. 16-22, 137.

31   The *Georgics*' translator was John Dryden.

32   Barrell, *The Dark Side of the Landscape*, p. 7; John Dixon Hunt, *Gardens and the Picturesque: Studies in the History of Landscape Architecture* (Cambridge MA: MIT Press, 1992), p. 228.

33   Malcolm Andrews, *The Search for the Picturesque: Landscape Aesthetics and Tourism in Britain, 1760–1800* (Aldershot: Scholar Press, 1989), p. 10; Christopher Hussey, *The Picturesque: Studies in a Point of View* (London: Frank Cass, 1983), p. 54; first published in 1927.

34   James Thomson, 'A Poem Sacred to the Memory of Sir Isaac Newton' in *The Seasons* (London: John Millan, 1730), p. 243. Refer to Jonathan Bate, 'Living with the Weather', *Studies in Romanticism*, 35, Fall (1996): 433, 437.

35   Thomson, *The Seasons*, p. 240.

36   Newton also appears in the Temple of British Worthies in Stowe's Elysian Fields, which Kent created in the 1730s.

37   Patrick Curry, *Prophecy and Power: Astrology in Early Modern England* (Cambridge: Polity Press, 1989), p. 161; Jankovic, *Reading the Skies*, p. 77.

38   John Claridge, *The Shepherd of Banbury's Rules To Judge of the Changes of the Weather, Grounded on Forty Years Experience* (London: W. Bickerton, 1744), p. 14. Refer to Jan Golinski, *British Weather and the Climate of Enlightenment* (Chicago and London: The University of Chicago Press, 2007), p. 72; Jankovic, *Reading the Skies*, pp. 153–155.

39   Tom Williamson, *The Archaeology of the Landscape Park: Garden Design in Norfolk, England, c.1680–1840* (Oxford: Archaeopress, 1998), p. 14.

40   Mrs Delany quoted in James, *Chief Justice Coke*, p. 295.

41   Walpole's eldest son, Robert, was actually appointed Ranger in 1726. Walpole's brother, Horatio, first Baron Walpole, owned the painting.

42   Sebastian Edwards, Andrew Moore and Chloë Archer, 'The Catalogue' in Andrew Moore (ed.), *Houghton Hall: The Prime Minister, The Empress and the Heritage* (London: Philip Wilson, 1996), p. 104.

43   Barrell, *The Dark Side of the Landscape*, pp. 36–37.

44   John Locke, *An Essay concerning Human Understanding*, ed. Peter H. Nidditch (Oxford: Clarendon Press, 1975), bk. 2, ch. 1, pp. 104–105; bk. 2, ch. 27, p. 342. First published in 1690.

45   Williamson, *The Archaeology of the Landscape Park*, p. 35; Tom Williamson, 'The Planting of the Park' in Moore, pp. 42, 44–45.

46   Hervey, 21 July 1731, quoted in Plumb, *Sir Robert Walpole: The King's Minister*, p. 88. Refer to John Cornforth, *Houghton, Norfolk* (Derby: Heritage House Group Ltd, 2007), p. 22; Field, *The Kit-Cat Club*, p. 312; J.H. Plumb, *Sir Robert Walpole: The King's Minister*, pp. 87–88; Porter, *English Society in the Eighteenth Century*, p. 59.

47   The stairs were later demolished. John Harris, 'The Architecture of the House' in Moore, *Houghton Hall*, p. 23.

48   Proposed by Colen Campbell and developed by Kent, Stone Hall was probably derived from Inigo Jones' Queen's House in Greenwich, 1635. Cornforth, *Houghton, Norfolk*, p. 17.

49   Indeed, the double-height hall fell out of fashion in the late 1740s as the influence of polite society became widespread and entertaining became less formal. John Cornforth, *Early Georgian Interiors* (New Haven and London: Yale University Press, 2004), p. 35.

50   John Dixon Hunt, *William Kent: Landscape Garden Designer* (London: Zwemmer, 1987), p. 57.

51   Anne Janowitz, *England's Ruins: Poetic Purpose and the National Landscape* (Oxford: Basil Blackwell, 1990), p. 5.

52   John Cornforth, 'The Genesis and Creation of a Great Interior' in Moore, pp. 32–34; Edwards, Moore and Archer, 'The Catalogue', pp. 110–111; Susanna Wade Martins, *Coke of Norfolk (1754–1842): A Biography* (Woodbridge: The Boydell Press, 2009), p. 51.

53   Cornforth, *Early Georgian Interiors*, p. 138; Cornforth, *Houghton, Norfolk*, p. 34.

54   Horace Walpole referred to in Margaret Jourdain, *The Work of William Kent* (London: Country Life, 1948), p. 70.

55   Burlington quoted in John Harris, *William Kent 1685–1748: A Poet on Paper* (London: Sir John Soane's Museum, 1998), p. 2.

56   Pope quoted Ibid., p. 2.

57   Plumb, *Sir Robert Walpole: The Making of a Statesman*, p. xii.

58   Making no mention of Gibbs and Campbell, and attributing only chimneypieces and ceilings to Kent, Ripley is credited as the architect and Ware as the draughtsman.

59   In 1728 Sir Matthew Decker mentioned 'arbours' in the two wilderness gardens but no garden buildings, quoted in John Cornforth, 'The Growth of an Idea', *Country Life*, 14 May (1987): 164.

60   Sir Robert Walpole quoted in Betty Kemp, *Sir Robert Walpole* (London: Weidenfeld and Nicholson, 1976), p. 135.

61 In 1728 Sir Thomas Robinson attributed the expanded park to Charles Bridgeman but it is uncertain how much of his design was realised. Williamson, *The Archaeology of the Landscape Park*, p. 50.

62 Thomas Coke quoted in James, *Chief Justice Coke*, p. 187.

63 Horace Walpole, *Correspondence*, ed. Wilmarth Sheldon Lewis (New Haven and London: Yale University Press, 1937), p. 43.

64 Quoted in D. P. Mortlock, *Holkham Library: A History and Description* (The Roxburghe Club, 2006), p. 76. Refer to James Lees-Milne, *Earls of Creation: Five Great Patrons of Eighteenth-Century Art* (London: Hamish Hamilton, 1962), p. 242.

65 Completed in 1733, the stables were most likely to Kent's design and his last major intervention at Houghton. There is no record of Kent visiting Holkham although it is very likely that he did so. Harris, 'The Architecture of the House', p. 22.

66 Little remains of Kent's gardens and garden buildings apart from the Triumphal Arch, Temple and Obelisk. Hardenberg, quoted in Leo Schmidt, Christian Keller and Polly Feversham (eds), *Holkham* (Munich: Prestel, 2005), p. 110; W. O. Hassall, 'Views from the Holkham Windows' in Frederick Emmison and Roy Stephens (eds), *Tribute to an Antiquary: Essays presented to Marc Fitch by some of his friends* (London: Leopard's Head Press, 1976), p. 310; Williamson, *The Archaeology of the Landscape Park*, p. 66.

67 Hardy in Schmidt, Keller and Feversham, *Holkham*, p. 139.

68 Refer to Matthew Brettingham Jr, *The Plans, Elevations and Sections of Holkham in Norfolk, The Seat of the late Earl of Leicester. To which are added, The Ceilings and Chimney-Pieces; and also, A Descriptive Account of the Statues, Pictures, and Drawings; Not in the former Edition* (London: T. Spilsbury, B. White and S. Leacroft, 1773), p. 7.

69 R. A. C. Parker, *Coke of Norfolk, A Financial and Agricultural Study, 1707–1842* (Oxford: Oxford University Press, 1975), pp. 12–23, 36.

70 Coke, letter to Matthew Brettingham Sr, 1734, quoted in Christine Hiskey, 'The Building of Holkham Hall: Newly Discovered Letters', *Architectural History*, 40 (1997): 148.

71 Supposedly by Coke, the poem is titled 'An Epistle from Ld. Lovell to Lord Chesterfield at Bath, Wrote by Mr. Poulteney'. William Pulteney was created Earl of Bath in 1742. Quoted in James, *Chief Justice Coke*, pp. 230–231.

72 Hunt, *Greater Perfections*, pp. 32–33.

73 Although Shaftesbury may not have predicted the picturesque garden he influenced its development. Anthony Ashley Cooper, third Earl of Shaftesbury, *Characteristicks of Men, Manner, Opinions, Times*, ed. Philip Ayres (Oxford: Clarendon Press, 1999), vol. 2, pp. 94 –101. Refer to David Leatherbarrow, 'Character, Geometry and Perspective: The Third Earl of Shaftesbury's Principles of Garden Design', *Journal of Garden History*, 4/4 (October-December 1984): 353.

74 Shaftesbury, vol. 2, p. 101; Newton, quoted in Schmidt, Keller and Feversham, *Holkham*, pp. 88–89.

Part two

Familiar buildings, unfamiliar readings

Nikolaus Pevsner, the connoisseur historian, began his book *An Outline of European Architecture* with the famous words: 'A bicycle shed is a building. Lincoln Cathedral is a piece of architecture'.[1] This notorious aphorism repeats a commonplace assumption that architecture – conceived as art-objects, as cathedrals and national monuments, as fine designs authored by great architects – is somehow more important than regular building – conceived as the kind of architecture that most of us inhabit most of the time. The authors of the four chapters collected in Part Two of this book, like many others, would challenge this distinction, preferring to include in the category 'architecture' many diverse ways in which people organise their relationships with each other and with the world.

Architecture – considered more broadly than Pevsner would allow – inevitably remains in progress and is never 'complete'. It is not assumed only to be the work of registered professionals. And the significant contributions of builders and inhabitants are recognised. Authorship is not decisive, and all buildings have multiple authors.[2]

Chapters collected here examine buildings whose designers are nameless in the context of 'high culture', or whose names have been largely forgotten. They examine architecture that might at first appear familiar in daily life. But, when closely read, the buildings being studied may seem less familiar after all. In different ways, they are charged unexpectedly with cultural politics and are redolent with cultural meanings. These chapters demonstrate that readings of seemingly familiar buildings can be just as insightful as readings of the famous buildings which architects and critics often prefer to talk about.

Flora Samuel, known for her writings on the canonical architect Le Corbusier,[3] here addresses three house extension projects in Cardiff, UK, all of which were built without the input of an architect. The three couples that commissioned these extensions seemed ambivalent – even hostile – to the possibility of employing an architect, who they assumed would be expensive, irrelevant and elitist. The three extensions describe a mainstream attitude to architecture in which the established figure of the architect is largely irrelevant; questioning what architects are for, and whether architects need to re-invent themselves for changing times.

Samuel Austin offers a reading of Hopwood Park motorway service area, which is sited on the M42 motorway on the edge of Birmingham, UK. Austin examines how the 'lounge space' of Hopwood Park operates. Its white surfaces, groups of sofas, clusters of lamps and display units on wheels support endless browsing. Signifiers from home, evocations of domesticity, are combined with wipe-clean surfaces and branded signage. Simultaneously welcoming and distant, familiar and uncanny, it comprises, Austin argues, a ubiquitous unplaceable present.

Diana Periton reads a familiar building from another place and time, embodying its own particular ideas of domesticity: a block of apartments constructed in suburban Paris in 1911. The architect of 67 *rue des Meuniers*, Louis Bonnier, is no longer well known, although he once led the office that oversaw regulation of the building process in Paris. The apartment block, Periton argues, transmits and transforms the customs and habits, the assumptions and expectations, which were also formalised into the city itself.[4] It was a 'component in a dynamic system', a 'living organism', whose order was 'part urged, part bestowed on its inhabitants', reminding them 'didactically, explicitly, of dignity and functional duty'.

The organisation of 67 *rue des Meuniers* bears interesting comparison with the alternative social orders studied by Jane Rendell in the chapter which concludes this part of the book. Rendell reads the Narkomfin Communal House, completed in Moscow in 1929, and the Corbusian Alton West Estate, completed in Roehampton, London, in 1958 as 'setting' and 'social condenser'. Following the psychoanalyst D. W. Winnicott, Rendell examines these configurations as 'transitional' objects and spaces 'located in the overlap between inside and outside'. Architectural ideas and ideals, she suggests, were lost in translation: between architect and inhabitant; between generations; and between different situations and cultures.

Necessary questions are raised by these readings. How relevant are architects to the seemingly familiar architecture that surrounds most of us most of the time? What are the important signifiers of 'home' in particular cultures, and how do they relate to the public sphere? Is domestic architecture ever personal or must it always inevitably be implicated in cultural politics? To what extent do people configure architecture and to what extent does it configure them? How does the act of reading architecture involve translation – between architects and inhabitants, between individuals and the cultures in which they live and work, and across cultures through time?

NOTES

1 Nikolaus Pevsner, *An Outline of European Architecture* (London: Penguin, 1998), p. 1.
2 Diane Harris, 'Social History: Identity, Performance, Politics, and Architectural Histories', *Journal of the Society of Architectural Historians*, 64, 4, December (2005): 421–423; Doina Petrescu, Florrian Kossak, Tatjana Schnieder, Renata Tyszczuk and Stephen Walker, *Agency: Working with Uncertain Architectures* (London: Routledge, 2009).
3 Flora Samuel, *Le Corbusier: Architect and Feminist* (London: Academy, 2004); Flora Samuel, *Le Corbusier in Detail* (London: Architectural Press, 2007); Flora Samuel, *Le Corbusier and the Architectural Promenade* (Basel: Birkhäuser, 2010).
4 The chapter expands on ideas developed by Periton with others in: Vittoria di Palma, Diana Periton and Marina Lathouri (eds), *Intimate Metropolis* (London: Routledge, 2008).

Chapter 6

Extension stories

Flora Samuel

This account focuses on the stories of three home extension projects in Cardiff, all of which were built without the input of an architect. Through these stories I will illustrate how the owners were, through the process of self build, able to produce extensions that are an affirmation of identity and a real source of pride. At the same time I will reveal serious concerns about the image of the architect in the minds of many people. The extensions indicate the irrelevance of the culture of architecture to the design of most homes in Britain and the irrelevance of architecture to much social science research on the home.

It is very difficult to find information on the subject of why so very few people choose to employ an architect to build or extend their homes in Britain. The Royal Institute of British Architects (RIBA) has no formal statistics on how many domestic clients choose not to use architects but K. MacInnes, has asserted that only 6 per cent of self builders contract an architectural firm.[1] Certainly, much domestic building work operates at the level of the black market and is unlikely to be included in official figures. This paper focuses on the reasons why many people in Britain choose not to employ an architect when embarking on the building of a house extension – on the benefits and drawbacks of this choice. It straddles two boundaries – that between the cultures of architecture and the social sciences and that between architecture and non-architecture, each with its own distinct methods, language and habitus (to use the sociologist Pierre Bourdieu's term). It is a difficult, but stolidly important, place to be.

This research raises questions about the interface between architectural culture and the social sciences, or rather the lack of interface between these two spheres that co-habited briefly in the 1970s but then retreated, bruised by the experience. Nowhere is this more evident than with research on the home. A great many of the recent books on this subject emanate from the social sciences, with architecture barely receiving a mention, perhaps because of a general lack of interest in architecture within the day-to-day lives of the public at large.

What follows is an account of three home extension projects built recently in the suburbs of Cardiff, the capital of Wales, with a focus on the networks of people behind the projects – 'architectural designers', builders, surveyors – who assist homeowners with the process of 'self build'.[2]

Three stories

I will chart the stories of three different extensions based on in-depth, semi-structured and conversational interviews I conducted, lasting roughly an hour, with their designers: David (financial adviser) and Rachel (part-time *Slimming World* consultant); Gareth (surveyor) and Belinda (part-time secretary, formally environmental scientist); and Pete (tax inspector) and Sara (part-time supermarket management).[3] My informants are all known to one another and they are all friends and acquaintances of mine. My foreknowledge of the couples would be both a benefit, because they would be more relaxed, and a problem because they would not want to offend me. I did not want the interviewees to feel constrained because they knew that I was an architect, albeit a lapsed one. They are all in their late 30s and occupy 'band 4' in the 2000 UK Census: 'administrative and secretarial occupations'. Each couple has two or three children, all under nine years of age, hence the need for home expansion. Whilst it might be tempting to describe the couples as 'ordinary', half of them are from the tiny percentage of people who, in the late 1980s, would have gone into higher education, and each couple's collective income is in excess of three times the national average. They are, thus, relatively wealthy and well-educated by British standards. Therefore, all would be in a good position to employ an architect.

The case study houses are all three bedroom semi-detached houses, built in the 1950s and rendered in pebbledash, on the same block and of relatively high value (£300,000–£400,000 in 2011). Rachel and David's is the largest extension, with a contract sum of roughly £100,000. It adds a single storey to the side and back, with a loft conversion in the roof to house a new bedroom and *en suite* bathroom (Figure 6.1). On the ground floor, the extra space provided by the building work has allowed for the expansion of the kitchen and dining room, a utility room and a little office to the side of the front door. Windows and doors are made of timber throughout, the kitchen floor is slate and the kitchen worktops are in granite. Belinda and Gareth's house is effectively a smaller version of the same. They have built a single storey extension at the back, repositioning and enlarging the kitchen and dining room in doing so and creating a downstairs WC and utility room at the centre of the plan. The contract sum in this case was roughly £40,000. Pete and Sara's extension is of similar scale: a widening of the extension to the side and the building of a room to replace the garage in the garden. While the couples professed that their projects had come out on budget, none of them had come out even remotely on time.

Forty-one per cent of the housing stock in the United Kingdom has been subject to at least one major alteration according to *The English Housing Conditions Survey*.[4] Cumulatively, such extensions have a profound effect on the built environment in even the most regulated of areas. Hand, Shove and Southerton argue that the pressure to extend 'is essentially social: it has to do with accomplishing and achieving what people take to be normal ways of life and normal forms of social interaction'.[5] The kitchen is fundamental: 'Kitchen extensions are not only about making space for consumer goods, but also about accommodating particular visions and images of domestic life.[6]

Figure 6.1 Rachel and David's extension which adds a single storey added to the side and back of their house, with a loft conversion in the roof including a bedroom and an *en suite* bathroom

When questioned about their objectives for the extensions, Rachel, David, Pete and Sara were unanimous in their choice of one word: 'space'. If pushed further, the first couple said that they wanted the house to 'work better', the second that they wanted to 'get our living room back'. Gareth and Belinda were more fulsome. They wanted a new kitchen; they wanted 'quality'; they wanted to overlook the garden; and, lastly, they wanted more space. Light had been a real area of concern for Gareth, who had worried that it would be too dark at the rear of the extended room. Rachel and David were remarkably pragmatic, expressing no interest in light, detail, feelings or any other values that might be promoted in architectural education.

Gareth and Belinda seemed to know more about particular design considerations and had the language to articulate them, possibly because they had sought out from magazines precedents of the kind of space they wanted to achieve. Having said this, Gareth referred to the project 'as just a bog standard extension – nothing groundbreaking' as though, perhaps, it would be pretentious to aspire to anything more. Gareth was particularly pleased with the utility and downstairs WC as places to keep things that spoiled the look of the rest of the house. I found this striking as, unlike Rachel and David, he had not listed making the house 'work better' as a concern.

None of the informants were entirely inexperienced in construction. Rachel's father, who had done several extensions himself, helped the couple, while Gareth, as a surveyor whose job is concerned with the rental of office space, had a good idea of the issues involved. He also received help from his father who is a builder. Pete and Sara had previously completed an earlier extension to their living room, an experience that informed this more recent work.

Self build versus architecture

The form of practice under consideration here is defined as 'self build' by mainstream magazines such as *Grand Designs* and *Homebuilding and Renovating*. In the UK context, all homeowners need to work through a series of hurdles before beginning work on-site – planning permission; building regulations approval and tender drawings with a written specification – each involving the production of particular information. They have the choice of employing an architect, a title protected by the statutes of the Architects' Registration Board (ARB) and the RIBA, or someone else, very often a technician or 'architectural designer'.[7] Armed with his or her CAD package this individual, very often, cuts-and-pastes-in standard windows, cavity walls and so on to produce planning permission drawings for a fee sometimes as little as £50. Such people are easy to find on the internet. The 'architectural designer' is also frequently brought in to cobble together the necessary information to get through the building regulations process, with the builder then leading the construction work. Frequently, the architectural designer and the builder are linked, sometimes contractually, giving the homeowners the feeling that they will work well together.

Questions about the variety and type of help sought by Rachel and David in preparing drawings revealed their degree of confusion about what had actually happened. They spoke most highly of a planning consultant (found through a family connection) who was reasonably priced, £100, and gave them what they felt to be good advice on how to get through planning. It took them a while to remember the profession of the first person that they employed to do the planning drawings. 'Oh yeah, that total dickhead [...] what were they?'; a quantity surveyor, as it turned out. In drawing the planning drawings, he 'got lots of things wrong and didn't listen', as a result of which he had to redraw the plans four times. They found him through a family connection because he was cheap. He charged them for three days work, but David, who saw him moving windows around on the computer, thought the job had probably taken him 'top end two hours'.

When asked if they actually understood the drawings, the response was a unanimous 'no' from David and Rachel because 'they were so bad'; and 'more or less not 100%' from Pete and Sara. The answer from Gareth was a categorical 'yes' – the answer from Belinda – 'not really'. Clearly, they had had to rely on words to communicate their desires and needs, trust playing a very big role.

Gareth and Belinda also used a quantity surveyor, a colleague of Gareth's, to draw up their plans, both for planning and building regulations, although

Gareth himself did the survey and spent a great deal of time sketching at the table with Belinda thinking through different options for the plan. The couple seemed reasonably satisfied with what Gareth's colleague had done although he had been very slow to do it. A structural engineer designed the foundations while the 'builder just made it solid'. Gareth himself had written the specification together with his quantity surveyor colleague.

Pete and Sara had gone down a rather different route. Some years ago, they had had their living room extended by a builder with an in-house 'architect'. They had worked with the same team at the start of their new extension. I asked them how they knew that the architect was an architect. 'Only because that was what the builder called him', was the response. Apparently he worked on these jobs in the evenings and weekends outside his usual full-time employment. He did all the drawings and the written specification for the couple.

In Rachel and David's case, the full plans submission for Building Regulations approval was completed by a structural engineer recommended by the builder who was, in the opinion of the couple, not cheap. Apparently he was very sloppy with his drawings, changing scale by accident as well as blocking up windows. More 'used to designing bridges than houses', the structural elements, in the opinion of the builder, had been vastly overscaled. What was worse, he had 'lied' on several occasions. The structural engineer also wrote the specification. When asked if they understood this document, the unanimous response was 'absolutely not'. However, the builder had gone through the paperwork with Rachel and David stating clearly what was and was not included in the tender price.

The most critical decision of the whole process was the choice of builder. Fortunately all the couples seem to have chosen well, as much of the process seemed to be reliant on the builder's skill and integrity. Four companies came to look at Rachel and David's job. The decision over who was employed was based on the builders 'attitude to Rachel' who knew she would have to 'put up' with these men in her house for several months. There was not a great deal of difference in the tender sums. They decided to employ a builder who her father had worked with on a previous occasion. In spite of this careful vetting, he had great difficulty in taking orders from Rachel, always deferring to David instead. It took three months of Rachel acting as project manager for the builder to accept her, as a woman, in the role. Rachel's method of managing the team was to write weekly lists of things that, in her opinion, needed to be done. David, meanwhile, handled the financial affairs. In general, they were happy with the input that they received from the builder who 'said when things wouldn't work' and 'changed things helpfully'. For example, he advised them to have a unified floor finish across the room that they were extending to make it feel more spacious. The couple did, however, recognise that they should not have taken his advice regarding the position of the *en suite* bathroom in the loft which he put on the rear elevation, blocking out light and the view of the garden in doing so, when it could have been positioned on the side.

Gareth and Belinda saw three different builders and took a great deal of care in following up personal recommendations. Their choice confined himself to issues of construction, advising the couple that it would be more straightforward to knock down part of the existing structure than to try to work with it, making changes to the floor slab and to the height and the pitch of the roof. Somehow – and Gareth and Belinda did not really seem to know how this had happened – the builder made a change from three to two velux windows (a sensible decision in my opinion as each window became associated with a particular living zone, though the implications for illumination could have been grave). Materials were chosen to match next door's extension, and for the builder's convenience.

Pete and Sara initially chose their builder because they had worked with him before but were disappointed when he pulled out of the project in favour of a larger job. They then sought prices from three contractors only to choose one that had been 'recommended by somebody in Church' because they 'felt that he knew what he was talking about'. They had left all the decisions about materials up to him, saying simply that they wanted them to 'blend in'. Although the project had not progressed much on site, their builder had already made suggestions about creating spaces for storage that they had found helpful.

All the couples interviewed recognised that special skills were needed for dealing with builders. Gareth had learnt that 'you have to keep on top of the builder – keep speaking to them'. Rachel had learnt the importance of planning ahead, anticipating when decisions would be needed, for example on positioning the electrics. In every case, the homeowners had been forced into unfamiliar and demanding roles that had made them to reflect on their own management skills and lack of authority when dealing with other people. Very often, they had to compromise on something that the builders had done without consultation so that, instead of feeling fully engaged with the evolution of their homes, they frequently felt both impotent and vulnerable.

Absenting the architect

Why didn't any of the couples employ an architect to assist with this stressful and expensive process? In the words of Gareth: 'I'm not sure how much an architect would add'. Clearly cost is a major issue – arguably the only issue. For Rachel and David, the imagined cost of an architect was important although they never actually enquired what that cost might be. Whatever the cost, it clearly was not going to be worth it in their opinion. The perception from the homeowners that I spoke with is that the use of an architect worries builders, who do not want to work with a complex contract or specification, rendering them less likely to want a job; the result being higher tender figures and a further financial disincentive for the potential client who is already daunted by the prospect of the architect's imagined fees.

I asked Rachel and David whether, if they were shown examples of extensions designed by architects and extensions designed by builders and technicians, they thought that they would be able to tell the difference. The answer was 'probably not' although Rachel did concede that works by architects might be more elegant in terms of materials as 'getting a decent finish out of builders was really difficult'. Both had seen an extension done by an architect on the other side of the road and they had not been impressed. When asked if they thought that architects made a difference to the way in which a space was designed, they had to think for quite a while, 'umm', before acknowledging that 'they might see things that you couldn't see' and also that the use of materials would probably be better. Pete and Sara did not think that an architect would make much difference on a 'project this size', but that maybe you could tell whether an architect had been involved from the 'windows, their shape and style' and the 'details' which might be 'out of the ordinary'. Rachel, David, Gareth and Belinda felt that there might be times when it was appropriate to employ an architect but that they themselves had not needed one because they had a 'good idea' about what they wanted. Although fond of literature and music, none have any manifest interest in the visual arts, as such it seems that they have little interest in the 'symbolic capital' associated by Bourdieu with aesthetic taste, the production of which is, in Dovey's terms 'the architect's key market niche'.[8]

From my reading of the magazine *Grand Designs*, I had thought that its instigator, Kevin McLeod, had done more in Britain to further the cause of architects than anyone else in recent years through the medium of his television programme of the same name, keenly viewed by most of my informants. My illusions were quickly dispelled, however, by Rachel who pointed out that whenever they showed an architect on *Grand Designs*, they were usually 'real prats'. She did however speak approvingly of the programme *Property Ladder* 'which makes you feel you can do without them'. Belinda felt that the architects on *Grand Designs* were quite pushy, citing the example of one female architect who had been 'quite miffed' when things had not gone according to her plans. Either way, it is always the owner not the architect that is placed at the heart of the process.

The respondents were unanimously negative about the public image of the architectural profession. When asked what architects could do to make themselves more employable, David thought that more should be done about marketing: 'we get stuff from double glazing salesmen through the door – why not architects?' For him, their lack of prominence on the high street was a real issue. Rachel made a face before saying 'well they seem to have a problem with their street cred at the moment'. It turned out that they did have a brief conversation with a 'creepy' architect who they felt to be too senior a member of his practice to be of much assistance to them. Gareth and Belinda found the idea of a percentage fee 'weird'; they would be 'scared' of it escalating.

When asked whether they were worried that the architect would take away the homeowners' control of the finished product, they said that it was not really a consideration. Gareth and Belinda said that they would have gone to lengths to find an architect that they got along with if they had decided to employ one. Ultimately, none of the informants could seen any value in using an architect in spite of the fact that, in each case, the building process had been very difficult and had taken much longer than anticipated. Indeed, there seemed to be no understanding that an architect might have been able to make the process more smooth and the product more efficient or more delightful, largely because of negative images of architects in the media.

To someone not familiar with reading plans and understanding the nuances of space, the CAD plans of the technician might not look so very different to those of the architect so there is no point in paying several hundred pounds for those. This issue is compounded by the question of whether people can really tell the difference between architect and technician designed space. My suspicion is that, very often, they can't. Whether this is because of nature or nurture is a very intriguing point that harks back to Plato and is one that exercised Le Corbusier, amongst other architects. For Bourdieu, however, the idea that aesthetic experience might in some way be innate or universal rather than social would be another of those misleading beliefs that keep arbiters of taste in their dominant roles.[9] Roni Brown, in her study of self builders, observes that 'Novelty, distinction, originality, and above all, a "total design concept" or "flow between aspects of the design", are not prerequisites of amateur home-making and building'. Instead, and perhaps paradoxically, 'the desire to achieve an individualised and personalised home, appears fundamental'.[10] In this way, much of what an architect might offer is rendered redundant.

The wide variety of material on the web and on the shelves of newsagents and libraries pertaining to the issue of home extensions does little to further the cause of the professional registered with ARB and a member of the RIBA. The architect is frequently depicted as an expendable figure who is perhaps of some use in the drawing of plans necessary for obtaining various statutory permissions. The RIBA seems to be its own worst enemy in promoting this idea. For example, in the RIBA published *Loft Conversions Guide*, the architect, 'the architectural technologist' or indeed the 'chartered surveyor' are all considered equal to the task of assisting the homeowner.[11] The unique selling point of the architect – design – is rarely given any recognition in books of this type, perhaps because it is so difficult to sell.

Paul Hymers, in his best-selling book *Home Conversion*, describes 'a good designer' as solely 'one who possesses the necessary skills of draughtsmanship and is familiar not only with the details of construction, but also with the problems and regulations relating to the work'.[12] At no point is there any mention of the words 'design' or 'quality'. Hymers describes the RIBA as a 'club', immediately endowing the chartered architect with an aura of elitism and adding several zeros to his or her envisaged fee in the mind's eye of the potential employer.

Conclusion

The extension stories discussed here illustrate a growing 'culture of amateurism';[13] potentially a sign of an emerging democratic culture in which the traditional role of the professional has been undermined. It seems to me that the work done by the homeowners was in some ways performative; in rebellion against the architectural profession, against professionals in general and everything that they stand for. This was reflected in the rather adversarial way that they talked about the profession of architecture.

Despite their complaints, it seems that the homeowners derived great benefit from participating fully in the design of the home. In maintaining control of the project, they were able to draw in and develop skills latent in their family, their networks and from their own past. Brown observes that the home owners are embarking on 'a creative journey that allows for reflexivity and personal discovery and the representation of autobiographic content in the materiality of the home'.[14] Indeed, it is the role of self building in the formation of identity that she emphasises in her study of self builders. In justifying her findings, she tries to correlate them with current thinking on the measuring of 'well-being' and illustrates how fundamental participation and creativity are to any definition of human needs. The issue of personal autonomy looms large in any measure of well being.[15] As every domestic architect knows, it is a delicate balance to steer a design without impinging on the clients' often changing desires. Although, to an outsider, the extensions described here might appear deeply generic, they are in fact highly personal to their owners. If, as Mary Douglas suggests, 'we had to choose an index of solidarity from the time-space structure of our homes, the strongest indicator would not be the stoutness of the enclosing walls but the complexity of co-ordination'.[16] It is, in some sense, the history of the extension project and its complexities that ties the house together.

Until recently, British people were taking an increasingly hands-on role in the alteration and maintenance of their homes. However, Helen Powell notes a recent change in attitude and behaviour caused, in part, by the recent recession.[17] In 2003, DIY was classified as a 'leisure' activity by the Office of National Statistics. It has, however, more recently been re-categorised as a chore alongside 'repairs and gardening'.[18] People are increasingly employing others to do work that they would previously have done themselves; a development that will presumably extend to the sphere of self build. Time has become an increasingly important commodity for the consumer. There is an opportunity here for architects to provide a service that works with, not against, homeowners' desires – if it isn't already too late and if the title architect is not already tainted beyond repair.[19]

NOTES

1   K. MacInnes, 'Here's One I Designed Earlier: How Architects Can Capitalise on the Growing Self Build/Market', *Architectural Design*, 64, (1994): xvi–xvii.

2   An early version of this research was first published as: Flora Samuel, 'Suburban Self Build', *Field*, 2 (2008): 111–125.

3   The names of the informants have been changed for publication.

4   EHCS, *The English Housing Conditions Survey* (London: Office of the Deputy Prime Minister, 2001). This information is omitted from the 2008–2009 version and so cannot be updated.

5   M. Hand, E. Shove and D. Southerton, 'Home Extensions in the United Kingdom: Space, Time and Practice', *Environment and Planning D:* Society and Space, 25, (2007): 668–681 (672).

6   Ibid.: 675.

7   Roni Brown, 'Identity and Narrativity in Homes Made by Amateurs', *Home Cultures,* 4, 3, (2007): 213–238. See also Roni Brown, 'Designing Differently', *The Self Build Home,* 21, 4 (2008): 359–370.

8   Kim Dovey, 'The Silent Complicity of Architecture' in Jean Hillier and Emma Rooksby (eds) *Habitus: A Sense of Place* (Ashworth: Aldershot, 2002), pp. 238–296 (288).

9   Pierre Bourdieu, *Language and Symbolic Power* (Cambridge: Polity, 1991), p. 16; Dovey, 'The Silent Complicity of Architecture', p. 289.

10 Brown, 'Identity and Narrativity': 213–238 (278).

11 Construction Products Association, *Loft Conversion Projects Guide* (London: RIBA Publishing 2010), p. 13.

12 Paul Hymers, *Home Conversion* (London: New Holland, 2003), p. 16.

13 C. Leadbeater, 'Amateurs: A 21st Century Remake', *RSA Journal,* June (2003): 22–25. Gary Beegan and Paul Atkinson, 'Professionalism, Amateurism and the Boundaries of Design', *Journal of Design History,* 21, 4, (2008): 305–313.

14 Brown, 'Identity and Narrativity': 278.

15 See for example: http://www.nationalaccountsofwellbeing.org/learn/measuring/indicators-overview.html [accessed: 14 March 2011].

16 Mary Douglas, 'The Idea of Home: A Kind of Space', *Social Research,* 58:1 (1991): 305–306.

17 Helen Powell, 'Time, television and the decline of DIY', *Home Cultures,* 6:1 (2009): 89–107 (93).

18 Office for National Statistics (2006), 'The Time Use Survey 2005'. Accessed on-line at www.statistics.gov.uk [accessed: 14 March 2011].

19 For a radical re-evaluation of the way in which architects interact with clients in a Canadian context see the work of John Brown and Housebrand, http://housebrand.ca/ [accessed: 14 March 2011].

Chapter 7

Lounge space: the home, the city and the service area

Samuel Austin

This essay is about Hopwood Park, a service area on Britain's M42 motorway, and what I call lounge space: a condition of being hosted without host that refigures relations between citizen and society. Hopwood Park's spaces are highly controlled, conforming to government regulations that mandate certain facilities and restrict most others,[1] and to a relentless retail logic that aims to maximise the operator's profits. The spatial language that shapes the highly controlled confines of the service area demands a closer reading.

At least since Robert Venturi, Denise Scott-Brown and Steven Izenour's *Learning from Las Vegas*, US roadside architecture has become a subject of fascination, while that of the UK has remained neglected.[2] The glamour and novelty of the first motorway service areas – only recently traced in architectural and cultural histories, with at least a hint of nostalgia for a golden age of car travel – have long been subsumed by a fine-tuned commercial logic in a market which is now dominated by just three nationwide operators.[3]

My focus here is on today's service areas, on Hopwood Park, but inevitably also on the many others that are barely distinguishable from it.[4] I will consider their relation to the 'formless' space of globalised capitalism that has been branded 'junkspace' by Rem Koolhaas, and to a contemporary condition of 'solitary contractuality' and 'non-human mediation' that Marc Augé describes as 'non-place'.[5] As an ever-present homely city, a lounge space owned by everyone and no one, Hopwood Park both resists and reorders precisely the specificities of place and time that recent histories have sought to recapture in the first decades of service areas.

Inside without outside, the outside within

Motorway service areas are accessible only by car. Early buildings evoked the modernity of the new roads with bridge and tower restaurants that overlooked the carriageways. During the 1970s and 1980s, sites turned away from an increasingly mundane and congested driving experience to simulate escape into the local place.[6] Recent service areas, by comparison, invoke very different associations less bound to road or rural context, neither local or national, but at once domestic and global.

Hopwood Park alludes to familiar urban spaces – if only via the sanitised and strategically organised form of the shopping centre. Several seemingly private retail units flank an ostensibly public space. Like a traditional European urban plan or contemporary mall, most service area buildings include both a high street – a linear space, primarily for movement – and a square – a more static space for assembling, in this instance, sitting and eating – with one widening into or (as at Hopwood Park) intertwined with the other. Such buildings, taking the form of 'Hi-Tech' sheds, are similar to the wide-span spaces of airport buildings, such as Foster + Partners' Stansted terminal. As Koolhaas and others have observed, airports have become cities of commerce and inevitably take urban forms.[7] Smaller and more tightly focused, the spaces of service areas seem more urban still (Figure 7.1).

The separate commercial units are bright and semiotically distinct, their identity clearly marked by signs and differences of interior fit-out, from floor, wall and ceiling materials to furniture and light fittings. Forming alcoves of various depths, shops are defined on three sides by walls lined with products, restaurants and cafés, by arcs of food-filled counters surrounded by signs. Here,

Figure 7.1 Hopwood Park: the internal street

walls are more dispensers than boundaries, where objects are advertised and offered for selection. The visitor is enveloped in the space of each brand. Although functionally predictable, what lies beyond this array is invisible and unknown. These are caves of consumption; interiors without exteriors. Through the shelved strata of each chamber, diverse resources seem to flow magically from a deep, impenetrable reserve, a bounty of technologised nature.[8] Each unit is very clearly owned, a private space dominated by one brand to the exclusion of others.

By contrast, the 'public' space between seems to evade identity, to express continuity and efface difference. Defined by the objects that surround it, but itself immaterial, there seems to be almost nothing to it. Two traits are particularly important here.

First, the space alludes to the outdoors. Exteriority is simulated by a reduction of enclosure: 'streets' tend to have glazed roofs in the manner of arcades, while 'squares' have full-height glazing to at least one side – two at Hopwood Park. The resulting space ostensibly has no walls, and often no ceiling either; it seems not to contain, only to open onto other spaces, be they branded units, external picnic areas or landscape views. This impression of outdoor space is supported, at some sites, by the inclusion of exterior fittings such as street lamps, canvas umbrellas, plants and trees, banners and large clocks.[9] At Hopwood Park, a deep, exposed roof structure with pendant lamps makes the closure of the space less abrupt. Although it occupies the largest volume, the 'street' or 'square' appears as an absence between presences, a leftover space subordinate to, and overshadowed by, the commercial enclosures that surround it, lacking any identity of its own.

Second, surfaces that remain are concealed or suppressed. In 'streets', 'squares' and other 'public' spaces, signs cover most of the few vertical surfaces – from the brand names and logos that mark out each unit, to adverts on columns and even above WC urinals. Any remaining walls, columns and floors tend to be finished in smooth, semi-reflective white materials. The absence of grain, together with bright, uniform lighting, avoids shadow and thus signs of depth, matter or presence. This ostensible lack of variation in texture and tone across different surfaces, and even between different materials, furthers the sense of immateriality and continuity: an apparent nothingness that fills every gap to unify the space, effacing any traces of material resistance.[10] This consistency of mute surface gives the appearance of neutrality and passivity; it is only there to accommodate the diversity of brands. As in Venturi, Scott Brown and Izenour's Las Vegas where 'symbol dominates space', signs appear to be the prime – perhaps the only – means of way-finding, the source of all meaning.[11]

Why white? Against bright signs, white recedes into the background, like the hazy horizon that enhances depth in Renaissance paintings. Alongside the suggestion of neutrality, there are implications of purity, virginity, naturalness, classical civility and utopia. Not nature, but like nature: a universal human context that claims the imagery of liberal democracy.[12] It promises spatial *carte blanche*, freedom of occupancy, use and movement: an openness that applies to brands as much as to visitors, as popular as it is apolitical.

This is ostensibly pure space, without any boundaries to define or exclude. It is only the brands that contain, only the brands that mark space. Not only do units have no windows or doors, their product displays and their furnishings, in many cases, extend out into the 'street'. There is no way to browse at distance; arrangements of stands physically impede the routes of visitors, while the seating and retail areas of cafés and fast-food outlets occupy large areas of the 'streets' and 'squares', their respective territories marked by barriers but also by floor surfaces, stands, tables and chairs in identifiable brand styles. While the brand's base, its own most 'interior' space, might be clearly indicated by bold signs, its extents become uncertain. With the multiple thresholds implied by furniture, finishes and signs, the border between 'outside' and 'inside', 'public' and 'private' is difficult to determine. This neutral, pure context seems to offer no resistance to occupation, to offer itself to appropriation by citizen brands as by outsiders. This is a city seemingly centred on the visitor, pouring out to meet him or her, ready to satisfy their desires. To a degree that surpasses the contemporary UK shopping centre, this is a street that is always open – and always full. In some areas, movement perpendicular to the route is easier than movement along it. More than a thoroughfare flanked by shops, it feels like a route cut through a single space of retail: the dense, contorted fit-out of a department store overlaid upon the linear space of an arcade (Figure 7.2).[13]

Figure 7.2 White space, branded chambers

This condition is different from the 'glittering-in-the-dark' of Las Vegas interiors described by Venturi, Scott Brown and Izenour – yet it is related. Rather than an 'interior oasis', another world within, service areas promise purification of the normal world outside. With no complex sequence of initiation – usually little more than a canopy and glazed draught lobby away from the car park – a seemingly naturally lit 'outdoor' street leads past artificially bright and colourful grottoes of recognisable brands. Unlike the casinos with their 'exaggerated enclosure' and layers of introversion, the service areas are hermetic while professing openness, caves offering prospect as well as refuge.[14] Like them, however, they are, in other ways, closed. Contrary to appearances, service areas are not public, and carefully policed. Access tends to be restricted and spaces are patrolled by multiple security cameras; power is concealed. As Koolhaas notes, 'Junkspace is authorless, yet surprisingly authoritarian'.[15] Despite apparent openness to difference, the brands admitted are limited; partly by commercial pressures, but also by official sanction to preserve the image of the whole. Moreover, those brands permitted tend to operate according to tight conditions.

If the role of owner is more disguised than in the Las Vegas casino, it is more comprehensive than in any urban context. Rather than separate shops run by different companies, the majority of brands are operated as franchises by employees of the service area. Here, ostensibly 'private' spaces are organised and controlled by the same company that owns the apparently 'public' spaces. The 'choice' between brands implied by the 'public' space thus conceals the sovereignty of the whole.[16]

Out of place, out of time

This 'outside' space within, characteristic of Hopwood Park and its siblings, occupies an ambiguous position. On the one hand, its presence is necessary – not only for practical reasons of shelter and thermal comfort. Its uniformity seems to guarantee that no single function or brand is dominant, to reassure that there is an overall organisation, a logical structure that connects coherently the different pieces, maintaining certain conventions. It is unusual for any elements associated with a brand – fixed or mobile – to encroach beyond its framing portal in any direction other than forwards. The separations between each unit define a virtual volume of space extending into the 'street' or 'square'. Though they may not be consciously read as such, floor patterns, column rhythms and cornices – whether imaged as classical or Art Deco; whether 'modern' curves and up-lighters or 'Hi-tech' ducts and diffusers – and changes of ceiling height mark the continuity of a route past and through the different commercial realms. On the other hand, however, this common space and structure, which ensures the unity and comprehensibility of the whole as well as the independence of each part, must be almost invisible; so generic as to be unnoticeable. That which is not branded and consumable, moveable and exchangeable, individuated and appropriable, is not to be seen.

This condition seems related to Augé's non-place, where everything points to something else and the particular loses its distinct identity. In another sense, however, identity is not lost, just concealed. The identity of the service area – as a host that orders and confines – is obscured behind the brands on offer. The focus is on recognisable signs that seemingly transcend the limits of place and time. As a particular place is variously obscured, abstracted and deferred, the visitor is placed within a seemingly universal context; what Koolhaas terms 'Public Space™'.[17]

The most prominent imagery indicates national or multinational brands, through logos but also through the qualities of unit fit-out: the healthy white and green glow of mini-supermarkets, the red and yellow super-sized menus of fast-food chains. These refer beyond the building, not only to other service areas but also to spaces within other building types in different contexts, from shopping centres to airports across the UK and beyond. In shifting the emphasis from building to unit, from host to hosted, there is also a movement from space to object. Attention is directed to products rather than the specific spaces or times of their encounter; away from the driving experience and the events or routine of the journey. Ubiquitous brands, with their breadth of existing, unplaced associations, are both everyday ornament, in the manner of wallpaper, and windows onto other worlds, like paintings. They signify normality, promise a familiar fix for diverse desires and evoke well-advertised fantasies beyond here-and-now.[18] Indeed, it is brands that ensure consistency of experience, not only across sites operated by the same company, but between those of different operators that even share some of the same franchises. While there are some variations depending on service area size, each company repeats a similar, limited, range of brands across their network of sites, typically arranged in roughly the same sequence: irrespective of variations in building form, the service area becomes generic space.

It follows that the main, in some cases the only, references to the host company are found outside. Bold signs for *Roadchef, Moto* or *Welcome Break* signify ownership of portals, but not the world within. As intermediaries, they mark entrances to a plural environment into which they seem barely to intrude. Exteriors may reference company colours. Inside, by contrast, in-house restaurants owned entirely by the company are represented as separate brands, in some cases with identities as distinct as those of other unit operators. Even on the outside, the operator's logo – distinct to the motorway – may be overshadowed by wall-size banners advertising the more ubiquitous brands that await within: a universal space, not of the road (Figure 7.3).[19]

Any representations of place point towards iconic sites not visible from the motorway, yet still seen from a position of automotive detachment. Welcome Break, for example, displays picturesque images of local places: historic spires at Oxford; Blackpool Tower at Charnock Richard. All are reproduced in high contrast, often from elevated, unreachable positions, cropped to exclude people or vehicles: timeless human artefacts, unpopulated and outside everyday life. Hopwood Park represents Birmingham with a juxtaposition of old and new landmarks: Future Systems' scaleless Selfridges store is seen beside the neo-gothic

Figure 7.3 Subtle hosting, the Hi-tech shed

spire of St Martin's Church. Usually at the entrance to service areas, these images confirm location, frame it like a postcard, but have little role in the internal experience.[20] The buildings offer barely any practical information about the locality; and menus and product ranges are standardised across each operator and franchise. Elements of the place and of other places are suspended within the neutral space, objectified and detached from context like museum exhibits. Hopwood Park and its relations market themselves as part of a ubiquitous space of global urban exchange; a safe distance from the complicated realities of locality and road, which must remain beyond the service area's outdoors within.

This resistance to location is accompanied by a suppression of differences in time. Whiteness and flat lighting do more than suggest a single, uniform space uninterrupted by particularities of place; they also defy the passing of time. It is always bright in Hopwood Park. Even at night, there are no dark corners. This defiance of diurnal rhythm allows the service area to inhabit an unplaceable present, an ever-presence. Flat screen televisions suspended above seating areas bring 24-hour news to diners. The time may be always displayed on screen, but the set and the format remain the same whatever the hour. This asserts a global present – up-to-date with world events, irrespective of local time. Neither 'retro' nor overtly futuristic, the buildings seem to defy their age. White suggests timelessness; an absence of pattern and colour that cannot go out of fashion. Surfaces are wipe-clean and the branding and fit-out of units can be regularly updated without disruption to the whole. Indeed, the buildings seem to embody a fear of time, with marks of the past concealed by regular refit.

If the space of the service area alludes to the gallery, it is not as a museum of all history, but as a constant vessel untouched by an ever-changing exhibition.[21] The service area thus seems to inhabit the illusion of eternal contemporaneity that Peter Eisenman traces in modern notions of zeitgeist: universal and of the moment, timeless yet up to date, beyond history.[22]

At home without domesticity: an everyday utopia

Hopwood Park in particular, and the British motorway service area in general, seems to promise an unchanging datum. A predictable experience irrespective of place or time, it conceals the very processes of travel it is there to accommodate. Such spaces have been linked to Michel Foucault's 'heterotopia': 'a sort of place that lies outside all places and yet is actually localisable', which, by containing conditions and events that do not fit normal society, stabilise existing structures and institutions of everyday life.[23] Like Foucault's cemeteries and sanatoria, brothels and circuses, contemporary service areas are 'heterotopic' in their containment of travel as a moment of destabilisation. Yet they are particularly uncanny (*unheimlich*) in that their relation to the 'home' is more ambiguous.[24] As brands suggest a trans-urban space, repeated with slight variations in 'public' spaces across the country and around the world, they also imply the comfort of home, or rather home-from-home: a stable place where every journey begins and ends, a place that escapes movement, or moves with you. Neither entirely homely or urban, service areas present a simplified and sanitised version of everyday life: a home without domesticity; a home in which you are always a guest without responsibility, comfortable without attachment. This may be seen, I will argue, as both a reflection and an inversion of the whiteness discussed above. Similarly generic and ubiquitous, this, too, disguises itself as difference.[25]

If service area 'squares' seem to be outdoor public space, they are also many lounges under one roof. 'Dining' areas are subdivided into 'rooms' of roughly domestic proportions by waist-high barriers, benches, bins and plants. These offer varied seating environments: from formal to informal, solitary to social, introverted to extroverted; for meeting, dining, relaxing, reading or working. Alcoves of sofas, clusters of armchairs, grids of dining chairs and rows of stools, each with a distinct type of table (rectangular, round, square or linear), define different relationships between those seated – so long as no more than a car-full want to sit together. Typically, each configuration coincides with a different floor finish and lighting condition that affect the tone, acoustics and apparent scale of the space. Carpets and up-lighters go with sofas, timber boarding and pendant lamps with dining chairs, tiles and spotlights with stools. As in a house, a range of activities and personal preferences are seemingly accommodated in different but related family-sized spaces (Figure 7.4).

In this reading, the city internalised becomes an adjunct to the home. With the service area's central 'public' space also a personalised lounge, the house engulfs the city. This lounge space juxtaposes a variety of homely spatial conditions with fresh and up-to-date products from supermarkets, cafés,

Figure 7.4 The many rooms of lounge space

newsagents and bookshops. The shops become limitless larder and bookshelf, automated cooker and kettle, arrayed around living-dining-study spaces where multiple desires may be satisfied without the need to go outside. On the condition of a financial transaction, there is no need to plan, to prepare or to clear up – to work. The service area seemingly offers the comfort and self-determination of the home without its responsibilities. It promises the freedom of choice and the anonymity of the city without the inconvenience of distance or the threat of otherness.

As micro city and macro house, Hopwood Park resists being read as an institution. It seems universal but not standardised, convenient rather than purposeful, familiar yet indeterminate. This experience is not an exception from the norm, not an escape from everyday routine, but its neutralisation and universalisation of the familiar: not eating out, but takeaway in a show home, or coffee-to-go in Ikea.

This condition of hybrid public and private signifiers, global brands in wide-span spaces, comfy chairs in front of TVs, is supported by a sensory environment that suggests intimacy through the multiplication of different semi-familiar features. Yet here, too, the limitations to this 'home-from-home' may be seen. This house of many lounges resists rest or complete privacy. With many partitions but no enclosures, the only internal doors are to toilet cubicles, and those are far from airtight. All 'private' chambers are occupied by brands. If this 'home' includes spaces for bodily relief and programmed play, what it lacks is quiet or intimate places. Apart from a small area for amusements,[26] which seldom involve much physical exertion, most of the 'rest' spaces at Hopwood Park and elsewhere are sedentary. Yet the rest they offer is far from sensory or secluded. Shops encircle seats, partitions are low and products often super-sized, so browsing never stops. There is constant background entertainment, something to be mentally, as well as physically, consumed. Indeed, the spaces seem to be designed to be comfortable, but only to a certain degree. Soft but upright chairs, short and firm sofas, gentle lamps in an already bright space, hinder sleep as they suggest relaxation. However passively, the visitor is expected to remain attentive. Consistent with the ever-presentness of the building's white space, no one must be allowed to dwell. With free parking limited to two hours and expensive thereafter, visits are not supposed to last long.[27]

This spatial quality – between home and city, dwelling and workplace, casual and formal – accommodates a breadth of users and events, from holidaying families to business meetings. It is a kind of common ground. Seemingly open, public, not owned – and yet reassuringly familiar – service areas have become, for some people, a place for dealing with difficult issues: for separated parents to exchange children; for confronting employees with tough decisions; for making the extraordinary seem ordinary.[28] As a leveller of differences, they ostensibly escape the spatial hierarchies and reduce the markers of wealth, power and position that would be present in the home or office.

The silent host

It is worth exploring this 'neutrality' further, this experience of being hosted without host. There is a connection with Jacques Derrida's discussion of unconditional hospitality in Immanuel Kant's 'Third Definitive Article of a Perpetual Peace'. Derrida draws attention to the relation between 'hospitality' and 'hostility', 'the undesirable guest which it harbours as the self-contradiction in its own body'. In his reading of Kant's text, the welcoming of the other always at the same time confirms the dominant position of the host who determines how far the offer extends. While hospitality may be 'a right, a duty, an obligation, the *greeting* of the foreign other as a friend', this is always only on condition that:

> the host, [*hôte*] the one who receives, lodges or *gives asylum* remains the *patron*, the master of the household, on the condition that he maintains his own authority *in his own home*, that he looks after himself and sees to and considers all that concerns him and thereby affirms the law of hospitality as the law of the household, *oikonomia*, the law of his household, the law of a place (house, hotel, hospital, hospice, family, city, nation, language, etc.), the law of identity which de-limits the very place of proffered hospitality and maintains authority over it, maintains the truth of authority, remains the place of this maintaining, which is to say, of truth, thus limiting the gift proffered and making of this limitation, namely, the *being-oneself in one's own home*, the condition of the gift and of hospitality.[29]

Here, the greeting of the outsider becomes the confirmation of the inside, of a defined place of ownership to which the host is entitled but the guest is not, unless they too accept the laws of that place, that home. Kant's unconditional hospitality 'self-deconstructs'.

From glazed façades and open shop units to comfy chairs in front of televisions and overspilling product displays, Hopwood Park reinforces an impression of unconditional hospitality, of being open to all without limitation. By seeming to exist only at the scale of the object rather than enclosure – in products and furnishings; in that which may be consumed – the service area conceals the authority, the structure, the place that makes the offer.

This is supported by an irregular and seemingly random arrangement of furniture – not all, but enough to disrupt the consistency of any single pattern. It makes the space appear unplanned, as though there is no single authority responsible for design – no system, no rules, no *demiurge*. Many product stands are on wheels so that they may be moved into circulation spaces during opening hours and then returned to be shuttered within units. This is, I suggest, not only a ploy to expand retail space beyond government stipulations but also a signifier of insubstantiality, a sign that the space is open to change. Through the various visual and audio entertainments on offer, the space is already noisy and active; there appears to be no compulsion to modify voice or behaviour. The individual's freedom to choose – between different routes, spaces, products, postures and actions – is seemingly preserved. So, the background condition of pure, neutral space, seemingly appropriated democratically by different brands, suggests a context that receives all without requiring anything in return. In this illusion of unconditional hospitality, it seems that no one there is to impose law or limit, no 'host' to make demands and nothing ostensibly asked of the 'guest'.

Yet there is a host. Not only do building details prescribe experiences, door-side detectors and cameras show that the host space is policed at its threshold (Figure 7.5). The laws of this hospitality become apparent in materials and finishes: robust, wipe-clean and scratch-resistant whiteness refuses marks of presence; thickly lacquered tables, chairs and wooden floors often in dark tones, stainless steel handrails and countertops and tiled floors, show little sign of wear. Similarly, there are very few opportunities for appropriation. Seats are no longer fixed (as they were in some 1970s and 1980s fit-outs) but are nevertheless arranged so tightly in partitioned zones, or are so heavy, that they are not easily rearranged. Objects might be moveable, but each clearly has its proper place; wheeled product stands are always returned each day to the same positions, often determined by changes in floor surface, with brakes applied. Shops may be closed but entertainments are always on, adverts always there. Visitors are addressed as consumers, not dwellers, who may use the space but not possess it, take only what is offered and only by giving something – their attention, at least – in return. This echoes the hospitality that Derrida describes: 'what it gives, offers, holds out, is the greeting which […] fold[s] the foreign other into the internal law of the host.'[30] Here, the host is not absent, just silent. And the laws they impose are disguised.

Figure 7.5 Signs, surveillance and instability at the threshold

The politics of lounge space

So how does this experience of silent hospitality relate to the conditions I described above, the overlaid signifiers of public and private, the homely city of many lounges? The visitor is, I have suggested, positioned between host and guest, sovereign and subject; a conflation of roles in which freedom is stressed and responsibility concealed. There is ostensibly no compulsion to provide or receive, to determine or conform – but neither is there any agency to compel others to do so. Instead of '*being-oneself in one's own home*', there is being-someone in a home that is at once no one's and everyone's. As home becomes city and city becomes home, the public is domesticated, the private opened up. There is the reassurance of a common structure: a universal condition countered by internal plurality; offering 'choice' between familiar spaces, objects and brands. This condition lies between uncertainty and prescription, avoiding both the unknown and the predetermined. Like the city, it is common ground, shared by all. But, like the home, it is centred on the individual subject. Here, two notions of stability are linked: one, societal, associated with spread risk, and conformity with a norm; the other individual and familial, with power and ownership.

This shared space is at once seemingly masterless and resistant to being mastered. The only authority appears not to be individual, institutional, local, or national, but global and timeless. In other words, it seems so ubiquitous that it is unplaceable, so universal it must be natural: hosting is deferred. As the company's name is elided by neutral space, the brands seem nebulous – ever-present but always only as proxy. Their headquarters, and even the conglomerates to which they belong, remain unknown. As service area buildings seemingly remove the multinational company from view, they ally themselves to a global space, to a common condition of sedentary consumption.

As Koolhaas notes, 'Junkspace is political'.[31] So is the lounge space of the service area, especially in its concealing of connectivity, of differences in place and time. The illusion of hospitality without host not only disguises power relations within the building; it conceals, beyond the horizon of whiteness, the international distribution networks, the other places, the cities and homes, the unequal global exchanges on which its seemingly unconditional 'welcome' depends. In lounge space, constraint is disguised as choice and choices appear without consequence. Agency is apparently neutralised. The other becomes invisible as the elsewhere turns into the city and the city into the home. Yet, in its extreme optimisation and efficiency, the way in which the service area harnesses promises of self-determination and choice through tropes of home and city always risks self-deconstruction. Perhaps visiting a service area – a lounge space – is uncanny precisely because it threatens to show up the uncomfortable interdependencies of globalised life that it tries so hard to efface.

NOTES

1   Department for Transport, *DfT Circular 01/2008: Policy on Service Areas and Other Roadside Facilities on Motorways and All-Purpose Trunk Roads in England* (London: TSO, 2008), pp. 12–13, 16–19.

2   Robert Venturi, Denise Scott Brown and Steven Izenour, *Learning from Las Vegas: The Forgotten Symbolism of Architectural Form* (1972), rev. edn (Cambridge MA: MIT Press, 1977). Reyner Banham's texts suggest institutional, socio-cultural and architectural reasons for the imbalance in attention. Compare 'Disservice Areas', *New Society*, 11 (1968): 762–763 with *Los Angeles: The Architecture of Four Ecologies* (1971) (Berkeley, CA: University of California Press, 2009).

3   David Lawrence, *Food on the Move: The Extraordinary World of the Motorway Service Area* (London: Between Books with Donlon Books, 2010); Peter Merriman, *Driving Spaces: A Cultural-Historical Geography of England's M1 Motorway* (Oxford: Wiley Blackwell, 2007).

4   Hopwood Park, operated by Welcome Break, opened in August 1999 near Bromsgrove in Worcestershire. It has strong similarities to the same operator's service areas at Oxford (M40, 1998) and South Mimms (M25/A1(M), 2000). Together with Moto's Donington Park (M1, 1999), they marked a new approach to service areas. See Jamie Doward, 'Motorway Meccas Get Mall Makeover: Service Areas Seem to Be Turning into Air Terminals', *Observer*, 22 August (1999), Business section, p. 6. The airport model continues to influence new service areas, redevelopments and extensions, including Roadchef's Norton Canes (M6 Toll, 2003) and Strensham South (M5, 2008), and Extra's Beaconsfield (M40, 2009).

5   Rem Koolhaas, 'Junkspace', in Rem Koolhaas/OMA-AMO, *Content: Triumph of Realisation* (Cologne; London: Taschen, 2004), pp. 162–171: 'Traffic is junkspace […] the entire highway system is junkspace, a vast potential utopia clogged by its users' (p. 166). 'The

traveller's space may [...] be the archetype of non-place': Marc Augé, *Non-Places: Introduction to an Anthropology of Supermodernity*, trans. by John Howe (London; New York: Verso, 1995), p. 86.

6   Lawrence, *Food on the Move*, pp. 42–91, 104–115.
7   See Koolhaas, 'Junkspace', pp. 166, 168. On building/airport becoming city, see 'Bigness' and 'Generic City', in Rem Koolhaas and Bruce Mau, *SMLXL* (New York: Montacelli Press), pp. 495–516, 1248–1264. On shopping centre as city, see Margaret Crawford, 'The World in a Shopping Mall' in Michael Sorkin (ed.), *Variations on a Theme Park: The New American City and the End of Public Space* (New York: Hill and Wang, 1992), pp. 3–30.
8   For associations of caves here turned to commercial effect, see Samuel Austin, 'Themes in the Architecture of the Cave', *Made*, 2 (2005): 80–91. On alcoves as a privileged space of intimacy, see Gaston Bachelard, *The Poetics of Space*, trans. by Maria Jolas (Boston: Beacon Press, 1994), pp. 130–132.
9   Such features, not present at Hopwood Park, are particularly prominent at Donington Park and Beaconsfield.
10 On the significance of smoothness, see David Leatherbarrow's discussion of 'picturesque roughness' in *Architecture Oriented Otherwise* (New York: Princeton Architectural Press, 2009), pp. 97–102.
11 See Venturi, Scott Brown and Izenour, pp. 7–9, 13, 116–117; also Augé, pp. 1–6, 94–96.
12 For associations of whiteness see David Bachelor, 'Whitescapes', in *Chromophobia* (London: Reaktion Books, 2000), pp. 9–49. On whiteness associated with classical civilisation and modern utopia, see Le Corbusier, trans. by F. Hyslop, *When the Cathedrals Were White* (New York: McGraw Hill, 1947).
13 On spatial, economic, cultural and historical formations of retail space, see Chiuhua Judy Chung *et al.* (eds), *Project on the City 2: Harvard Design School Guide to Shopping* (Cologne: Taschen, 2001). On spatial strategies to increase consumption, see Jon Goss, 'The "Magic of the Mall": An Analysis of Form, Function and Meaning in the Contemporary Retail Built Environment', *Annals of the Association of American Geographers*, 83, 1 (1993): 18–47 (29–35).
14 Venturi, Scott Brown and Izenour, *Learning from Las Vegas*, pp. 49–50, 55.
15 Koolhaas, 'Junkspace', p. 168. On control of private 'public' spaces, see David Chaney, 'Subtopia in Gateshead: The Metro Centre as a Cultural Form', *Theory, Culture and Society*, 7 (1990): 49–68; Crawford, 'The World in a Shopping Mall', pp. 22–27; Goss, 'The "Magic of the Mall"', pp. 25–28, 37–43; Mark Gottdiener, *The Theming of America: American Dreams, Media Fantasies, and Themed Environments*, 2nd edn (Colorado; Oxford: Westview Press, 2001), pp. 145–189. On space and power, see Michel Foucault, 'Panopticism', in *Discipline and Punish: The Birth of the Prison*, trans. by Alan Sheridan (New York: Random House, 1995), pp. 195–228.
16 On the rise of franchises and brands in service areas, see Lawrence, *Food on the Move*, pp. 94–111, 123–124, 134–135.
17 Augé, *Non-Places*, pp. 94–101; Koolhaas, 'Junkspace', p. 168. On anonymous space, see Andrew Wood, 'A Rhetoric of Ubiquity: Terminal Space as Omnitopia', *Communication Theory*, 13, 3 (2003): 324–344. Mark Gottdiener notes a trend away from overt theming to more subtly allusive mall environments, pp. ix–x, 182–183. This contrasts with the increasingly distinct experiences of branded stores, and icon buildings. See Anna Klingmann, *Brandscapes: Architecture in the Experience Economy* (Cambridge MA: MIT Press, 2007).
18 On objects as part of systems of symbolic exchange, see Jean Baudrillard, *The System of Objects* (1968), trans. by James Benedict (London: Verso, 1996).
19 When Welcome Break changed its motorway signage to 'Welcome Break KFC', circumnavigating restrictions on roadside advertising, the company reported increased sales of up to 30%. [n.a.], 'News in Brief', *Forecourt*, August 2005, p. 4.
20 For the political implications of distanced views, see Roland Barthes, 'The *Blue Guide*', in *Mythologies*, trans. by Annette Lavers (New York: Noonday Press, 1972), pp. 74–77 (p. 76): 'To select only monuments suppresses at one stroke the reality of the land and that of its people, it accounts for nothing of the present, that is, nothing historical, and as a consequence,

the monuments themselves become undecipherable, therefore senseless.' The imagery of Hopwood Park is significant. An instant icon, Selfridges's sinuous façade of circular discs reflects and reframes aspects of context, while allowing little connection at human scale between inside and outside.

21 For whiteness as seemingly neutral space out of place and time, with allusions to sacred spaces, see: Brian O'Doherty, *Inside the White Cube: The Ideology of the Gallery Space* (Berkeley, London: University of California Press, 1999).

22 Peter Eisenman, 'The End of the Classical: The End of the Beginning, the End of the End' (1984), in Kate Nesbitt (ed.), *Theorizing a New Agenda for Architecture: An Anthology of Architectural Theory 1965–1995* (New York: Princeton Architectural Press, 1996), pp. 212–227 (pp. 216–218).

23 Foucault, 'Of Other Spaces: Utopias and Heterotopias', in Neil Leach (ed.), *Rethinking Architecture: A Reader in Cultural Theory* (London: Routledge, 1997) pp. 350–356 (p. 352). Foucault presents a less concrete notion of 'heterotopia' in his preface to *The Order of Things: An Archaeology of the Human Sciences* (London; New York: Routledge, 2002), pp. xvi–xxvi, stressing their power to destabilise the status quo. On the resulting ambiguities and architectural interpretations of 'heterotopia', see Henry Urbach, 'Writing Architectural Heterotopia', *Journal of Architecture*, 3 (1998): 347–354.

24 Sigmund Freud, 'The "Uncanny"' (1919), in *Art and Literature*, The Pelican Freud Library, 14, ed. by James Strachey (London: Penguin, 1990), pp. 335–376.

25 On interrelations between home, consumer culture and global politics, see Beatriz Colomina, Annmarie Brennan and Jeannie Kim (eds), *Cold War Hot Houses: Inventing Postwar Culture, from Cockpit to Playboy* (New York: Princeton Architectural Press, 2004).

26 Regulations impose a limit of 100m². See *DfT Circular 01/2008*, p. 17

27 Many sites have a small 'lodge' beside the main building, adding a further commercial logic to the limited offer of rest: sleep is possible, but only at extra cost. On service area products, see Lawrence, *Food on the Move*, pp. 160–161.

28 Bryony Coleman, 'Chieveley, My Nemesis', *Guardian*, 2 October 2002, section G2, p. 13; 'Pull over, Fill up and Start Work', *Guardian*, 15 May 2002, section Office Hours, p. 2; Daniel Normark, 'Tending to Mobility: Intensities of Staying at the Petrol Station', *Environment and Planning A*, 38 (2006): 241–252. Such ritual significance has prompted critiques of 'non-place'. See Peter Merriman, 'Driving Places: Marc Augé, Non-Places and the Geographies of England's M1 Motorway', *Theory, Culture and Society*, 21 (2004): 145–167.

29 Jacques Derrida, 'Hostipitality', trans. by Barry Stocker and Forbes Morlock, *Angelaki*, 5.3 (December 2000), pp. 3–18 (pp. 3–4). Italics original.

30 Derrida, 'Hostipitality', p. 6.

31 Koolhaas, 'Junkspace', p. 167.

Chapter 8

The architecture of urban life: 67 *rue des Meuniers*

Diana Periton

In a quiet neighbourhood of eastern Paris, in the cleft of a valley where the *rue des Meuniers* (Mill Road) meets the *rue de la Brèche aux Loups* ('Escape Route of the Wolves') is a solid, calmly assertive building of yellow-grey brick (Figure 8.1). The rhythm of the windows, the near equality of its eight storeys, its single door and the disciplined exuberance of its brickwork serve together to mark it out as a housing block designed to give dignity to occupants of moderate means. Carved stone plaques on either side of the door indicate that it was built in 1911, and that the architect was Jacques Bonnier (Figure 8.2). But the Bonnier archives make clear that Jacques' father, Louis, was in fact largely responsible; the aim of the attribution was to launch Jacques' architectural career, through a building whose developer-client was another family member, Louis Bonnier's cousin Jules Cuisinier.[1]

Louis Bonnier's name is no longer well known. In 1911, he had just been made administrative director of Paris' *services d'architecture, des promenades et plantations, de la voirie et du plan de Paris*.[2] It was his municipal office that oversaw regulation of the building process, from the scale of the individual building to that of the street and the city as a whole. In 1912–13, Bonnier would become involved in drafting the first development plans for a 'greater Paris', a Paris made conceivable in a new, unbounded way by the decision to demolish the city's nineteenth-century ring of fortifications.[3] In 1919, he would help to establish France's first school of urbanism, and its journal *La Vie Urbaine* ('Urban Life'), both of them dedicated to the study of the processes by which the city is formed and transformed.

Earlier, Bonnier had been an inspector for the *casier sanitaire*, the sanitary record office, charged with reporting to the city authorities on the state of Parisian housing stock and its density of inhabitation in relation to the incidence of tuberculosis. He was the principle author of the 1902 *Règlements de voirie*, an updated version of legislation to manipulate and control the proportions of new buildings in Paris, whether for reasons of health and safety or from an aesthetic point of view. The rules dictated maximum building heights according to width of street, permissible depth of balconies and other projections as well as dimensions of courtyards and windows in relation to habitable rooms. They were devised to bring more light and air into new buildings than their predecessors. More provocatively, they were contrived to encourage variety and 'movement' in street façades.[4] Bonnier claimed that such rules result directly

Figure 8.1 67 *rue des Meuniers,* Paris XIIe

from the 'state of society'; they are 'the codification, the record, of tomorrow's customs and habits – even of today's'. It is the role of the architect, as '*véritable artiste*', to interpret them creatively.[5]

This chapter studies Bonnier's housing block at 67 *rue des Meuniers* to explore how a building interprets, and thus both transmits and transforms the customs and habits, assumptions and expectations that engender it. The building was commissioned by a private developer but it conforms to regulations that have their origin in 'the need to limit the liberty of the individual in view

Figure 8.2 Entrance door, 67 *rue des Meuniers*, Paris XIIe

of the general interest', wrote Bonnier; the land-owner is not so much '*chez lui*' when he develops his plot, as '*chez nous*', participating in something shared. Customs and habits – the prevailing 'general interests' – once codified into building regulations are then treated as the inevitable disciplining framework of a skill to be mastered by the architect, rather as bricks impose a discipline on the skill of the bricklayer who constructs the façade. The rules that dictate the permissible depth of balconies and projecting windows are interpreted to compose here a façade that is both angular and gently rippling (it has the desired 'movement'); combined with those that insist on the set-back of the upper floors, they are taken up to create a veritable cityscape of loggias and dormers, with 'chimney breasts and party walls [...] that contribute to the play of silhouettes against the sky'.[6] Inside the building, rules and expectations that between them dictate the number of rooms required and their uses, their minimum sizes and their level of sanitation are again in play, respected and manipulated in Bonnier's contribution to the constitution of a new building type, the *immeuble d'habitation à petits loyers*, or low-rent housing block.[7] In their turn, the working families it houses, who aspire here to live '*bourgeoisement*', by conforming to civic conventions simultaneously transform them.

   For Bonnier, these rules and conventions, both written and unwritten, are guarantors of the transmission of culture. To practice architecture is to interpret them creatively, in order to sustain that culture, and also to develop and improve it. Influenced by Bonnier's multiple roles, this chapter considers his building as the manifestation, not simply of architectural practice, but also of urban practice, of ongoing involvement in the making and re-making of the city.

A disciplined *art nouveau*?

Bonnier's building is hard to label in terms of architectural style. Its most prominent characteristic – its 'brickiness' – is in marked contrast to the cut stone of bourgeois Paris, or the render fashioned to look like stone of the block that faces it across the street. Architectural historian François Loyer suggests that, in the 'social housing' that began to appear on undeveloped sites across eastern and southern Paris at the turn of the twentieth century, architects sought to assert values different from those of the standard appearance of bourgeois decorum. Loyer mentions the visible commitment to hygiene's demands for the circulation of air, manifest in the planted courtyards open to the street that make many of these blocks so recognisable.[8] Bonnier's building hides its courtyard but flaunts its brickwork; brick is not used humbly, or economically, but sculpturally, with a controlled exuberance, as if to proclaim a new, formerly unrecognised, status for its inhabitants in their daily lives. 'The aesthetic effect of the overhangs, of the play of shadows and light', wrote Bonnier, 'is not a luxury for the people, but a need, and a right; it has the same status as hygiene'.[9]

   The desire to give aesthetic pleasure and architectural expression to a section of society previously ignored by the profession is implicitly linked, by Loyer and others, to the more general search for a 'modern style', a style that would find its sources of invention beyond the repeated adaptation and manipulation of already-codified historical models.[10] Loyer classifies Bonnier as a 'regionalist', for whom the constants that architecture reinterprets are of those of the '*longue durée*' of the place in which a building is rooted: the materials that the place provides, the visual relationship of building to landscape that has evolved, and the way of life – the collective culture – that the landscape engenders.[11] The *rue des Meuniers*, until the 1870s simply the Mill Path, winds low along the edge of the steep-sided vallée de Fécamp, where grazing lambs were once wolves' easy prey. But, by 1911, this valley was hemmed in – to the south by the great swathe of railway lines that end in the *Gare de Lyon* and the goods' yards of Bercy; to the north by the more local *chemin de fer de Vincennes* with its attendant depot – and its stream had been paved over. Citadel-like, Bonnier's building does not so much expound its existing site as establish it in its new conditions. It seems to seek to provide solidity for this liminal zone that is no longer rural, not fully industrial and struggling to be a neighbourhood. Contemporary photographs show the building rising up across the cobbled street, framed between bakery and pharmacy (both shops are still there); they tend to edit out the shacks, barely two storeys high, that abut its party walls.

The other stylistic label associated with Bonnier is that of *art nouveau*; its 'restless dynamism of organic form' again a rejection of the conventions of period styles.[12] For the 1900 Paris World Exhibition, Bonnier had proposed some exuberantly flowing, draped and sprouting garden kiosks of indeterminate construction. Compared to these, the façade of the *rue des Meuniers* building, despite the plasticity of its upper levels, has been austerely disciplined. But Bonnier's links were not only with the promoters of France's languidly rococo school of *art nouveau* that dominated the 1900 Exhibition, officially sanctioned for its pacifying charm. They were also with writers, painters and musicians for whom the 'new art' demanded acute awareness, an open-ness to the liberating, unsettling force of intense feeling provoked by encounters with places, objects or raw materials – artists for whom it was 'one of the most noble of social forces, one of the most exhilarating means by which the properly human personality grows freely'.[13] In 1893, Bonnier had built a seaside villa for Belgian composer Georges Flé on the northern French coast, near the picturesque cluster of summer cottages that he had completed a year earlier for members of his own family. Here, recitals of Émile Verhaeren's vibrant and uneasy symbolist poems, set to music, were performed – poems in which the landscape became an '*état d'âme*', a projected state of the soul.[14] And here, painter Théo van Rysselberghe experimented to produce painfully iridescent pointillist scenes of the dunes. Both Verhaeren and van Rysselberghe were involved in the *Section d'Art* of the *Parti Ouvrier Belge*, the Belgian Worker's Party, which called for 'moral and intellectual transformation' as much as for social and economic change.[15]

In 1895, Bonnier had made alterations to an eighteenth-century Parisian town house for art dealer Siegfried Bing to turn it into the commercial gallery that gave *art nouveau* its name. Bing's *Maison de l'Art Nouveau* was conceived as a series of domestic rooms, furnished and decorated with pieces specially commissioned from sculptors and painters working together with designers, craftsmen and manufacturers. Van Rysselberghe designed a ceramic-tiled fireplace in the dining room choreographed by Henry van de Velde, where Paul Ranson painted the wall panels and Edouard Vuillard decorated the porcelain plates. In a balconied internal hall, formerly the courtyard, one-off exhibitions – of Edvard Munch's lithographs and etchings (branded a scandal when shown earlier in Berlin), or of Constantin Meunier's bronze sculptures of labouring coalminers – were displayed amongst potted palms, beneath a translucent vault of irregular, hand-blown glass bricks, part of Bonnier's reorganisation.[16]

Bonnier's interventions at the *Maison de l'Art Nouveau* had a deliberate, elemental awkwardness to them, quite unlike the decorative fluidity of his 1900 garden pavilions. From the street, he gave the over-scaled main doorway a broad, flat, rectilinear frame of dark-painted wood (Figure 8.3). Inside it, a stiff panel declaring the gallery's name was pulled down like the partly lowered fire shutter to a stage, almost crushing two huge clumps of sunflowers, in painted plaster, which stood on either side. When the gallery opened, one critic wrote that the sunflower 'motif [...] is perhaps not the best of ideas; the foliage and flowers produce rather drooping forms [...] But its originality is uncontestable'.[17] Another found that the 'large fragments of broken glass' (the weakly glimmering glass block screen of the entrance door itself, deep inside the opening) gave the garish, south-facing golden sheaves a 'bewildering backdrop'.[18] Like Verhaeren's 'wrinkled flowers which bend, carrying – as well as their regrets – their riches, on dry stems', they patiently stood guard over the potentially transformative world of the 'new art' within.[19]

Figure 8.3 *Maison de l'Art Nouveau*, Paris IXe

Figure 8.4 Frieze above entrance door, 67 rue des Meuniers, Paris XIIe

The extent to which Bing's collaborators were motivated by the emancipatory, even revolutionary possibilities of the 'new art', and to which his establishment was simply part of the official promotion of beautiful objects, has been discussed elsewhere.[20] Either way, the 'organic ensembles' of its carefully assembled rooms were a far cry from the *rue des Meuniers*' attention to minimum dimensions, and the washable white paint of its communal areas that render dirt visible and germs easily dispersed.[21] But the façade of the housing block shares something of the composed awkwardness of the *Maison de l'Art Nouveau* and, over the door, the motif of the sunflower reappears, albeit in a very different guise (Figure 8.4). The doorway here seems too small, a single narrow slot cut deep into the otherwise uninterrupted concrete base of the building. Above the low cast iron lintel, four small sunflower heads, picked out in pointillist mosaic of yellow and orange, peer out from beneath four diminutive brick vaults which also support a shallow concrete canopy. Neither brick nor concrete projects far enough to shelter visitors. Instead, it is the sunflowers themselves, facing north-east, which are protected, almost hidden. In return, they keep still, mute watch over the entrance to the citadel, guardians that allow the fantastical cityscape to bloom above. They are the building's only figurative ornament.

Crafts, arts and *métiers*

One of the goals of *art nouveau* was to bring about a unification of art and craft, to abolish the distinction between high and low art by imbuing crafted objects with the status of art.[22] At the *Maison de l'Art Nouveau*, artists worked with craftsmen, and craftsmen as artists, to make functional pieces intended to bring 'aesthetic joy' and 'noble emotions' to all those who came in contact with them.[23] In 1899, Bing's building was further altered, probably by Bonnier, to accommodate workshops where all could work in concert.[24] Cabinet-maker Niederkorn gave public demonstrations of his working processes.[25] Art, made an intimate part of everyday life, would 'blend with it, penetrate it, impregnate it' – so wrote Roger Marx, inspector of French museums, influential art critic, and campaigner for the revitalisation and diffusion of craft at the turn of the twentieth century.[26]

For Marx, art, like nature, animates matter. Nature and art together constitute an 'indivisible whole'; the same 'devoutness, the same ideal, arouses both the earth and that which is built on it' as together they 'fashion the outlines of our motherland'. *Art nouveau* and regionalism become indistinguishable, as nature and culture are rendered reciprocally dynamic in the making of our environment, both following what Marx described as the 'primordial law of the adaptation of means to ends'. Art is 'the visible and durable expression of the character and state of mind of a people'. Yet its ends are not static – art is also a 'means of action'. The artist-maker takes up those means to play an active, activating part in society's 'eternal metamorphosis'.[27]

For Bonnier, as for other French architects associated with *art nouveau*, construction itself is a quasi-natural phenomenon. Loyer notes that most of these architects were disciples of Viollet-le-Duc, for whom construction emerged as the almost inevitable outcome of a place's materials and way of life.[28] In line with Marx, Viollet-le-Duc's followers subtly shifted the emphasis to highlight the role of the architect-as-artist, able to tap into and to manipulate the generative joint forces of nature and culture. Bonnier spoke of the artist's duty to understand the purpose of his work – its 'destination' – and to know his materials; for it is in forming matter to a purpose that art 'gives birth to feeling'. For each material, the artist – whether architect or artisan – must know 'its origin, its nature'. He must know 'its elasticity, its texture, […] colour and patina'. He must know its conduct, faced with external forces – its resistance to climate, and the way it interacts with others. He must know how it can be treated – forged, moulded, cut, assembled. He must know how much it costs. More than that, declared Bonnier, 'the artisan must not just *know* the matter that he works with, he must *love* it', and not with the 'timid, distant love we attribute to knights for their ladies in medieval romance' but with 'ardent love […] his caresses spiced with triumphant energy' (Figure 8.5).[29]

Bonnier's description of the artist-artisan's labours touches on those of John Ruskin or William Morris, for whom the process of making is itself an 'aesthetic joy', a 'noble act'. But Roger Marx accused Ruskin (and the English as a whole) of having 'too much enthusiasm for muscular vigour'. Ruskin, he said, 'sacrifices inspiration to the practice of a trade' by insisting that all manual workers be considered artists.[30] French *art nouveau*'s adaptation of the English Arts-and-Crafts movement's emphasis on making did not share Ruskin's abhorrence of the division of labour. Instead, Marx – and also Bonnier – accepted that division as an inevitable part of collective work in which labourer, artisan, artist and, ideally, industrialist and developer too, strive together for the same goal. Art itself, filtered through the inventive, interpretive powers of the artist,

Figure 8.5 *La Semaine des Constructeurs* ('Builders' Weekly'). Cover by Louis Bonnier

establishes a 'close solidarity' between them.[31] At the *rue des Meuniers*, that artist is the architect. It is he who has shaped the construction to its purpose. In his drawings, it is he, before the metal-worker, who has identified every tie-rod (literally drawing attention to the building's warehouse genealogy), just as he, not the bricklayer, has first meticulously set out the energetic antics of the bricks.[32]

So if Bonnier called the architect sometimes a 'specialist technician', sometimes an artisan, it was in order to highlight the 'higher goals' that the true architect, as '*véritable artiste*', must also pursue.[33] Although he will need to start with a 'methodical training' and must aspire to a 'complete education' (defending the new title of '*Architecte diplômé par le gouvernement*', Bonnier stressed the slow, iterative process by which the novice gains competence and expertise across many fields), the architect-as-artist must ultimately transcend what can be taught, and find his own 'personal solution to eternal ideas'.[34] He has a calling, but it is not that of the hopelessly romantic artist without practical interest. Instead, it is that of someone who, ceaselessly, perfects his ability to determine and assimilate people's needs and give them material expression, and who does this through syntheses that cannot be achieved merely by the application of principles. For this, wrote Bonnier, 'is what distinguishes him from the engineer'.[35]

Bonnier's portrayal of the architect, culled here from several sources, in its emphasis on understanding that cannot be reduced to a method and on judgement that relies on experience, seems to search for a way to describe that architect's practical wisdom, his sheer involvement with the situation in which he works and acts.[36] Yet, at the same time, Bonnier assumed that good judgement, if it is to go beyond the codifications of the engineer, must be that of the individual artist-genius who transcends all particular knowledge. Bonnier turned the situation – the 'customs and habits' of society, the ongoing life of the city – into a project, for which the artist must discover 'personal solutions', his own creative syntheses of purpose and matter. The contradictions in his description of architectural practice – the confusion over whether culture is a project for achievement or a situation in which the architect participates – were not Bonnier's alone. The *Code Guadet*, adopted by the *Société Centrale des Architectes* in 1895, similarly pointed towards the importance of judgement born of involvement when it insisted on architecture's status as a liberal profession whose experienced practitioners act freely within society for both client and society as a whole. But it, too – by defining the architect as part technical expert, part artist – went on to confine such judgement to specialist expertise, whether technical or aesthetic.[37]

What is more, even as architects themselves struggled to pin down their role through diplomas and codes, their practices were further disciplined, by shifting assumptions about the nature of building and of city-making. Increasingly specialised construction processes rendered material synthesis a question more of co-ordination than creative invention. Increasingly explicit and extensive building regulations limited scope for interpretation. The new methods of the burgeoning social sciences – of sociology or human geography – were brought to bear on architecture's understanding of place and way of life. In his post as *Directeur administrative des services d'architecture* [...] *et du plan de Paris*, Bonnier was fully implicated in these changes. His 1902 *Règlements de Voirie* asked that buildings conform to 'formal prescriptions, precisely applicable'; although, deduced from custom and habit, they were intended to pre-empt 'unsanctioned jurisprudence' on the part of architects and regulators.[38] His co-written reports for the *casier sanitaire* sought to specify conditions necessary to healthy housing 'with the rigour of a theorem'.[39] These codifications left little room for judgement of any kind, scant latitude for the '*véritable artiste*'.

La vie urbaine

In his work for the City of Paris, Bonnier was a *fonctionnaire*. During the 1870s, Maxime du Camp's six-volume survey of the city, *Paris, ses organes, ses fonctions, sa vie*, had identified the city as an organism constituted by a series of systems – post and transport systems; water supply and sewage systems; crime and the criminal justice system; poor and the social care system; systems of education and religious observance – all of which worked together to uphold urban life. 'Paris being a great body', he wrote, 'I have tried to make an anatomical study of it […] to show Parisians [how …] their administrative organs function'.[40] It was the political economist Turgot who, in the 1770s, first used the word *fonctionnaire* to describe someone inserted to maintain the smooth functioning of the state's systems.[41] And Turgot, again, was amongst those who began to emphasise productive work as the source of national wealth, and hence to re-evaluate the role of the labourer. Enlightenment *philosophes* together started to re-define the nation's classes in a way that was no longer concerned predominantly with political or legal rights but instead with productive contribution.[42] Labouring, instead of being dismissed as merely menial, might also be virtuous. The labouring class, too, had a *'fonction publique'*.[43]

Stone *bas-reliefs* depicting labourers – a carpenter, a blacksmith – serene and busy in work that supports a loving and ordered family life often mark the entrances of otherwise brick-built 'social' or 'workers' housing' that began to appear in Paris at the turn of the twentieth century (Figure 8.6). They are examples of the preparatory-level, didactic art that Roger Marx proposed would allow the labourer to discern 'the dignity inherent in his task, and […] the duty it sets out for him'.[44] The housing was built by philanthropic institutions as part of a campaign to address '*la question ouvrière*', the incipient threat to urban order that the labouring class' unstable way of life was feared to pose. Detailed studies by Pierre du Maroussem published in the 1890s – part of the new science of social economics – attempted to identify and analyse the 'genus' that was the labouring class by focusing on various of its known 'species', such as Parisian carpenters and cabinet-makers.[45] They drew attention to the increasing alienation of the labourer as the structure of guilds and apprenticeships broke down and the journeyman became an independent day-labourer or piece-worker. They also highlighted the aspirations of that labourer to intellectual freedom and the trappings of a bourgeois lifestyle. In du Maroussem's case study, the carpenter's wife is no longer content to wear a bonnet, she must have a hat with a feather; the carpenter himself has dispensed with the Bible and instead has a bookshelf displaying Karl Marx's *Capital*. 'Workers' housing' of the 1900 onwards acknowledged some of these aspirations by providing pared-down versions of bourgeois apartments for its occupants (unless it was pitched at entry level when a special plan-type, based on a rural dwelling, was devised).[46] It sought at the same time to divert others, by rendering each block a harmonious community of workers, proud of their manual trades – proud, that is, of their particular '*fonction publique*' in the social order.

Figure 8.6 Frieze above entrance door, Fondation Rothschild housing, *rue de Prague*, Paris XIIe. Sculptor: L. Drivier, 1908

The plans of the fifty-three dwellings in Bonnier's building on the *rue des Meuniers* echo those of the philanthropists' more overt 'workers' housing'. Whether two- or three-roomed, each has a labelled dining-room, the clear indication of civilised family life (Figure 8.7). Each has a small but separate kitchen. The properly ventilated WC – now obligatory for all new apartments – conforms to the maximum dimensions permissible in low-cost housing, devised to prevent the room's misuse.[47] One of the flats on each floor has a dedicated *toilette*, where hat with feather can be properly arranged. Similar to its philanthropic counterparts, Bonnier's building is a 'little city'. Less autonomous than they (it has no laundry, no crèche, no workshops), it is still self-contained architecturally; its chimneys command the sky like the towers of a medieval hill-town, accessed through a single gate. Like them, it is a component in a dynamic system, taking its place between railway maintenance yards and goods depots, between local trade school and tobacco factory, between pharmacy and bakery. But while an order, a decorum, is part urged, part bestowed on its inhabitants, those inhabitants are not reminded didactically, explicitly, of dignity and functional duty. The reticent sunflowers peering out above the doorway hint instead at the city's transformative possibilities – for such flowers capture what sunlight there is, and turn it into seeds of gold.[48]

'*La vie urbaine*', the urban life that Bonnier and his colleagues would later make an object of specific study, is the life of the city understood as a 'living organism' that 'evolves both in time and in space'.[49] Its functions, and its structures, evolve with it, as do the customs and habits, assumptions and expectations of the genera and species that constitute it. But its evolution is unpredictable, simultaneously destructive and full of hope. 'In these cities', wrote poet Verhaeren, 'everything shifts – horizons themselves are on the march [...] All that was just and sacred will seem strange'. 'In these cities', he incanted, 'where crowds surge and sweat and toil [...] I feel my heart swell, exalt within me; I feel it ferment, and multiply'.[50] As artist, Bonnier flirted gingerly with the transformatory force of this 'organism as powerful as it is fragile', while as *fonctionnaire* he regulated and tamed it, to produce at 67 *rue des Meuniers* a rigorous, carefully controlled dream world, stilled, ebullient, and tense.[51] In either case, culture – and the city it engenders – has become not so much something in which we actively, freely participate, but a quasi-natural, unstoppable life force to which we are all in thrall.[52]

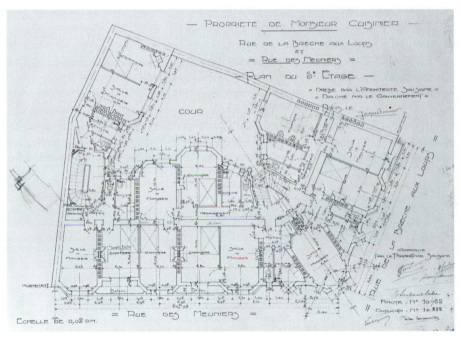

Figure 8.7 Fifth floor plan, 67 *rue des Meuniers*, Paris XIIe

NOTES

1 Bernard Marrey, *Louis Bonnier 1856–1946* (Liège: Mardaga, 1988), p. 71.
2 Louis Bonnier archive, SIAF / Cité de l'architecture et du patrimoine / Archives d'architecture du XXe siècle, 035Ifa302.
3 Commission d'extension de Paris, *Considérations techniques préliminaires* (Paris: Imprimerie Chaix, 1913).
4 Louis Bonnier, *Conférences faites dans l'hémicycle de l'Ecole Nationale des Beaux-Arts les 22 et 29 octobre 1902 sur les 'Règlements de Voirie'* (Paris: Charles Schmid, 1903), p. 12.
5 Ibid., pp. 3–4 and 32.

6   Ibid., pp. 3 and 12.

7   See title block on drawings, Louis Bonnier archive, 035Ifa59. Bernard Marrey, in *Archives d'architecture du XXe siècle*, ed. Maurice Culot (Liège: Mardaga, 1991), p. 93, claims 67 *rue des Meuniers* as 'the archetype for future low-rent housing'.

8   François Loyer, *Histoire de l'architecture française: de la révolution à nos jours* (Paris: Mengès, 1999), p. 415.

9   Bonnier, *Règlements*, p. 12.

10   See e.g. Claude Loupiac, 'Les prémices de l'architecture moderne, 1889–1914', in Gérard Monnier (ed.), *L'Architecture moderne en France*, tome 1, 1889–1940 (Paris: Picard, 1997).

11   Loyer, *Histoire de l'architecture française*, p. 228.

12   Debora Silverman, *Art Nouveau in Fin-de-Siècle France* (Los Angeles and London: University of California Press, 1989), p. 1.

13   Jules Destrée, *Art et socialisme* (Brussels: Bibliothèque de Propagande Socialiste, 1896), p. 1.

14   William Rees, *French Poetry 1820–1950* (Harmondsworth: Penguin, 1990), pp. 362–363; André Gide, *Emile Verhaeren* (Liège: Lampe d'Aladdin, 1927), pp. 23–24.

15   Destrée, *Art et socialisme*, p. 1.

16   John Rewald, *Post-Impressionism* (1956) (London: Secker and Warburg, 1978), p. 481; Gabriel Weisberg, *Art Nouveau Bing* (New York: Harry N. Abrams, 1986).

17   Louis-Charles Boileau, *L'Architecture*, 11 January 1896, quoted in Marrey, *Louis Bonnier*, p. 36.

18   Arsène Alexandre, *Le Figaro*, 28 December 1895, quoted in translation in Weisberg, *Art Nouveau Bing*, p. 80.

19   Emile Verhaeren, 'L'Heure Torride' in *Almanach* (Brussels: Dietrich, 1895), illustrated with woodcuts by Théo van Rysselberghe.

20   Silverman, *Art Nouveau*, particularly chapter 14, 'Maison de l'Art Nouveau Bing', pp. 270–283.

21   Silverman, *Art Nouveau*, p. 273; Louis Bonnier archive 035Ifa59. The plans show room dimensions and sometimes calculate areas. Sketches check that minimum corridor widths can be achieved. Regulations required that '*habitations à bon marché*', in order to receive certain tax breaks, should have white painted or chalk-whitenable communal areas – see *Préfecture du Département de la Seine, Comité de patronage des habitations à bon marché et de la prévoyance sociale, Règlements de salubrité, 21 juin 1910*, article 14 (a marked-up copy is in the Louis Bonnier archive, 035Ifa319/1). Bonnier's concerns as inspector for the *casier sanitaire*, and the evidence of the building itself, suggest he thought these precautions advisable at 67 *rue des Meuniers*.

22   Silverman, *Art Nouveau*, pp. 1, 8, etc.

23   Anatole France, preface to Roger Marx, *L'Art social* (Paris: Fasquelle, 1913), p. vi.

24   Weisberg, *Art Nouveau Bing*, pp. 143–145.

25   Marcel Morot, 'Notes sur l'Art Nouveau – Entreprise de S. Bing à la fin du XIXe siècle', Bonnier archive 035Ifa311/1. Morot worked with Bing from 1888 to 1904.

26   Marx, *L'Art social*, p. 4.

27   Ibid., pp. 4–5, 13.

28   Loyer, pp. 190 and 229; see e.g. Eugène-Emmanuel Viollet-le-Duc, *Histoire de l'habitation humaine* (Paris: Hetzel, 1875).

29   Louis Bonnier, notes for 'Conférence faite à l'Hôtel de Ville de Versailles, 1922: L'Art Moderne', Louis Bonnier archive 035Ifa301/1.

30   Marx, *L'Art social*, pp. 10–11.

31   Ibid., pp. 4, 13, 27–29.

32   See Louis Bonnier archive, 035Ifa59. His *Groupe Scolaire*, 1908–1911, a building in Paris' XVth arrondissement containing both a primary school and a secondary school with a focus on learning a trade, turns some bricks outwards to reveal brickmakers' marks that become part of the decorative scheme of the façade.

33   Bonnier, *Règlements*, pp. 1 and 32; 'Rapport de Louis Bonnier [...] au IVe congrès international d'architectes à Bruxelles en 1897' in *Bulletin du Société des Architectes Diplomés par le Gouvernement*, no. 1, 2e série, 1898, p. 32.

34 Louis Bonnier, *A propos d'un groupe scolaire* (Paris: Librairie centrale des Beaux-Arts, 1913), pp. 8, 9; 'Rapport de Louis Bonnier', pp. 17–32.

35 'Rapport de Louis Bonnier', p. 11; *Groupe scolaire*, pp. 6–7.

36 See Hans-Georg Gadamer, 'What is Practice? The Conditions of Social Reason', in *Reason in the Age of Science*, trans. Frederick G. Lawrence (Cambridge MA: MIT Press, 1981), pp. 69–87.

37 Loyer, *Histoire de l'architecture française*, pp. 205 and 415. Julien Guadet reminded architects that they practiced '*une profession libérale et non commerciale*'.

38 Bonnier, *Règlements*, p. 14.

39 Paul Juillerat and Louis Bonnier, *La tuberculose et l'habitation*, report presented to the 'Congrès International de la Tuberculose', Paris, October 1905.

40 Maxime du Camp, *Paris, ses organes, ses fonctions, sa vie* (Paris: Hachette, 1869–1876), vol. I, p. 5.

41 Anne-Robert-Jacques Turgot (1727–1781) was Louis XVI's finance minister in the 1770s. It is Emmanuel Le Roy Ladurie, in *La ville classique* (Paris: Seuil, 1981), p. 288, who credits him with using the word *fonctionnaire* in this way.

42 Félix Ponteil, *Les classes bourgeoises et l'avènement de la démocratie* (Paris: Albin Michel, 1968), p. 13.

43 Lucien Fèbvre, 'Travail, évolution d'un mot et d'une idée', *Journal de Psychologie Normale et Pathologique*, 1948, p. 22. Fèbvre is quoting Cabet. See also Richard Sennett, *The Craftsman* (London: Allen Lane, 2008), p. 92.

44 Marx, *L'Art social*, p. 42.

45 Théodore Funck-Brentano, 'Préface' in Pierre du Marroussem, *La question ouvrière* (Paris: Arthur Rousseau, 1891), vol. 1, p. 12.

46 The two housing types were labelled 'Henri Becque' and 'Emile Zola'. The first makes one of its principle rooms a dining room and has a separate kitchen. The second, for those needing initiation to a bourgeois lifestyle, has a *salle commune* – a kitchen-dining room – as its principle room. See Loyer, p. 416.

47 On the top floor – conforming strictly to regulations – are three one-roomed apartments for '*célibataires*' which share a WC. Each still has its own kitchen.

48 See M. E. Warlick, *Max Ernst and Alchemy* (Austin: University of Texas Press, 2001), p. 264.

49 'Avertissement', *La Vie Urbaine*, nos.1–2, 1919, p. 1.

50 Emile Verhaeren, 'La Foule' in *Les visages de la vie* (1899) (Paris: Société du Mercure de France, 1908).

51 Louis Bonnier, 'La Population de Paris en mouvement', *La Vie Urbaine*, nos.1–2, p. 51.

52 See Hannah Arendt, *The Human Condition* (Chicago and London: University of Chicago Press, 1958), p. 117 ff.

Chapter 9

The setting and the social condenser: transitional objects in architecture and psychoanalysis

Jane Rendell

This chapter focuses on 'transitional' objects and spaces, located in the overlap between inside and outside. I position next to one another textual accounts of two specific kinds of transitional objects and spaces – the setting of psychoanalysis and the social condenser of architecture – in order to create a place of potential overlap in the mind of the reader. One textual strand is located in psychoanalysis and charts a particular set of ideas around transitional objects and spaces. It starts out with D. W. Winnicott's notion of the transitional object of the first relationship, and the transitional space it occupies between the internal psyche and external world; moving to André Green's work on the setting, a homologue, in his own words, for the analytic object positioned at the space of overlap between analyst and analysand, inside and outside; before returning to Sigmund Freud, the originator of psychoanalysis, to reflect on how the first object is also the lost object in his work on mourning and melancholia; in order to introduce Jean Laplanche's critique of Freud's distinction between word-presentations which exist in the conscious mind, and thing-presentations which exist in the unconscious, and his own concept of the 'enigmatic message' and thing-like presentations, those objects which signify 'to' someone rather than 'of' something.

The other textual strand of the essay is grounded in architecture and examines transitional objects and spaces in terms of the social condenser, a foundational principle in Moisei Ginzburg and Ignatii Milinis's Narkomfin Communal House (1928–1929) in Moscow, a building whose design was influenced by Le Corbusier's five point plan, but which in turn inspired aspects of Le Corbusier's *Unité d'Habitation* (1947–1952) in Marseilles thirty years later. Certain principles of the *Unité* were then adopted and adapted in the public housing schemes of the post-war Welfare State in the United Kingdom, specifically by the London County Council Architects Department in the Alton West Estate, Roehampton, London SW15 (1954–1958).

My aim is not to explain the relation between these three architectural spaces, the architects and cultures that produced them and those that inhabited them, but to position the transition from one architectural space to another, next to a sequence of theoretical insights drawn from psychoanalysis concerning the transitional spaces which exist in the relationships between a subject and his/her objects. The overlapping space between architecture and culture operates on many levels, through the triangular structures which take place between subject and object; perhaps between an architect and his/her imagined and/or built objects; or in the relation between one building and another in the space mediated by the user and the historian; and on the page, between the critic who writes and the reader who comes later to experience those words.

The transitional object or object of the first relationship (1951)

> I have introduced the terms 'transitional object' and 'transitional phenomena' for designation of the intermediate area of experience, between the thumb and the teddy bear, between the oral erotism and true object-relationship, between primary creative activity and projection of what has already been introjected, between primary unawareness of indebtedness and the acknowledgement of indebtedness.[1]

The focus of the theory of object relations created and developed by the Independent British Analysts is the unconscious relationship that exists between a subject and his/her objects, both internal and external.[2] In continuing to explore the internal world of the subject, their work can be thought of as a continuation of Freud's research, but there are also important differences, particularly in the way that the instincts are conceptualised and the relative importance assigned to the mother and father in the development of the infant. Evolving the concept of an object relation to describe how bodily drives satisfy need, Freud theorised the instincts as pleasure-seeking, but Ronald Fairbairn, an influential member of the Independent Group, suggested instead that they were object-seeking, that the libido is not primarily aimed at pleasure but at making relationships with others. For Melanie Klein too, objects play a decisive role in the development of a subject and can be either part-objects, like the breast, or whole-objects, like the mother. But whereas for Freud, it is the relationship with the father that retrospectively determines the relationship with the mother, for Klein, it is the experience of separation from the first object, the breast that determines all later experiences.[3]

Following on and also developing aspects of Klein's work, Winnicott introduced the idea of a transitional object, related to, but distinct from, both the external object, the mother's breast, and the internal object, the introjected breast. For Winnicott, the transitional object or the original 'not-me' possession stands for the breast or first object, but the use of symbolism implies the child's ability to make a distinction between fantasy and fact, between internal and external objects.[4] This ability to keep inner and outer realities separate, yet inter-related, results in an intermediate area of experience, the 'potential space', which Winnicott claimed is retained and that, later in life, contributes to the intensity of cultural experiences around art and religion. Winnicott discussed cultural experience as located in the 'potential space' between 'the individual and the environment (originally the object)'. In Winnicott's terms, for the baby this is the place between the 'subjective object and the object objectively perceived'.[5]

> This potential space is at the interplay between there being nothing but me and there being objects and phenomena outside omnipotent control [...] I have tried to draw attention to the importance both in theory and in practice of a third area, that of play which expands into creative living and into the whole cultural life of man. This third area has been contrasted with inner or personal psychic reality and with the actual world in which the individual lives and that can be objectively perceived. I have located this important area of *experience* in the potential space between the individual and the environment, that which initially both joins and separates the baby and the mother when the mother's love, displayed as human reliability, does in fact give the baby a sense of trust, or of confidence in the environmental factor.[6]

The Narkomfin Communal House, Moscow (1928–1929)

> Low voltage activity and a weak consciousness would be focused through the circuits of these 'social condensers' into high-voltage catalysts of change, in the habits and attitudes of the mass population.[7]

The concept of the social condenser was developed through the theoretical and then practical work of the Russian constructivists in the 1920s. Quoting artist Aleksei Gan – 'the capitalist towns are staunch allies of counter-revolution' – architectural historian Catherine Cooke describes Gan's belief that the existing design of cities did not allow the social form of the revolution to flourish. She goes on to suggest 'a logical implication', that if one were to design the right kind of space, this would promote the new kind of society: 'if a "misfitting" environment can obstruct social change, a "fitting": one can foster it. If spatial organisation can be a negative catalyst, it can also be a positive one'. [8] Cooke discusses how the notion of the social condenser invented and promoted by the constructivists had to be, following Gan, actively 'revolutionary' and, according to its subsequent development by architect and theorist Moisei Ginzburg, must 'work' materially.[9]

This constructivist design methodology was developed in the designs for apartment types 'A-F' for STROIKOM, the Russian Building Committee, and then realised in six schemes, including the Narkomfin Communal House in Moscow, designed by Ginzburg with Milinis in 1928–1929.[10] In Victor Buchli's fascinating in-depth ethnographic study of the Narkomfin, he underscores the importance of generating a new socialist *byt*, or daily life, domesticity, lifestyle or way of life, for architectural designers in this period.[11] He explains how OSA (Union of Contemporary Architects), headed by Ginzburg, 'sought to address the issue of the new *byt* by creating an entirely new rationalized architecture and material culture based on communist theories of industrialized production and on patterns of consumption guided by socialist ethics.'[12]

Buchli discusses how the original programme for the Narkomfin included four separate buildings: a living block with three types of living unit following the STROIKOM guidelines (F, 2-F, and K types, along with dormitory units), the communal block (with a kitchen, dining room, gymnasium and library), a mechanical laundry building and a communal crèche, which was never built. Buchli explains that the Narkomfin was a 'social condenser' of the transitional type. This meant that the accommodation allowed for both pre-existing bourgeois living patterns (K and 2-F units) and fully communist F units.[13] The main distinction between the two was that the former included kitchens and a family hearth while the latter was primarily a sleeping unit with minimal facilities for preparing food, since cooking and eating were to take place in the communal block. Buchli stresses that this variety was not an expression of tolerance, but rather reflected the OSA belief that architecture had a transformative power, capable of 'induc[ing] a particular form of social organisation', and that the intention was that the building would help ease those following bourgeois living patterns into adopting socialist ones.[14]

> The Narkomfin Communal House was not designed as a fully fledged *Don Kommuna* but as a 'social condenser' of the transitional type.[15]

The analytic object, or the space of 'overlap' demarcated by the analytic setting

> When I put forward the model of the double limit [...] Two fields were thus defined: that of the intrapsychic on the inside, resulting from the relations between the parts comprising it, and that of the intersubjective, between inside and outside, whose development involves a relationship to the other.[16]

In psychoanalytic theory, the main conditions of treatment, following Sigmund Freud, include 'arrangements' about time and money, as well as 'certain ceremonials' governing the physical positions of the analysand (lying on a couch and speaking) and the analyst (sitting behind the analyst on a chair and listening).[17] Freud's 'rules' for the spatial positions of the analytic setting were derived from a personal motive – he did not wish to be stared at for long periods of time, but also from a professional concern – to avoid giving the patient 'material for interpretation'.[18]

In a discussion of Freud's method, Winnicott distinguished the technique from the 'setting in which this work is carried out'.[19] In Winnicott's view, it is the setting which allows the reproduction of the 'early and earliest mothering techniques' in psychoanalysis.[20] While Italian psychoanalyst Luciana Nissin Momigliano describes how Winnicott 'defined the "setting" as the sum of all the details of management that are more or less accepted by all psychoanalysts',[21] Argentinian psychoanalyst José Bleger redefined Winnicott's term setting to include the totality of the 'psychoanalytic situation' – the process – what is studied, analysed and interpreted – and the non-process or frame – an institution, which he argues provides a set of constants or limits to the 'behaviours' that occur within it.[22] Other analysts have used slightly different spatial terms to describe the setting. For Laplanche, it is a double-walled tub, where the outside wall is contractual but necessary for preserving the inner wall, which is subject to the uncertainties of the analytic process,[23] and, for Green, it is a casing or casket which holds the 'jewel' of the psychoanalytic process.[24]

Green, who uses both Freudian and Winnicottian concepts in his work, considers the analytic setting a 'homologue' for what he calls the third element in analysis, the 'analytic object' which, in his view, 'corresponds precisely to Winnicott's definition of the transitional object'[25] and is formed through the analytic association between analyst and analysand.[26]

> The analytic object is neither internal (to the analysand or to the analyst), nor external (to either the one or the other), but is situated between the two. So it corresponds precisely to Winnicott's definition of the transitional object and to its location in the intermediate area of potential space, the space of 'overlap' demarcated by the analytic setting.[27]

Unité d'Habitation, Marseilles (1947–1952)

> Narkomfin's elevation on round reinforced concrete columns was certainly influenced by him [Le Corbusier]. In turn, Le Corbusier in the late 1940s used Narkomfin's split-level duplex apartments in his famous *Unités d'Habitation.*[28]

The 'slab block' of the *Unité d'Habitation* in Marseilles was designed by Le Corbusier and built between 1947–1953. The *Unité* is 17 stories high and houses approximately 1,600 people in 23 different flat types. Its intricate section of interlocking two-storey apartments with double-height living spaces incorporates a *rue intérieure* every three floors. The *Unité* originally included 26 communal facilities: an internal street of shops with a laundry, post office, pharmacy, barbers, a hotel and restaurant and a health centre on floors 7 and 8; and, on the top floor, a kindergarten and nursery, leading to a garden on the roof, with a swimming pool for children and a gymnasium.[29]

The *Unité* draws on many aspects of Le Corbusier's earlier research and work, built and unbuilt: the vertical gardens of the *Immeuble-Villas* (1922), for example, and the five point plan – comprising *piloti*, free façade, open plan, ribbon windows and a roof garden – which was developed through the 1920s[30] as well as the urban scale projects of *La Ville Contemporaine* (1922) and *La Ville Radieuse* (1935), and first realised in the *Villa Savoye* (1929–1931).

Le Corbusier made visits to the Soviet Union in the mid to late 1920s to study the latest architecture,[31] and was inspired by a number of aspects of the Narkomfin design including its innovative section with its central axis: the *rue intérieure*, the variable range in possible apartment types (including one with a double-height living space), and the provision of communal facilities. In mutual acknowledgement, Ginzburg and other Soviet constructivists in the early 1920s had read articles by Le Corbusier[32] and references to Le Corbusier's five-point plan are evident in the design of Narkomfin.[33]

To focus on the creative overlap between the two schemes in terms of the borrowing of innovative architectural design features from each other is interesting, but to consider this alone could serve as a distraction from the important tensions that existed between Le Corbusier and Ginzburg in terms of their political positions, and the differing ways in which they understood the relation between architecture and revolution. Both Ginzburg and Le Corbusier were advocates of the machine but if, for Le Corbusier, technology's role was to support capitalism and to make it more efficient and rational, for the Russian constructivists, including Ginzburg, the radicalisation of architecture through new industrialised forms and processes was celebrated in order to develop the newly formed Bolshevik state based on socialist principles.[34] Architectural historian Jean-Louis Cohen, who has studied Le Corbusier's relation to Soviet architecture in great depth, notes that, in 1928, at the first OSA conference, Ginzburg criticised Le Corbusier's design solutions, noting they were 'poorly defined' and 'purely aesthetic'.[35] While for Ginzburg, at least in 1928, architecture could provoke revolution, for Corbusier, architecture's purpose was to take the place of revolution:

Architecture or Revolution. Revolution can be avoided.[36]

The generalised triangular structure with variable third

> The object is thus situated in two places: it belongs both to the internal space on the two levels of the conscious and the unconscious, and it is also present in the external space as object, as other, as another subject.[37]

Green notes that the transitional space of the setting has a 'specificity of its own', which differs from both outside and inner space.[38] Michael Parsons, in a commentary on Green's work, draws attention to his understanding of the analytic setting not as a static tableau but as a space of engagement, not as 'just a representation of psychic structure' but as 'an expression of it'.[39] Parsons explains that for Green: 'It is the way psychic structure expresses itself, and cannot express itself, through the structure of the setting, that makes the psychoanalytic situation psychoanalytic'.[40]

Green understands this as a spatial construction, as the 'generalised triangular structure with variable third'.[41] In Green's work, triadic structures do not have to be Oedipal in the traditional sense; they incorporate Winnicott's transitional space between mother and child, mediated by the choice of a 'not-me object'. In conversation with Green, Gregorio Kohon suggests that he is trying to 'make sense of this mad passion for the mother within an Oedipal constellation, but the mad passion for the mother does not include the mother at all. It only includes the unknown object of bereavement, which can be the text created, or the painting, or the piece of music'.[42]

In *Shadow of the Other*, Jessica Benjamin has argued that the dialogue between mother and child can take the place of 'Jacques Lacan's third term that breaks the dyad'. Instead of thinking of the maternal dyad as a trap with no way out, Benjamin understands the dialogue itself to be a third co-created by two subjects.[43] She maintains that while the intrapsychic perspective continuously reverses through identification, the intersubjective view aims to create a third position 'that is able to break up the reversible complementarities and hold in tension the polarities that underly them'.[44] Rather than a person located outside the dyad, the third may therefore be considered a function, for example, to symbolise. And as Green emphasises:

> the structure is triangular but it doesn't mean that it is Oedipal. The third can be, for instance, art.[45]

Alton West Estate, Roehampton, London SW15 (1954–1958)

In England, the *Unité's* intricate plan was simplified into a stack of identical maisonettes. The '*rue intérieure*', or internal access corridor, was replaced by the traditional English access balcony, which also was cheaper than the internal staircase access of the new point block type, and which made possible a greater economy in lift provision.[46]

Alton West consists of 65.89 acres of housing comprising 1,867 dwellings located in 98.64 acres of parkland. The dwellings are grouped into five types, namely, 12-storey point-blocks of flats, 11-storey slab-blocks of maisonettes, 4-storey slab-blocks of maisonettes and terraces of single-storey housing for old people. The tall blocks are located in three clusters, two of point-blocks and one of slab-blocks, with the lower buildings distributed between them.[47] Community facilities were originally provided in the form of schools (nursery, primary and comprehensive), a surgery, shops and a library.[48]

Architectural historian Nicholas Bullock has outlined how Corbusier's *Unité* was a point of reference for the architects of the London County Council in the 1950s and that while, for example, the architects of Alton East at Roehampton were advocates of New Humanism, those of Alton West were 'pro-Corbu'.[49] Bullock refers to the hot debates held in London pubs over the adoption of the principles of the *Unité*, and how these were linked to divergent socialist views and attitudes to Soviet communism.

Bullock notes that, in the translation from the *Unité* to Alton West, certain key design features were lost including the communal spaces, double-height living rooms and central access corridor. Miles Glendinning and Stefan Muthesius suggest that it was for economic reasons that the traditional English access balcony replaced the *rue intérieure*. [50] A loss in translation was also registered in terms of the reduction of shared facilities including the roof garden, and a criticism made of the scheme at the time was that the separation of different dwelling types had produced a lack of coherent structure at a community level:

> If communities are to exist in high buildings, then it is necessary that there are community and service activities related to the group structure of those communities.[51]

Thing-like presentations or the 'waste' products of translation

> In melancholia the relation to the object is no simple one; it is complicated by the conflict due to ambivalence [...] In melancholia, accordingly, countless separate struggles are carried on over the object, in which hate and love contend with each other [...] The location of these separate struggles cannot be assigned to any system but the *Ucs*, the region of the memory-traces of *things* (as contrasted with *word*-cathexes).[52]

The psychoanalytic concept of the lost object is introduced in the work of Freud in relation to two stages of loss; first the loss of the mother's breast and then her whole person.[53] Freud defines mourning as a reaction to the loss of a loved person or ideal, but notes that while there is nothing about mourning that is unconscious, 'melancholia is in some way related to an object-loss which is withdrawn from consciousness'.[54]

Critical of the way Freud opposes thing-presentations and word-presentations,[55] Laplanche proposes a process of translation–repression comprising two phases. The first involves 'inscription' or the 'implanting' of what he calls 'enigmatic signifiers', messages,[56] from the mother that contain aspects of her unconscious, and the second entails the reactivation of certain traumatic signifiers which the subject attempts to bind or symbolise.[57] Failure to do this results in the repression of residue elements that are not capable of signifying or communicating anything but themselves. Laplanche calls these untranslatable signifiers 'thing-like presentations' (*représentation-chose*) in order to show that the unconscious element is not a representation or trace of an external thing. 'Thing-like presentations' are not representations *of* things, but representations that are *like* things.

For Laplanche, 'the passage to the unconscious is correlative with a loss of referentiality'.[58] In his account, repression – the negative side of the translation of the enigmatic message – produces dislocation.[59] It is an effect of the process of repression, 'a partial and failed translation', that the 'preconscious presentation-of-the-thing (*Sachvorstellung, représentation de chose*) is transformed into an unconscious presentation-as-a-mental-thing (*représentation-chose*) or thing-like presentation, a designified signifier'.[60] Laplanche describes this unconscious residue as having a 'reified and alien materiality'.[61] As a message it signifies 'to' someone rather than 'of' something since, despite the loss of its signified, this thing-like presentation can still communicate to an addressee, verbally and non-verbally, through gesture.[62] As John Fletcher maintains, Laplanche's model of translation-repression rethinks the problem of unconscious representation by understanding repressed elements, not as memories or copies of past events, but as remainders or 'waste' products of translations.[63]

> For in between the primary intervention of the other and the creation of the other thing in me, there occurs a process called repression – an extremely complex process comprising at least two stages in mutual interaction, and leading to a veritable dislocation/reconfiguration of (explicit and implicit-enigmatic) experiential elements.[64]

The Narkomfin, again, but from somewhere else

The fact that Narkomfin failed in its function as communal housing also explains why it has been neglected over the years. The building never achieved the communality that Ginzburg intended for it: the balcony on the first floor intended for conversation quickly became storage space; the roof garden was never completed and the communal dining room barely used. By the mid 'thirties the canteen was being little used and was closed. People used their small kitchen niches in their own apartments. The increasing paranoia of Stalin's Russia affected the inhabitants of Narkomfin, after all they worked together and lived together. The Finance Commissariat was one of the more dangerous places to work in the 1930s and there were denunciations which led to arrests in Narkomfin.[65]

While Bullock has focused on describing the loss of certain design principles vital to Le Corbusier's *Unité* in the process of reformulating the project for London's public housing provision, he fails to mention the debt that both the *Unité* and Alton West owed to the Narkomfin. This omission of reference to the Narkomfin, and its social condenser, results in an argument that defines the relation between architecture and revolution in Le Corbusier's terms and vacates the political imperative – defined in terms of the revolutionary – at the heart of the design. Yet the process of retracing those elements which have been lost, that have slipped through the two-phase translation – from Moscow to Marseilles, and then from Marseilles to London – is perhaps not simply one of re-finding those objects discarded because the recipients did not value them for their original political and cultural context. There is also the issue of their reception by their receivers and the associated processes of repression and dislocation to consider.

According to Buchli, by 1930, there was a call in the Soviet Union for the rapid proletarianisation of the architectural profession; and VOPRA, a group opposing OSA, called for the admission of students of proletarian origin over those of bourgeois origin, attacking constructivism for its formalism and developing instead a distinctly Stalinist style based on classicism. The full socialisation of the family life planned for in schemes such as Narkomfin was condemned and a publication, *Concerning Work on the Restructuring of Everyday Life*, demanded the reassessment of *byt* reform and only partial socialisation. The Council of People's Commissars was to produce proposals for the design of settlements with individual houses for workers and, although laundry facilities, dining rooms, bathhouses, schooling and day care were to be collectivised, the attempts in projects like the Narkomfin to socialise child rearing and make the family home more minimal were criticised. Instead, the 'segregated petit-bourgeois hearth where nuclear families would live and rear their children was to remain intact'.[66]

Buchli argues that, under the pressure of an increasingly hostile government, the Narkomfin was considered part of the discredited left and 'Trotskyite' thinking, and the *pilotis* taken as a sign of constructivism.[67] By the mid 1930s, the area under the *pilotis* was filled in with apartments with prerevolutionary plans, the communal block was altered, the bridge connecting communal block and living block was sealed off and converted into labourers' dormitories, and the laundry facility was reworked into offices. Under this external pressure, Ginzburg himself began to turn in on himself, criticising his own work and denying the value of the socialist and revolutionary principles which governed his early design of the Narkomfin. Buchli quotes him as commenting on the design that:

The forms of socialist life were not understood in dialectic terms, in movement, but in some sort of uniform and unchanging order [...] only in the sleeping cabins is the self allowed to develop.[68]

Winnicott's transitional object, again, but in a different place

> To use an object the subject must have developed a *capacity* to use objects. This is part of the change to the reality principle.[69]

In his 1968 paper 'The Use of an Object', Winnicott describes how 'relating may be to a subjective object, but usage implies that the object is part of external reality'.[70] For Winnicott, to use an object is to take into account its objective reality or existence as 'a thing in itself' rather than its subjective reality or existence as a projection. The change from relating to using is for him significant, it 'means that the subject destroys the object': that the object stands outside the omnipotent control of the subject, recognised as the external object it has always been.[71]

But what does it mean to 'use' an object – a concept, a building – rather than to relate to one? Commenting on the potential use of the concepts contained in this essay by Winnicott, Juliet Mitchell argues that if one does not use theory, all one can do is apply it or question it 'within its own terms'.[72] She argues, following Winnicott, that to use a theory we have to destroy it; and that when it survives it 'will be in a different place',[73] one where it is independent and therefore charged with the capacity of a 'use-object'.[74]

What kind of transitional object is the Narkomfin? Maybe it is too simple to think of it as a lost object or an object whose loss is to be mourned. In response to the Stalinist regime, its initial value was repressed by its architect and dislocated; and, later in the two-phase translation of its elements *en route* from Moscow to London, via Marseilles, the social condenser was repositioned as residual waste. Yet, as a thing-like presentation, as a message, it still communicates to its addressee, signifying 'to' us rather than 'of' the thing that has been lost. Perhaps the reconfiguring of its original principles in the *Unité* and Alton West, is not only a loss then, or a lack of recognition, but might be better considered a destruction, which has allowed the Narkomfin to resurface in a different place. Might it be possible to use this lost object, not by questioning it within its own terms or by applying it, but by charging it with the capacity to reactivate a new version of the social condenser for today?

> This sequence can be observed: (1) Subject *relates* to object. (2) Object is in process of being found instead of placed by the subject in the world. (3) Subject *destroys* object. (4) Object survives destruction. (5) Subject can *use* object.[75]

NOTES

1   D. W. Winnicott, 'Transitional Objects and Transitional Phenomena: A Study of the First Not-Me Possession', *International Journal of Psycho-Analysis*, 34 (1953): 89–97, 89.

2   Gregorio Kohon (ed.) *The British School of Psychoanalysis: The Independent Tradition* (London: Free Association Books, 1986) p. 20. The British School of Psychoanalysis consists of psychoanalysts belonging to the British Psycho-Analytical Society, within this society are three groups, the Kleinian Group, the 'B' Group (followers of Anna Freud) and the Independent Group.

3   Klein describes the early stages of childhood development in terms of different 'positions'. The paranoid schizophrenic position characterises the child's state of one-ness with the mother, where he or she relates to part-objects such as the mother's breast, as either good or bad, satisfying or frustrating. See Melanie Klein, 'Notes on Some Schizoid Mechanisms' (1946) in *Envy and Gratitude and Other Worlds 1946–1963* (London: Virago, 1988) pp. 1–24. This position is replaced by a depressive stage where in recognising its own identity and that of the mother as a whole person, the child feels guilty for the previous aggression inflicted on the mother. See Melanie Klein, *Love, Guilt and Reparation and Other Works 1921–1945* (London: The Hogarth Press and the Institute of Psycho-Analysis, 1981).

4   Winnicott, 'Transitional Objects and Transitional Phenomena', see in particular pp. 89 and 94. See also D. W. Winnicott, 'The Use of an Object', *The International Journal of Psycho-Analysis*, 50 (1969): 711–716.

5   See D. W. Winnicott, 'The Location of Cultural Experience', *The International Journal of Psycho-Analysis*, 48 (1967): 68–372, 371. See also D. W. Winnicott, *Playing and Reality* (London: Routledge, 1991).

6   Winnicott, 'The Location of Cultural Experience', 371–372.

7   Catherine Cooke (ed.) *Russian Avant-Garde: Art and Architecture: Special issue of Architectural Design*, 53, 5/6 (1983): 42.

8   Cooke, *Russian Avant-Garde: Art and Architecture*, 38.

9   Catherine Cooke, *Russian Avant-Garde: Theories of Art, Architecture and the City* (London: Academy Editions, 1995), p. 118.

10 Cooke, *Russian Avant-Garde: Art and Architecture*, 44–45. See also Victor Buchli, *An Archaeology of Socialism* (Oxford: Berg, 2000).

11 Buchli, *An Archaeology of Socialism*, p. 23.

12 Victor Buchli, 'Moisei Ginzburg's Narkomfin Communal House in Moscow', *Journal of the Society of Architectural Historians*, 57, 2 (1998): 160–181, 161.

13 Buchli notes that the original design was the A-1 *Don Kommuna* entered in a competition and exhibition of *Don Kommuny* organised by OSA in Moscow in 1927: Buchli, 'Moisei Ginzburg's Narkomfin Communal House in Moscow', 179, note 13. According to Gary Berkovich, the architects of this 1927 design were Anatolii Ladinskii and Konstantin Ivanov, under direction of their professor Andrey Ol'. See Gary Berkovich, 'My Constructivism', trans. by Gary Berkovich and David Gurevich, extracted from the book of memoirs *Human Subjects*. Excerpts from 'My Constructivism' were first published in the *Inland Architect* magazine, 25, 8 (1981): 8–19. See http://www.e-noosphere.com/Noosphere/En/Magazine/Default. asp?File=20080108_Berkovich.htm [accessed: 12 April 2011].

14 Buchli, 'Moisei Ginzburg's Narkomfin Communal House in Moscow', 162.

15 Buchli, 'Moisei Ginzburg's Narkomfin Communal House in Moscow', 162.

16 André Green, 'The Intrapsychic and Intersubjective in Psychoanalysis', *Psychoanalysis Quarterly*, 69 (2000): 1–39, 3.

17 Sigmund Freud, 'On Beginning the Treatment (Further Recommendations on the Technique of Psycho-Analysis I)' [1913] *The Standard Edition of the Complete Psychological Works of Sigmund Freud, Volume XII (1911–1913): The Case of Schreber, Papers on Technique and Other Works*, translated from the German under the general editorship of James Strachey (London: The Hogarth Press, 1958), pp. 121–144, p. 126 and p. 133. For a detailed description of Freud's consulting room, see Diana Fuss and Joel Sanders, 'Berggasse 19:

Inside Freud's Office', Joel Sanders (ed.) *Stud: Architectures of Masculinity* (New York: Princeton Architectural Press, 1996), pp. 112–139.

18 Freud, 'On Beginning the Treatment', p. 134.

19 D. W. Winnicott, 'Metapsychological and Clinical Aspects of Regression Within the Psycho-Analytic Set-Up', *International Journal of Psycho-Analysis*, 36 (1955): 16–26, 20.

20 Winnicott, 'Metapsychological and Clinical Aspects of Regression', 21.

21 Luciana Nissin Momigliano, 'The Analytic Setting; a Theme with Variations', *Continuity and Change in Psychoanalysis: Letters from Milan* (London and New York: Karnac Books, 1992), pp. 33–61, pp. 33–34. Momigliano points out that in Italy the term 'setting' is used in the Winnicottian sense to 'indicate a safe and constant framework within which the psychoanalytic process evolves', whereas in Anglo-Saxon language this is currently called the 'frame'.

22 José Bleger, 'Psycho-Analysis of the Psycho-Analytic Frame', *International Journal of Psycho-Analysis*, 48 (1967): 511–519, 518.

23 The French term used is '*baquet*'. See Jean Laplanche, 'Transference: its Provocation by the Analyst' (1992) translated by Luke Thurston in ed. by John Fletcher *Essays on Otherness*, (London: Routledge, 1999), pp. 214–233, p. 226, note.

24 The French word used is '*écrin*'. See André Green, *Key Ideas for a Contemporary Psychoanalysis: Misrecognition and Recognition of the Unconscious* (London: Routledge, 2005) p. 33, note.

25 André Green, 'Potential Space in Psychoanalysis: The Object in the Setting', Simon A. Grolnick and Leonard Barkin (eds) *Between Reality and Fantasy: Transitional Objects and Phenomena* (New York and London: Jason Aronson Inc., 1978), pp. 169–189, p. 180.

26 André Green, 'The Analyst, Symbolization and Absence in the Analytic Setting (On Changes in Analytic Practice and Analytic Experience) – In Memory of D. W. Winnicott', *International Journal of Psycho-Analysis*, 56 (1975): 1–22, 12.

27 Green, 'Potential Space in Psychoanalysis', 180.

28 Franziska Bollerey and Axel Föhl, 'Architecture of the Avant Garde: Icons and Iconoclasts', p. 46. See http://www.maps-moscow.com/userdata/part_01.pdf [accessed 12 April 2011].

29 For the initial designs, see Le Corbusier, *Oeuvre complete 1938–1946* (Zurich: Les Editions d'Architecture, 1946), pp. 172–187. See also Alban Janson and Carsten Krohn, *Le Corbusier, Unité d'habitation, Marseilles* (London and Stuttgart: Axel Menges, 2007).

30 Le Corbusier developed his five-point plan through publications in the journal *L'Esprit Nouveau* from 1921 and his book *Vers une architecture* first published in Paris in 1923.

31 Jean-Louis Cohen, *Le Corbusier and the Mystique of the USSR: Theories and Projects for Moscow 1928–1936* (Princeton: Princeton University Press, 1992).

32 Cooke, *Russian Avant-Garde: Art and Architecture*, 38–9 and Cooke, *Russian Avant-Garde: Theories*, p. 122.

33 For example the debt Le Corbusier's Unité owes the Narkomfin is noted by numerous critics and historians. See also 'An interview with Richard Pare, photographer and expert on Soviet Modernist architecture', by Tim Tower, http://www.wsws.org/articles/2010/nov2010/pare-n13.shtml [accessed: 12 April 2011].

34 Cohen quotes in detail a letter to Moscow architects published in *Stroikelnaia Promyshlennost* in 1929 where El Lissitzky puts forward a strong critique of Le Corbusier, identifying some key problematics of his approach, for example, his understanding of architecture as a 'buffer between the producer/entrepreneur and the consumer/inhabitant', his position as a Western artist, and thus individualist, his interest in the building as showpiece rather than a place to be lived in, and his formal preference for classicism. See Cohen, *Le Corbusier and the Mystique of the USSR*, pp. 107–109.

35 Cohen, *Le Corbusier and the Mystique of the USSR*, pp. 114–115.

36 See Le Corbusier, *Vers une architecture* (1923). For comparison, see also Moisei Ginzburg, *Style and Epoch* (1924), trans. by Anatole Senkevitch (Cambridge MA: MIT Press, 1983). Richard Pare argues that here Corbusier takes the luxury liner and the private villa as his examples; while Ginzburg takes the warship and the communal house. See 'An interview with Richard Pare'.

37 Green, 'The Intrapsychic and Intersubjective in Psychoanalysis', 3.

38 André Green and Gregorio Kohon, 'The Greening of Psychoanalysis: André Green in Dialogues with Gregorio Kohon' in Gregorio Kohon (ed.) *The Dead Mother: The Work of André Green* (London: Routledge, 1999), pp. 10–58, p. 29.

39 Michael Parsons, 'Psychic Reality, Negation, and the Analytic Setting' in *The Dove that Returns, The Dove that Vanishes* (London: Routledge, 2000); Kohon, *The Dead Mother*, pp. 59–75, p. 74.

40 Parsons, 'Psychic Reality', p. 74.

41 Green and Kohon, 'The Greening of Psychoanalysis', p. 53.

42 Green and Kohon, 'The Greening of Psychoanalysis', p. 53.

43 Jessica Benjamin, *Shadow of the Other: Intersubjectivity and Gender in Psychoanalysis* (London: Routledge, 1998) p. 28, note 5. Benjamin originally made this argument in Jessica Benjamin, 'The Omnipotent Mother: A Psychoanalytic Study of Fantasy and Reality' in *Like Subjects/ Love Objects* (New Haven: Yale University Press, 1995) pp. 81–113, especially pp. 96–97.

44 Benjamin, *Shadow of the Other*, p. xiv.

45 Green and Kohon, 'The Greening of Psychoanalysis', p. 53.

46 Miles Glendinning and Stefan Muthesius, *Tower Block: Modern Public Housing in England, Scotland, Wales and Northern Ireland* (London and New Haven: Yale University Press, 1994), p. 58.

47 [n.a], 'Alton Estate (W) Roehampton Lane, London, SW15', *The Architect's Journal* (5 November, 1959): 461–478.

48 [n.a], 'Housing at Priory Lane, Roehampton, SW15', *Architectural Design* (January 1959): 7–21.

49 Nicholas Bullock, *Building the Post-War World: Modern Architecture and Reconstruction in Britain* (London: Routledge, 2002), pp. 102–107.

50 Glendinning and Muthesius, *Tower Block*, p. 58.

51 [n.a], 'Housing at Priory Lane, Roehampton, SW15', 21.

52 See Sigmund Freud, 'Mourning and Melancholia' (1917) in *The Standard Edition of the Complete Psychological Works of Sigmund Freud, Volume XIV (1914–1916): On the History of the Psycho-Analytic Movement, Papers on Metapsychology and Other Works*, (London: The Hogarth Press, 1955), pp. 237–258, pp. 255–256.

53 See Sigmund Freud, 'Three Essays on the Theory of Sexuality' (1905) in *The Standard Edition of the Complete Psychological Works of Sigmund Freud, Volume VII (1901–1905): A Case of Hysteria, Three Essays on Sexuality and Other Works* (London: The Hogarth Press, 1955) pp. 123–243 and Sigmund Freud, 'Beyond the Pleasure Principle' (1920) in *The Standard Edition of the Complete Psychological Works of Sigmund Freud, Volume XVIII (1920–1922): Beyond the Pleasure Principle, Group Psychology and Other Works* (London: The Hogarth Press, 1955), pp. 1–64. See also Freud, 'Mourning and Melancholia'.

54 Freud, 'Mourning and Melancholia', pp. 255–256.

55 Jean Laplanche, 'A Short Treatise on the Unconscious' (1993), trans. by Luke Thurston, *Essays on Otherness*, ed. by John Fletcher (London: Routledge, 1999), pp. 84–116, p. 92, note 20.

56 Laplanche explains that he uses the term message since it indicates the non-verbal as well as the verbal, and also because, unlike language, it does not 'efface the alterity of the other in favour of trans-individual structures'. See Jean Laplanche, 'The Unfinished Copernican Revolution' (1992) trans. by Luke Thurston in *Essays on Otherness*, ed. by John Fletcher (London: Routledge, 1999) pp. 52–83, p. 73. Like Laplanche, André Green has taken issue with Jacques Lacan's formula: 'the unconscious is structured like a language'. Green posits that the unconscious 'is structured like an affective language, or like an affectivity having the properties of language'. Green's position, again following Freud's, is that if the unconscious, opposed to the pre-conscious, is constituted by thing-presentations as Freud suggests then what is 'related to language can only belong to the pre-conscious'. See Green 'Potential Space in Psychoanalysis', 186 and Green and Kohon, 'The Greening of Psychoanalysis', p. 24.

57 Laplanche, 'A Short Treatise', p. 93.

58 Laplanche, 'A Short Treatise', p. 90.

59 Laplanche, 'A Short Treatise', p. 104.

60 Jean Laplanche, 'The Drive and its Source-Object: its Fate in the Transference' (1992) trans. by Leslie Hill in *Essays on Otherness*, ed. by John Fletcher (London: Routledge, 1999) pp. 117–132, pp. 120–121, note 6.

61 Laplanche, 'The Drive', pp. 120–121, note 6.

62 Laplanche, 'A Short Treatise', p. 91. John Fletcher notes that in 'signifying to' Laplanche is 'alluding to' Jacques Lacan, who distinguised between a signifier of something, a meaning or signified, and a signifier to someone, an addressee. See Laplanche, 'A Short Treatise', p. 91, note 18, editor's comment. Laplanche refers explicitly to Lacan's model of language but dismisses it as 'only applicable to a perfect, well-made, univocal language' and takes up instead the 'full extension' Freud gives to language which includes gesture and other kinds of expression of psychical activity. Laplanche, 'A Short Treatise', p. 92.

63 John Fletcher, 'Introduction: Psychoanalysis and the Question of the Other' *Essays on Otherness*, ed. by John Fletcher (London: Routledge, 1999) pp. 1–51, p. 37.

64 Laplanche, 'The Unfinished Copernican Revolution', p. 71, note 37. Here the reader is referred to Jean Laplanche, *New Foundations for Psychoanalysis* [1987] trans. by David Macey (Oxford: Basil Blackwell Ltd., 1989), pp. 130–133.

65 See http://www.opendemocracy.net/od-russia/clementine-cecil/narkomfin-building-life-after-luzhkov [accessed: 12 April 2011]. Clementine Cecil is a journalist and co-founder of MAPS, Moscow Architecture Preservation Society, a society dedicated to preserving the architectural heritage of Moscow. http://www.maps-moscow.com/?chapter_id=232 [accessed: 12 April 2011].

66 Buchli, 'Moisei Ginzburg's Narkomfin Communal House in Moscow', 165.

67 Buchli, 'Moisei Ginzburg's Narkomfin Communal House in Moscow', 177.

68 Buchli, 'Moisei Ginzburg's Narkomfin Communal House in Moscow', 175.

69 Winnicott, 'The Use of an Object', p. 713.

70 Winnicott, 'The Use of an Object', p. 715.

71 Winnicott, 'The Use of an Object', p. 713.

72 Juliet Mitchell, 'Theory as an Object', *October*, 113, Summer (2005): 29.

73 Mitchell 'Theory as an Object', 29–38, 32.

74 Mitchell, 'Theory as an Object', 33.

75 Winnicott, 'The Use of an Object', p. 715.

Part three

Redolent details, insightful documents

This third part of the book shifts from the scale of landscapes and buildings to the scale of details and documents. The chapters collected here show that scale is no impediment to insightful reading; that even the smallest, or most superficially negligible, detail or document can yield cultural insights when closely read.

In his famous essay 'The Tell-the-tale Detail', Marco Frascari has argued that the detail is the 'minimum unit of architectural signification', showing how a detail can be a microcosm of the whole, and how the detail can impose its order on the whole.[1] Michael Cadwell has extended this argument in his accomplished book *Strange Details*, showing how four projects by famous architects (Carlo Scarpa, Frank Lloyd Wright, Mies van der Rohe and Louis Kahn) re-thought elementary principles of construction to make dense, intense worlds out of their details, whose after-effects have been contagious.[2]

Cadwell also examines four details in his essay here, in order to test contemporary ideas about sustainability in architecture. He pursues four lines of inquiry – 'the line of the wall, the line of the ground, the line of effects, and the line of vision' – in four projects by Renzo Piano, Steven Holl, Neutelings Riedijk and OMA. He echoes David Leatherbarrow's opening call for a rich cultural reading of building construction and performance, for a rich ecological dynamic that is not set up in opposition to a narrow technical understanding. Architecture 'arises from a dense cultural atmosphere', Cadwell reminds us, and contemporary sustainable technologies are too often 'entrenched in the world they wish to displace'.

Mhairi McVicar's essay pursues a meeting between two detailing ideologies first introduced in Cadwell's chapter: the confrontation on the campus of IIT in Chicago between the Commons Building, attributed to Mies van der Rohe, and its more recent addition, the McCormick Tribune Campus Center, attributed to Rem Koolhaas and OMA. At IIT, the original structure – the epitome of high modernism, obsessively planned on its rectilinear Cartesian grid, exquisitely jewelled to millimetric tolerances in steel and sheet glass and hailed for its constructional 'honesty' – meets OMA's rambunctious, loose, polemical architecture obsessed with shape and form. McVicar presents an almost forensic reading of two details that are in close proximity here – an exposed structural steel column at the Commons and a ceiling detail at the McCormick Center – to tease out the alternative architectural values and ideas of precision that they embody.

Turning from details to documents, the subsequent chapter by Katie Lloyd Thomas considers the specification of glass, examining instructions for the selection and installation of that material in an 1835 specification (for an asylum for the blind in Bristol) and a 2005 specification (for a supermarket in London, designed by Chetwoods Architects). While such technical documents are conventionally assumed to be separate from the cultural work of architecture, she shows how the recent shift towards performance specification is only made possible by a vast nexus of industrial, scientific, regulatory and design practices which, in turn, reconfigures the capacities of materials such as glass.[3] In the case of new parliamentary buildings, for example (and echoing Wainwright's discussion in Chapter 3), these glass performances are seen to produce new, and increasingly social, mediations which challenge the modernist rhetoric of transparency, and whose implications should be recognised more widely.

The idea of contemporary architectural practice, where architects work on drawings and specifications remote from the building site, is frequently assumed to have come about with the introduction of paper to Europe in the fifteenth century. Paul Emmons and Jonathan Foote examine a fascinating early plan drawing – the sole drawing ascribed to scholar and architect Leon Battista Alberti – made as part of an unrealised project for a thermal bath at the Palazzo Ducale in Urbino. They read this somewhat austere drawing for evidence of Alberti's habits and techniques, examining how familiar site practices appear to have been translated onto paper, and considering how the drawing might have been translated into construction. Echoing Leatherbarrow and Cadwell, the authors emphasise that plans are cultural constructions rather than merely technical descriptions, and that – not least through drawing – contemporary 'practice' remains rooted in the ethical judgements of what was once called 'practical philosophy'.

The final chapter in the third part of the book, by Hugh Campbell, moves from the documents which anticipate construction to the documents which architects arguably prize most in interpreting the result: photographs. He reads two recent architectural photographs: a picture by photographer Candida Höfer of the *Neues Museum* in Berlin (designed by David Chipperfield and Julian Harrap); and a picture by Walter Niedermayr of the Glass Pavilion at the Toledo Museum (designed by SANAA). Such images, Campbell suggests, are often imagined as portraits, but he questions whether architecture is 'as ripe for portraiture as the self'. He argues that architectural photographs need not be as partial or misleading as they are commonly assumed to be, suggesting that photographs *can* match-up to architecture's complex material presence.

Again, these chapters ask pertinent questions. How can the architectures of details and documents be read in the same ways as built architecture? How can materials and details be understood as dynamically integral to cultural ecologies? How do architectural details participate in cultural politics? How do the conventions of drawing and specification participate in cultural politics? How are site practices translated into drawing, and how are drawing practices translated onto site? Do the documents employed to anticipate and describe architecture necessarily rely on built architecture for their value?

NOTES

1   Marco Frascari, 'Tell-the-tale Detail' in K. Nesbitt (ed.) *Theorizing a New Agenda for Architecture: An Anthology of Architecture Theory 1965–1995* (New York: Princeton Architectural Press, 1996), pp. 498–515 (p. 498).
2   Michael Cadwell, *Strange Details* (Cambridge MA: MIT Press, 2007).
3   Katie Lloyd Thomas (ed.) *Material Matters: Architecture and Material Practice* (London: Routledge, 2006).

Chapter 10

Four lines

Michael Cadwell

Sustainability will exert as much pressure on architecture in this century as industrialisation did in the previous century. This now seems inevitable. Population growth, consumer culture, and global warming are converging with wide-ranging consequences: the economic consequences of decreasing energy supplies; the political and social consequences of petrodictatorships and civic unrest; and the environmental consequences of climate change and plant and animal extinction. Any significant response to these conditions requires government intervention and energy technologies beyond architecture's purview, yet architecture must do its part to address energy and resource conservation.[1] The technical imperative of sustainability has replaced the technical imperative of industrialisation.

Notwithstanding the urgency of sustainability and the difficulties of its address, sustainability's greatest challenge to architecture is cultural not technical. Technical imperatives lend themselves to the narrow prescriptions of utility – the same prescriptions that architectural criticism has spent the last fifty years attacking for, among other things, leading to our current environmental impasse. If architecture is to be sustainable, it must be ecological – a thick zone of cultural engagement rather than a thin line of technical progress.

Architecture arises from a dense cultural atmosphere. Le Corbusier, for example, argued for the technical advances of the reinforced concrete frame in his Dom-ino House, yet he was also committed to the formal potential of the frame's abstract vocabulary of point, line, and plane. Mies van der Rohe was similarly invested in the steel frame, but his buildings do not celebrate steel structure so much as dissemble the structure of perspective. Even Louis Kahn, who often harnessed architecture to technical inevitability – 'what a brick wants'[2] – produced buildings late in his career that celebrate fleeting effects – 'on a grey day it will look like a moth; on a sunny day like a butterfly.'[3] Technology plays a role in these cases, but it never does so alone.

If sustainability is to generate anything other than rote responses, therefore, it must be integral to architecture's cultural role of constructing new worlds. If we consider architecture as the ecology of interdependent systems with cultural implications, rather than the production of independent objects with technical agendas, then we must reconsider long held conventions.[4]

I offer four conventions in support of this argument: *the line of the wall, the line of the ground, the line of effects,* and *the line of vision.* These lines pose technical challenges of envelope, foundation, material transformation, and spatial configuration. Technique is necessary in each case, but not sufficient. Affect trumps technique because it is technique's goal; affect is technique rendered as intelligible experience. What is primary, therefore, is the ecological affect of a conventional boundary's thickening into a thick zone of exchange – a wall, for example, experienced as a conduit rather than a barrier. I will focus on the wall of Renzo Piano's Tjibaou Cultural Centre, the contrasting groundworks of Steven Holl's Stretto House and Bloch Building, the opposing effects of Peter Zumthor's Baths at Vals and Neutelings Riedijk's Netherlands Institute for Sound and Vision, and the optics of OMA's McCormick Tribune Campus Center – in each case, an ecological dynamic is experienced whether or not sustainability is a primary concern.[5]

The line of the wall

The Jean-Marie Tjibaou Cultural Centre (1998) extends along a strip of land that separates a lagoon from the South Pacific on the island of New Caledonia. Ten ballooning pavilions punctuate the Centre's linear organisation. Recalling the huts of the indigenous Kanak people to which the Centre is dedicated, the pavilions are circular in plan and wrapped with slim iroko wood members (Figure 10.1). The basketry bows in section; horizontal slats face the arcing ribs that couple with straight inner ribs supporting a sloping roof. A thicket of galvanized steel ties and struts weave inner and outer ribs into a flexible, yet resilient structure. The internal envelope nests behind the straight ribs, its modular panels of wood, metal, and glass addressing daylight, ventilation, acoustics, and storage.

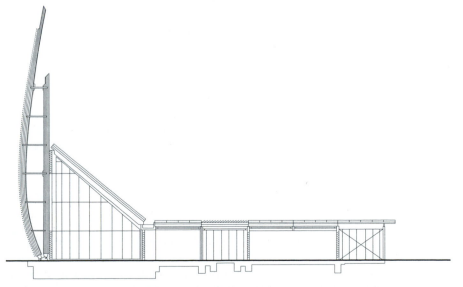

Figure 10.1 Jean-Marie Tjibaou Cultural Centre, section

The Centre's wall is no longer a wall in the conventional sense of a barricade against wind and rain. Granted, modern construction is more often layered rather than monolithic, its visible face masking structure and an elaborate sequence of vapour and thermal barriers. However, the Centre's wall pulls these layers apart, swelling to articulate what a conventional wall suppresses. A façade's thin veneer becomes a diaphanous windscreen, a venting airspace becomes a spacious chimney, and a backup wall of weatherproofing becomes transparent to the entire assembly.

More air than material, the wall is more conduit than barrier. It vents habitable spaces to its leeward side, pulling in cool ocean breezes at its base, drawing them over the stabilising thermal mass of its concrete substructure, and exhausting warmer air at its top. The wall's louvres adjust to wind velocities, even neutralising air pressures during cyclones. Lively air carries the smell of the ocean and lush vegetation and the aftertaste of salt. On the exterior, the pavilions seem both an abstraction of the landscape, their cylindrical forms and wooden construction referring to the trees of adjacent hills, and a part of that landscape, these same forms swelling at midsection and dissolving into feathered tops that wave and hum in the wind. The exchange of building and landscape is absorbed into the everyday experience of the Centre, as sensations of touch, smell, taste, and sound reinforce visual sympathies.

In spite of this reciprocity, the Centre's construction systems posit a duality. If the Centre's wood and steel enclosure complements its concrete substructure, they remain discrete systems. Indeed, this division has been a recognised strategy since the nineteenth-century writings of Gottfried Semper, whose diagram of a Caribbean hut delineated tectonic systems dealing with the sky (the wood frame and woven envelope) and stereotomic systems dealing with the ground (the earthwork and hearth).[6] Even a modern high-rise building aligns with these terms: foundation as earthwork, core as hearth, steel or concrete structure as frame, and curtain wall as envelope.

An ecological understanding suggests a different approach, however. If we are to navigate a dynamic world of interdependent systems, then negotiating differences is more helpful than insisting on polarities. In architectural terms, this involves a shift from wall as barrier to wall as conduit. In perceptual terms, the shift from barrier to conduit undercuts the dualism of solid and void, and suggests a merger of building and landscape. If the perceptual implications of a wall's horizontal separation of inside and outside extend to the ground plane's vertical separation of earth and sky, then the possibility of an aerated ground presents itself.

The line of the ground

Two buildings by Steven Holl are interesting in this regard. The Stretto House (1991) is, among other things, an application of Semper's diagram. Stretto's concrete foundation steps down its pastoral site, measuring the earth's slope and reaching beyond the house's perimeter with low walls that gauge topography. Standing on this earthwork is a succession of tall rectangular volumes enclosed in concrete block and trimmed with native limestone. These bars, or hearths in Semper's lexicon, provide lateral stability for the steel frame that dots the open spaces stretching between them and supports the curved roofs sailing above. As a final touch, the open spaces' defining envelope is a tapestry glass, hand-sanded aluminum, and acid-reddened brass, stitched together by mullions and control joints. Holl's office produced an axonometric drawing of the house that articulated a stereotomic system of foundation and bars anchoring to the earth, and a tectonic system of frame, envelope, and roof floating in the air above (Figure 10.2). The diagram could not be clearer.

The strategy of flowing space and rectilinear bars reappears at the Bloch Building; Holl's addition to the Nelson-Atkins Museum of Art in Kansas City (2006). The original building, a handsome symmetrical Beaux Arts block, defines its interior with simple geometries that extend to the exterior with an entry court to the north, and a vast lawn that drops to the river to the south. Holl's addition lies along the eastern boundary of the site, humouring the original by deflecting its axial thrust. Stretto's bars are now an entry volume

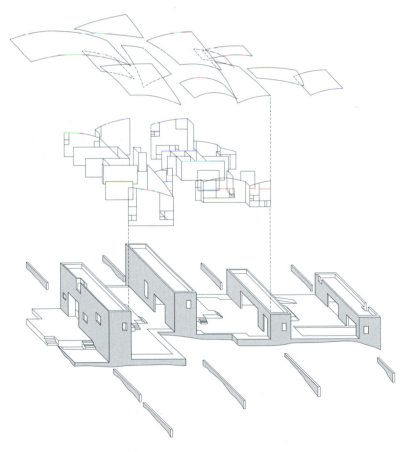

Figure 10.2 Stretto House, axonometric

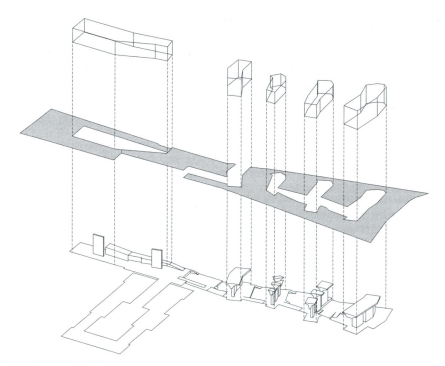

Figure 10.3 Bloch Building, axonometric

oriented north-south with four volumes oriented east-west stepping down the site, measuring the space flowing between. However, the Bloch volumes are not solid masonry bars but luminescent glass lenses, and the fluid space between them does not rest upon the ground but folds into it (Figure 10.3).

Holl often refers to the Bloch's relationship with the Nelson-Atkins in metaphorical terms, as feather and stone, the addition's light glass wall acting as a foil to the solid masonry wall of the original.[7] As built, the glass wall does not lend itself to such clear oppositions. Conventional glazing affords thin transparencies and brittle reflections, while contemporary assemblies proffer delicate veils – none of these effects are in evidence. Instead, the Bloch's wall appears as a translucent thickness, one that deep openings for doors and windows verify.

Construction drawings reveal that two rows of channel glass planks interlock to form the outer wall, while a second double row of planks seal the interior envelope. The pressurised cavity between the two rows adjusts to temperature fluctuations and houses artificial lighting, remote-controlled sunshades, steel structure, and service access. Unlike a conventional curtain wall, but like the stone wall of the Nelson-Atkins, the glass planks are load bearing and resist wind loads. Unlike a conventional bearing wall, however, the glass wall has a void at its centre. The Bloch wall, that is, follows neither the skeletal logic of tectonic construction nor the monolithic logic of stereotomic construction. Instead, it combines attributes of both logics with a glass wall that is, in fact, wider than the stone wall of the Nelson-Atkins.

As the lenses step down the site, they bracket a series of sculpture courts above and galleries below; galleries that eventually spill into the lawn. Now oriented to accept north and south light, the lenses' laminated glass eliminates ultraviolet radiation and encloses the exfoliations of flat-stemmed ductwork that rise from the floor to support the roofs. Strange half-vaults bend and sway, beckoning northern light and deflecting southern light. Hollow vaulting, muted shadows and subtle colouration give rise to the uncanny perception of a solid shaft of light, and diffuse the easy oppositions of solid and void, earth and sky.

The ground is no longer a stable referent. The ground is above the galleries (the sculpture courts), at the same level as the galleries (the lawn to the west), and below the galleries (the service entry to the east). The galleries neither lock to the earth like a stone, nor hover above it like a feather. Instead, the galleries aerate the ground, filling it with light and air.

Manipulated daylight animates this strange combination of material and light. Daylight literally and figuratively illuminates; yet the detailing of glass and plaster constructs these effects. The line of effects, that is, swerves from nature to culture, from an appreciation of natural forces to an acknowledgement that this appreciation is constructed and more capacious constructions are always possible (the Bloch Building is, after all, a museum). Underscoring this swerve, the lenses emit a soft white glow at night, as if the earth might hold daylight's nocturnal twin.

The line of effects

The Thermal Baths at Vals in Switzerland, designed by Peter Zumthor (1996), also invest in effects, although of a different sort. Embedded in an Alpine mountainside, the baths encase themselves in massive walls. The broad slabs of gneiss stone that face these walls are integral to the reinforced concrete structure (Figure 10.4, left). Gneiss also defines the surrounding landscape; its jagged outcroppings break the thin veil of vegetation on distant mountain peaks. Stacked as long bands parallel to the earth, the gneiss cladding evokes the site's stratification, while its 15-centimetre module matches the stair risers. Where the piers give way to the roof's requirements for differential movement, narrow expansion joints extend above the roof's grass surface. Capped with minimal skylights, the joints direct sunrays to slice into the stone caverns below.

The Baths' harsh relief contrasts with the Bloch's subtle modulation of natural light. Material never merges with light at the Baths, just as space never merges with ground. The Bloch offers a new experience of the ground, the Baths hide beneath it. Harvesting materials from the site and constructing them to recall that site's stratification, the Baths suppress the mechanics that make that effect possible and repress the recognition that the organising agent is man – literally, the gait of man. The line of effects stiffens with its own pretence.

A similar stone appears at the Netherlands Institute for Sound and Vision at Hilversum (2006), designed by Neutelings Riedijk Architects. The Baths and Institute could not be more different in siting (ancient Alpine remove versus

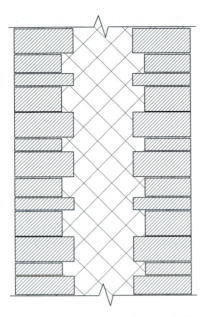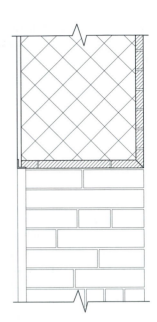

Figure 10.4 Baths at Vals wall section (left) and Netherlands Institute for Sound and Vision wall section (right)

recovered suburban plot) and programme (restoration of the body versus persistence of media) and the two stones – both slate, both tautly coursed – resonate with these differences. The Institute's slate is a tile, its bald face pasted to the structure behind, whether that surface is horizontal (and recalls the slate's origin) or vertical (and denies it). At joints, the tile flaunts its thinness, bevelling its meagre 20 millimetre dimension to appear even thinner (Figure 10.4, right). Most tellingly, as the building descends below grade and into the archive's circulation canyon, the offices' glass curtain wall follows uninterrupted, and a reflected light betrays the canyon's deep thresholds. A goofy orange glow trips chthonic associations with a cartoon's irreverence.

The detailing of the Baths is exquisite, concealing mechanical connections while addressing gravity, thermal movement, waterproofing, and insulation. Yet, what the Baths conceal with maximum effort, the Institute reveals with minimum distraction. This is particularly true of the Institute's rainscreen. Its banal bolted steel armature neither requires excessive craft nor distracts from the coloured glass that it supports. Celebrity portraits emboss the glass smeared with brilliant reds, yellows and blues.[8] The effects are startling. From a distance, the cubic volume of the building merges with blue skies and sunsets, while at evening suggesting a giant TV set glowing in the living room of a tract house. Moving closer, colour dissolves into a hallucinogenic cloud, one that loosens vision's grasp. Closer still, flickering figures arise from the slurry of colour. The Baths refuse such play, as resolute from a distance as they are in close-up.

The Institute basks in artifice: a lurid materiality achieved through technically advanced processes and joined with nonchalance. Yet, the Institute's elision of sunset and TV screen suggests that coloured glass, metal mullions, and suburban Dutch muck are a part of a large ecology rather than intruders. Not content to swerve the line of effects, the Institute bends the line back on itself like a snake swallowing its tail.

The line of sight

The McCormick Tribune Campus Center at the Illinois Institute of Technology also swallows the line of effects, much as it thickens the line of the ground, yet these are not the only lines that the Center reconsiders. Throughout the controversy surrounding its design and construction (1998–2003), Rem Koolhaas maintained that 'I do not respect Mies, I love Mies.'[9] Arguing that additional programs had mangled the original Commons, that mechanical retrofits had scarred it, and that urban dissipation had stranded it, Koolhaas contended that preservation efforts were too little too late. In spite of accusations of 'wanton defacement,'[10] OMA's alternative is a reconsideration of Mies in terms of form, context, material, and, most profoundly, in terms of sight.

As deployed by Mies, the orthogonal form and its transparent envelope offer the paradoxical combination of Olympian remove and heightened attention. The McCormick presents an orthogonal form, but compresses it vertically and horizontally. Chicago's elevated transit line buckles the McCormick roof at its third point, pressing down on the space beneath and releasing it to the east and west (Figure 10.5, above). As if responding to this pressure, the McCormick's floor stutters into successive levels that treat the ground as a negotiated thickness rather than, as with Mies, elevating above the ground.

Between the compressed roof and the thickened ground, three spatial operations are at play (Figure 10.5, below). The first is a nine-square organisation that follows the module of the Commons, which nests in the McCormick's northeast corner. Following the logic of compression, three north-south bands of programme compact the nine-square: student activities to the east; public amenities to the west; and recreational facilities between. Individual functions either reinforce the nine-square (as with the student advising block) or provide a finer grain to the bands (such as with the public meeting rooms, theatre, and ballroom). Cutting through both organisations is a third: the paths that link student housing to the east and academic buildings to the west. Although generated by OMA's study of pedestrian movements across the site, these lines are also a rotation of the nine-square, much as the banding of program is a horizontal version of the vertical bands celebrated by *Delirious New York*. Whatever the precedent, formal dexterity masks deadpan pragmatism and produces the frisson of incommensurable adjacencies: students play ping-pong as a metal transportation tube bursts through the ceiling above.

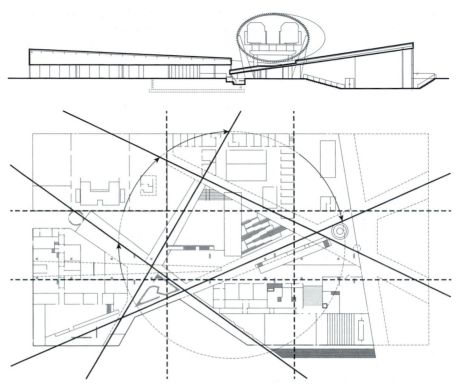

Figure 10.5 McCormick Tribune Campus Center section (above) and plan (below, unbuilt elements are dotted)

The material palette's cinematic range of effects and moods heightens the collision of programmes. Most prominent among OMA's strategies for 'bringing the colour back to Mies'[11] is the orange panelite wall that marks the State Street entry and folds inward to the public ballroom and auditorium. Here, as elsewhere in the building, the material is casual in its attachment and blurs the distinction between artifice (the sandwich of coloured plexiglass and aluminum honey-comb) and nature (the panelite's hot, solar glare). Similarly, the ubiquitous gypsum wallboard ceiling exposes its spackled joints and grass-green finish, and the liquid polish of the concrete floor alternates between a sandy wash and a turquoise gloss. A scattering of effects proliferate this hybridised background: the acidic sheen of the computer bar, the endless mirrorings of the University Club, and the pixellated portraits of the founder's wall, to name just a few.

Four gardens complement the building's spatial compressions and material bedazzlements. While Mies' buildings typically force the occupant to the perimeter and direct views outward, the McCormick blocks the perimeter and directs views inward. The gardens relieve the interior by allowing daylight to penetrate deep into the building, while insisting that they are a part of, rather than an antidote to, material artifice. Thus: a watergarden's blue glass blocks sit in river-run gravel and the liquid reflections of their storefront enclosure; a tree court couples a prosaic evergreen with stumps gathered as furniture; and indigenous prairie grasses bracket the cafeteria, floating in a tray above it to the south and flipping to the vertical on the northern embankment so that even the horizon is a negotiated rather than absolute condition.

The repeated appearance of the gardens' raked ground – sand, gravel, and soil – recalls the contemplative mood of Japanese gardens. Like Japanese gardens, the McCormick gardens shun production and participation. Contemplation is a misnomer, however. We rarely see the gardens frontally and they are never our destination – we see them tangentially on our way someplace else. Equivalent rather than exceptional events within the building, the gardens take part in the building's thickness rather than stand apart from it.

For the building is, above all else, thick. It is compressed between collapsed ceiling and buckling ground, riddled with orthogonal patterns, sliced by diagonal circulation, and dense with material effects. Thickness thwarts singular lines of sight. A dizzying array of reflections engulfs the University Club, for example, and even when one point of view dominates, such as looking northward in the Welcome Center, perspective dissolves with the competing grids of ceiling, wall, and structure and the reflective glare of panelite, glass, gypsum, and concrete. More often, such as looking southward from the recreation band's northern end, several lines of sight compete: the panelite path to auditorium and ballroom, the glazed prow of the radio control room, the diverging markings of transportation tube, gypsum ceiling, and concrete floor, and, beckoning in the distance, sunlight in the hanging garden and the atomic glow from the computer station. These lines never release to a vista, but dissipate into a thickness that seems without end. Visual saturation subsumes optical tricks.

Here, too, OMA loves, but does not respect, Mies. Mies' buildings deploy the orthogonal grid as a device that allows us to concentrate on our surroundings, and – as those surroundings wave off perspective's order – question perspective as a mode of concentration. The McCormick, on the other hand, compresses and slices the orthogonal frame so that our vision splits into many possible concentrations. Mies slays perspective, distrusting its singularity. OMA flays perspective, countering the singular with the multiple.

Thickness

The Tjibaou Centre's voluminous wall, the Bloch Building's aerated ground, the Netherlands Institute's hybridised materiality – in each case, what was once a line becomes a thick zone of exchange. At the McCormick Center, vision itself thickens as a single point of view splinters and is absorbed. Tjibaou, Bloch, and Institute offer new fluid worlds that erode conventional divisions between inside and outside, earth and sky, nature and culture. The McCormick offers a new way to see these worlds, not as one coherent system, but as an ecology of many systems, sometimes diverging and sometimes converging.

All these buildings have sustainable strategies. Tjibaou's envelope is attuned to South Pacific air currents and the earth's thermal mass reduces the Bloch's energy requirements. The Institute is perhaps the most inventive and economical: articulating programme elements as blocks that are conditioned independently, packing these blocks into a cube with an optimal surface to volume ratio, doubling this efficiency by burying the bottom half of archival storage, and leveraging these efficiencies for a public space that need not be conditioned and is wrapped with the cube's luminous rainscreen. Even at the McCormick, gardens reduce artificial lighting demands and, as originally designed, mechanical ventilation requirements as well.[12]

What distinguishes these buildings is that sustainability is incorporated into a larger cultural practice: they change our world. Sustainable buildings may offer important technical advances, but their affects, and the subjects they create, are too often entrenched in the world they wish to displace. If sustainability has taught us anything, it is that subjects have economic, political, social, and environmental consequences. The consequences of the Tjibaou, the Bloch, the Institute, and the McCormick may be less predictable than those promised by buildings devoted only to sustainability, but new worlds are more hopeful than false promises.

NOTES

1   The summary of our environmental impasse comes from Thomas L. Friedman, *Hot, Flat, and Crowded: Why We Need a Green Revolution – and How it Can Renew America* (New York: Farrar, Straus and Giroux, 2008), pp. 3–49.
2   Kahn's lecture at Pratt University in Alissandra Latour (ed.) *Louis I. Kahn, Writings Lectures, Interviews* (New York: Rizzoli, 1991), p. 323.
3   Kahn's description of the Yale Center for British Art is in Jules David Prown, *The Architecture of the Yale Center For British Art* (New Haven: Yale University Press, 2009), p. 45.
4   The definition of architecture as the ecology of interdependent systems, rather than the independence of technological objects comes from Carol Burns, 'High Performance Sites,' in Carol Burns and Andrea Kahn (eds) *Site Matters* (Routledge: London, 2005).
5   Parts of this chapter develop ideas from my essays: Michael Cadwell, 'Faxes from the Future', *Hunch: The Berlage Institute Report*, 12, 2009; Michael Cadwell, 'Grand Transparent', *Domus*, 904, June, 2007; Michael Cadwell, 'Two Stones', *Log*, 12, Spring/Summer, 2008.
6   Gottfried Semper, *The Four Elements of Architecture and Other Writings* (Cambridge: Cambridge University Press, 1989), pp. 101–129.
7   See, for example, Jeffrey Kipnis, *Stone and Feather: Steven Holl Architects / The Nelson Atkins Expansion* (New York: Prestel, 2007), p. 47.
8   Neutelings Riedijk developed the glass in collaboration with the artist Jaap Drupsteen, the Institute of Industrial Technology Eindhoven, and glass manufacturer Saint Gobain.
9   Rem Koolhaas, 'Miestakes' in Phyllis Lambert (ed.) *Mies in America* (New York: Abrams, 2001), p. 720.
10 John Vinci, 'IIT Plans Forget History,' *Chicago Tribune*, March 20, 2000.
11 Rem Koolhaas as interviewed by Lynn Becker. See http://www.lynnbecker.com/repeat/OedipusRem/koolhaasint.htm [accessed: 15.07.11].
12 According to Sarah Dunn, who was OMA's project architect through schematic design.

Chapter 11

'God is in the details'/'The detail is moot': a meeting between Mies and Koolhaas

Mhairi McVicar

'God is in the details', Mies van der Rohe was quoted as saying in 1959.[1] 'Issues of composition, scale, proportion, detail are now moot', countered Rem Koolhaas in 1995.[2] These two contrasting ideologies of the architectural detail meet at the Illinois Institute of Technology, Chicago, where Mies' Commons shopping centre, completed in 1954, is now adjoined by Koolhaas' McCormick Tribune Campus Center, completed in 2003 (Figure 11.1).

When the 1998 competition entry for the McCormick Tribune Campus Center at IIT, designed by Koolhaas' Office for Metropolitan Architecture (OMA), proposed to subsume Mies van der Rohe's Commons Building, there was an outcry – perhaps predictably – among parts of the Chicago architectural community.[3] Koolhaas responded with the essay 'Miesstakes', arguing that the

Figure 11.1 OMA's McCormick Tribune Campus Center (left) adjoining Mies van der Rohe's Commons (right). Illinois Institute of Technology Campus, Chicago

Commons could be read as either 'surprisingly accommodating' or as a 'pathetically martyred icon'.[4] As well as listing and illustrating numerous interior and exterior adaptations – or degradations – which the Commons had accommodated in the five decades since its construction, Mies – Koolhaas claimed – was 'uninterested' in the construction of the Commons, his apparent lack of direct involvement in this specific work rendering it more accommodating to adaptation than other works in the Miesian *oeuvre*.

Despite the architects' rhetoric, there are numerous similarities in the architectural practices according to which each detail was conceived and constructed. In both cases, neither Mies nor Koolhaas were physically present during daily construction. Both led growing architectural practices at the time of construction, which were undertaking multiple projects in multiple locations. Both projects were required to balance the economic pressures of a limited budget against ambitious aims to market IIT to prospective students. Both architectural practices delegated construction drawings and site supervision to associate architects, collaborating with complex organisational structures of clients, building contractors, sub-contractors and suppliers during construction. And, in each case, the work was shaped by underlying architectural ideologies which challenged the role of the architectural detail in contemporary architectural practice.

I will read here two details – a junction in exposed steel at Mies' IIT Commons building, and a greenboard ceiling detail which recurs throughout Koolhaas' McCormick Tribune Campus Center – for their insights into the cultures of architectural practice which produced them.

Perfection and roughness

Following the announcement of Koolhaas and OMA's competition win, the Chicago architectural press set out its own agenda for evaluating the success of the proposal. 'IIT Center: Success will be in the details'[5] declared Blair Kamin, architectural critic for the *Chicago Tribune*, suggesting that the project – taking on the legacy of Mies in Chicago – could only be judged in Mies' terms at the scale of the architectural detail. The project's success, Kamin argued, would depend upon whether Koolhaas could 'translate a brilliant idea into a finished building that upholds the Chicago tradition of elevating construction into art'. Suggesting that OMA were known for 'crude details' rather than 'jewel like precision', Kamin wrote that 'Mies raised pragmatism and problem-solving to an art: he was the poet of practice.'[6] While the *Chicago Tribune* proposed assessing the McCormick Tribune Campus Centre according to the expectations of 'perfect' detailing, Koolhaas' writings argued that the elevation of construction into art could no longer be accommodated within the scales and complexities of contemporary architectural practice. 'The "art" of architecture', Koolhaas had previously asserted, 'is useless in Bigness.'[7]

'Bigness' had been defined by Koolhaas as a condition of structures taller, deeper, bigger than ever before, requiring social and programmatic reorganisation and revisions to the processes of architectural production. The makers of 'Bigness', Koolhaas wrote, are:

> *a team* (a word not mentioned in the last 40 years of architectural polemic). Beyond signature, Bigness means surrender to technologies; to engineers, contractors, manufacturers; to politics; to others.[8]

Accepting the complexity and multiplicity of global networks, he suggested that architects can no longer hope to control production at the scale of the detail. Yet quality in contemporary architectural practice has become defined, contractually, through construction drawings and specifications as a perfect alignment between the architects' instructions and the constructed result. Any unspecified discrepancy is typically rejected as an error or omission, to be feared and avoided. This definition is relatively recent, as Nigel Hiscock observed in *Wise Master Builder*, noting that the constructed layouts of thirteenth-century cathedrals were routinely 'little short of chaotic'.[9] Irregularities from inaccurate or unstable drawings, inaccurate interpolations of dimensions and imprecise setting-out did not imply poor quality work, but were instead accepted as the inevitable circumstances of physical reality. Rather than perfect adherence to a geometric ideal, mediaeval architects did not, Hiscock observed, 'set out to achieve such degrees of accuracy, or were able to, or necessarily shared the modern concept of precision'.[10]

'Modern concepts of precision' in architectural production mirror the emergence and consolidation of the architectural profession. Following a separation of design from construction which began in the fifteenth century,[11] the professionalised architect has become, by self-definition, increasingly distanced from construction, particularly in the last 150 years. Simultaneously, the emergence of large speculative builder and developer organisations, the development of new building typologies, materials and construction processes, and the creation of new specialised consultants has combined to create a complex, multi-layered, globally scaled construction industry. It could be argued that architectural design now consists in interfacing pre-existing, standardised components, as David Leatherbarrow has observed.[12] In this practice culture, the architectural detail has emerged as instrumental in attempting to control operations in the field. 'In one sense', Edward Ford proposed in his study of the *Details of Modern Architecture*, 'detailing was born when craftsmanship died.'[13]

Precision in detailing, David Pye argued in *The Nature and Art of Workmanship*, is intrinsically linked to the idea of control and craft in architectural construction. 'Let us provisionally give the name "perfect" workmanship to that in which the achievement seems to correspond exactly with the idea', Pye proposed: 'let us on the other hand give the name "rough" to workmanship in which there is an evident disparity between idea and achievement.'[14] A perfect alignment is assumed to assure quality; a rough alignment to threaten it. Yet, Pye argued, 'perfect' workmanship may be lifeless and mechanical, while 'rough' work may permit a craftsman to improve a detail according to site conditions.

Any architectural detailing thus demonstrates, unavoidably, a stance towards perfection or roughness.

The polemic surrounding the McCormick Tribune Campus Center's engagement with the Commons highlights varying expectations for the capacity of the architectural detail to act as a controlling device in architectural practice. Controlled 'roughness' at the McCormick Tribune Campus Center appears alongside controlled 'perfection' at the Commons. Read in conjunction with the cultures of architectural practice that produced them, the two constructed details considered here can be understood as alternative responses by architectural firms to the pressures of global industrial production.

1953: the Commons shopping centre

The first detail I will discuss is constructed at the IIT Commons building, 3200 South Wabash, Chicago (Figure 11.2). It consists of an exposed structural 8WF32 steel column painted with Detroit Graphite Co.'s Prime-Rite and Iron-Gard Finish coats,[15] separated by a half-inch tolerance of caulking and mortar from buff-coloured brick infill panels and 12 gauge steel frame plate glass windows supplied by Hope Windows, Inc (Figure 11.3).[16]

This detail embodies the systematic refinement of one idea through decades of work. The Commons student centre was the fourteenth building to be built as part of the Campus Masterplan for the Illinois Institute of Technology, the most extensive commission of Ludwig Mies van der Rohe's career following his emigration to the United States in 1937. The commission to construct a campus, realised over two decades, had afforded Mies the opportunity to develop a 'slow unfolding' of ideas; a theme he had spoken and written about repeatedly. 'Every decision', he suggested, 'leads us to a definite clarification of principles and values'.[17] Mies' claim that architecture responded to an epoch shaped by economy and technology was put to the test by the scale, economies and aspirations of an American campus.[18] In this culture, the delegation of a corner detail at the Commons to others would be precisely controlled by a detailing approach which – in the absence of the genius designer – permitted no deviation.

Writings about Mies frequently emphasise his physical presence in the design and construction of his work. 'If he had little formal training, he earned his own calluses,'[19] wrote Franz Schulze, highlighting Mies' education at the *Gewerberschule* in Aachen and his apprenticeship on local building sites. Mies was happy with this interpretation, recalling his pride in obtaining his journeyman's licence as a bricklayer as a young man.[20] Skilful photography contributed to the consolidation of this narrative. Mies was famously recorded 'supervising' the masons on-site at the Farnsworth House and at 860–880 Lake Shore Drive. During the construction of the Commons, however, Mies was conspicuous by his absence.

Figure 11.2 OMA's McCormick Tribune Campus Center (left) meets the east façade of Mies van der Rohe's Commons (right)

Figure 11.3 North façade of Mies van der Rohe's Commons

Koolhaas has suggested that, twelve years after work began on the IIT masterplan, Mies was 'uninterested' in the Commons, leaving 'the design to Gene Summers, the project architect'.[21] Certainly, there is little evidence to suggest that Mies had a significant role in the Commons' construction. Correspondence indicates that the project was handled by Summers until 1953 before being passed variously to Joseph Fujikawa, Myron Goldsmith and architectural intern David Haid. Construction drawings were completed not by Mies himself, nor by his office, but by associate architects Friedman, Alschuler & Sincere, a practice who had previously collaborated with Mies' office on IIT's Wishnick Hall. However, Mies' absence at the Commons might not be understood as a lack of interest if the Commons itself is understood not as an individual building but as an iterative application of an ideology developed and refined in response to the pragmatic yet ambitious context of Chicago.

Having begun rebuilding itself only a week after the devastating fire of 1871,[22] Chicago had declared itself unbeaten, treating its almost complete demolition as little more than an opportunity to rebuild a modern city of unprecedented scale at unprecedented speed. The steel frame would play a key role in this. A powerhouse of steel production by geographic fortune, sited at the confluence of ore, coal and limestone supply, Chicago had been the site of the first steel production in the USA in 1865.[23] By 1954, while the Commons was under construction, Chicago was one of the principal iron and steel producers in the world, generating a quarter of the nation's output.[24] In Chicago, Colin Rowe has suggested, the steel frame convinced as fact whereas in Europe it had effectively remained an idea.[25] In Chicago, a city which offered unlimited potential, knowledge and skill in steel, Mies, too, would convert ideas into facts as he slowly, systematically tested steel construction and tolerances at the IIT campus.

Conceived in wartime, aspirations for the newly formed IIT were ambitious yet pragmatic, demanding simplicity and flexibility.[26] Mies' aspiration to unite order and stability would be set against the global uncertainty of war and the more immediate local chaos of an urban slum surrounding the campus. A 24-by-24 foot grid ordered every aspect of the design according to the disparate needs of classroom, laboratories, drafting studios and furnishings, contained within a limited palette of construction materials. The first building constructed on the IIT campus in 1941, the Metals and Minerals Research Building, was reviewed as 'neither a masterpiece nor an exemplar of IIT buildings'[27] but rather as an adjustment to new ground rules; with the establishment of a limited threefold palette of structural steel, buff coloured brick infill panel and plate glass which would be repeated throughout IIT over the next two decades. Successive buildings – Alumni Memorial Hall, Perlstein Hall, Wishnick Hall – each refined the relationships between these three components, consecutively testing and refining the architectural detail; expressed most famously in the multiple sketches developed by Mies' office which exhaustively tested alternatives for a steel and brick corner. Twelve years into the construction of the IIT campus, this limited palette was applied to the one-storey-plus-basement pavilion design for the Commons shopping centre, commissioned in January 1953 according to a resolutely pragmatic brief.[28] Speed drove the project, as did economy. By July of that year, excavation had begun while Friedman, Alschuler & Sincere's construction drawings were still in progress.[29] Projected to cost $350,000, or 75 cents per cubic foot, [30] 'these were', Mies later recalled, 'the cheapest campus buildings anywhere in the States'. While the Commons may have been guided by pragmatic efficiencies, historian Kevin Harrington has suggested that the Commons, as a pavilion, is significant as one of the three typologies which dominated Mies' career – high rise, long span and pavilion – with each project undertaken by the office claimed to have demonstrated another step towards resolving the problem of a specific typology. The attitude in Mies' office, Harrington suggests, 'was that all of these problems are liable to the finest possible solution'.[31]

'Today', Mies was later to write, 'our epoch is mothered by technology and economy [...] Refined solutions of our problems which express these forces of our time are, in fact, art.'[32] The IIT campus epitomised this belief. A precisely edited palette of steel, glass and brick applied repeatedly over two decades culminated in a systematic approach to the detail which could – confidently – demand precise tolerances in construction. Steel, by its nature, permits little deviation, requiring tolerances as low as three-sixteenths of an inch. Plate glass in a steel frame is similarly unyielding, leaving the buff brick infill panel with no choice but to submit to the steel frame with only half an inch of tolerance either side. Writing of the curriculum at the IIT School of Architecture, which Mies also developed, he had once advocated the 'clarifying principle of order, which leaves no room for deviation'.[33] Mies would now delegate control through a detail which permitted room for deviation.

Mies' absence at the Commons can then be understood in the light of a refined solution to a precisely stated problem. Control depended not on Mies' personal presence, but instead by the presence of a widely appreciated, long-developed, edited, iterative process. This process – understood as raising the repetitive refinement of functional, economic, standardised components to an art – offered an answer to the problems encountered by a growing architectural practice working on multiple projects in a context driven by technology and economy. A detail defined by slow unfolding would delegate the demand for 'perfect' details to a team. The McCormick Tribune Campus Center, fifty years later, would also operate through teamwork. Here, the team would be called to answer the problem of detailing a 'rough' finish.

2003: the McCormick Tribune Campus Center

The second detail I will discuss is a ceiling detail which recurs throughout the McCormick Tribune Campus Center. It began as a precisely detailed plywood finish which was to be applied over a layer of Type X taped greenboard (a variety of plasterboard) to meet City of Chicago code flame spread ratings. When 'value-engineering' required a 'big-ticket' item to be removed from the scope of work to reduce costs, the plywood was targeted as a superfluous layer. It was omitted to leave only the greenboard below. Rather than applying a conventional paint finish, the designers proposed leaving the surface of the greenboard unfinished with exposed taped joints and fastener heads.[34] This finish, classified as 'Level 2' by the Gypsum Association, is typically used 'in garages, warehouses, and other places where appearance is not a primary concern'.[35] Here, in a work understood as significant architecture, adjacent to Mies, this 'rough' finish would be of great concern; demanding the elevation of a rough surface to a finish which would not only answer the expectations of a global team of architects, builders, engineers, clients and consultants, and global architectural critics but which would respond critically to the challenges of *Bigness* as formulated by Rem Koolhaas in *S,M,L,XL*.

In that book, Koolhaas had, as noted above, observed that 'the detail is moot' (Figure 11.4). In this context, the practice of 'rough' detailing – exemplified by the exposure of 'Level 2' greenboard – would serve both to accommodate and express the uncertainties, complexities and possibilities of contemporary construction. 'Rough' has multiple meanings: a raw, unfinished state, or imprecision. In Pye's definition, 'rough' equates to accommodation; the individual builder is permitted to adapt an instruction according to the actualities of the material or site. The McCormick Tribune Campus Center demonstrated rough detailing in all three senses. Control of a rough detail was here delegated to the on-site design and construction team, negotiating the rapidly changing conflicts between a tight budget and an ambitiously complex palette of unconventional materials in unconventional assemblies, hovered over by the aura of Mies and the Chicago architectural community's expectations about detailing.

In 1997, IIT commissioned a report from Chicago-based firm Holabird & Root Architects to develop a competition programme for a new student centre on a campus, which had doubled in size but still only housed half the 6,000 students anticipated by Mies' masterplan proposals.[36] In lieu of a small, densely populated campus, the campus was now large and sparsely populated. Responding to reports that students found the campus 'dull and uninteresting', and that they wanted 'a richer architectural vocabulary, as well as a variety of architectural styles and colors',[37] IIT set about 'Renewing the Mies Campus'.[38] Koolhaas and OMA's winning competition entry responded with an explosive collage of materials and colours, controversially subsuming Mies' muted palette of steel, glass and brick.

To reintroduce urban density on the campus, OMA condensed programmatic, spatial and material diversity, creating an internalised dense urban environment laden with complexities and ambiguities, as a counterpoint to the order that Mies had once overlaid on a chaotic urban environment. Materials of varying colour, texture, layering and graphics were either custom-made or conventional components were applied in unconventional assemblies. Plastic decking from oil rigs became a façade system, for example. Custom stainless steel flooring, derived from OMA's New York Prada store, was later patented by the contractors who installed it.[39] Such unconventional materials and unconventional assemblies resulted in construction sections of varied thicknesses and tolerances sitting side-by-side within three steel and concrete structural systems, meeting in what a project architect at Holabird & Root termed 'slop joints';[40] a term not commonly encountered in Chicago architectural circles.

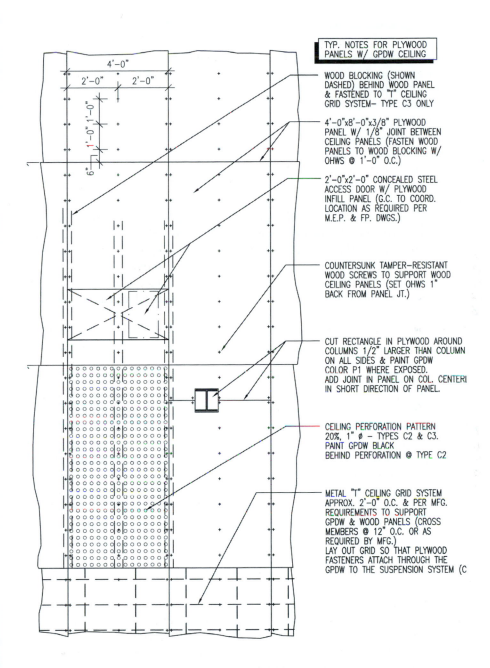

TYP. NOTES FOR PLYWOOD
PANELS W/ GPDW CEILING

WOOD BLOCKING (SHOWN
DASHED) BEHIND WOOD PANEL
& FASTENED TO "T" CEILING
GRID SYSTEM- TYPE C3 ONLY

4'-0"x8'-0"x3/8" PLYWOOD
PANEL W/ 1/8" JOINT BETWEEN
CEILING PANELS (FASTEN WOOD
PANELS TO WOOD BLOCKING W/
OHWS @ 1'-0" O.C.)

2'-0"x2'-0" CONCEALED STEEL
ACCESS DOOR W/ PLYWOOD
INFILL PANEL (G.C. TO COORD.
LOCATION AS REQUIRED PER
M.E.P. & FP. DWGS.)

COUNTERSUNK TAMPER-RESISTANT
WOOD SCREWS TO SUPPORT WOOD
CEILING PANELS (SET OHWS 1"
BACK FROM PANEL JT.)

CUT RECTANGLE IN PLYWOOD AROUND
COLUMNS 1/2" LARGER THAN COLUMN
ON ALL SIDES & PAINT GPDW
COLOR P1 WHERE EXPOSED.
ADD JOINT IN PANEL ON COL. CENTERI
IN SHORT DIRECTION OF PANEL.

CEILING PERFORATION PATTERN
20%, 1" Ø - TYPES C2 & C3.
PAINT GPDW BLACK
BEHIND PERFORATION @ TYPE C2

METAL "T" CEILING GRID SYSTEM
APPROX. 2'-0" O.C. & PER MFG.
REQUIREMENTS TO SUPPORT
GPDW & WOOD PANELS (CROSS
MEMBERS @ 12" O.C. OR AS
REQUIRED BY MFG.)
LAY OUT GRID SO THAT PLYWOOD
FASTENERS ATTACH THROUGH THE
GPDW TO THE SUSPENSION SYSTEM (C

15 ENLARGED PARTIAL CEILING PLAN
TYPICAL PLYWOOD PANELS

A13-2   1/2"=1'-0"

Figure 11.4 Unbuilt proposed detail of plywood ceiling, later replaced by an exposed 'Greenboard' ceiling. Detail 15, 081-A13.2 drawn by Holabird & Root Architects, Chicago.

Chicago Tribune critic Blair Kamin had suggested that, to meet Chicago expectations of perfect detailing, the involvement of a 'renowned' Chicago firm would be required.[41] The ideology of the 'moot' detail would be mediated by the detailing reputation of Holabird & Root, a venerable Chicago firm who had collaborated as associate architects with Mies at IIT. The joint venture between OMA in Rotterdam and New York and Holabird & Root in Chicago also involved a worldwide team of consultants: structural engineers in London; a lighting consultant in Seattle; mechanical, electrical and plumbing engineers, a civil engineer, acoustic consultant, security consultant and a landscape architect in Chicago; graphic designers in New York; and graphics consultants in Boulder, Colorado.[42] Despite the attentions of this extended team, Kamin – echoing Koolhaas' assertion that Mies had been uninterested in the Commons – asserted that Koolhaas' physical presence would influence the potential quality of the project: 'No one else', Kamin wrote:

> so vividly personifies the globalisation of the practice of architecture and, perhaps, the danger inherent in that phenomenon. One day Koolhaas is in Chicago. The next day, he is in Ann Arbour, Mich. Then he's in New York. Then Germany. Then Rotterdam. [...] he is savvy enough to say of the IIT Campus center, 'I fully intend to be involved in this building myself and to make sure it's not a hit-and-run situation'.[43]

However, Koolhaas would not be present for daily construction. Like Mies at the Commons, detailed supervision was delegated to the team. In contrast to the precisely refined details which controlled the Commons site in Mies' absence, control would be negotiated on-site. A former OMA employee, Mark Schendel of Studio Gang, was brought in as a site architect to negotiate between OMA, Holabird & Root and the global team of consultants, clients and builders. He described his role as continually tracking in real-time the changes to details on the site caused by value engineering.[44] No matter how comfortable a construction crew had become in knowing a set of drawings, Schendel recalled, 'they were constantly being faced with new details that sometimes were very difficult to co-ordinate with existing conditions on the site'.[45] As predicted by Koolhaas, the drawn detail was to become moot when confronted with the rapidly changing demands of a complex project and its shifting budget.

The ceiling detail as constructed was, however, precisely controlled and crafted. Following the omission of the plywood ceiling finish, instructions issued by the design team, during construction, specified precisely the supposedly 'rough' greenboard finish: specifying the width of taped joints, the spacing of fixings and the size of the joint compound squares covering the fixings. No boards were to be cut, save where the rectangular boards met the angular geometry of the building's perimeter. Mock-ups in the Commons building tested varying sizes of joint compound squares and taped seams. Plumbers were instructed not to pencil their customary notes and dimensions on the exposed greenboard. Care was taken to avoid fingerprints on the delicate paper surface of this rough material and a clear low-sheen protective coat was applied to protect it against staining and marks. Accustomed to constructing a rough underlay to be covered with a final finish, the builders were re-trained as finish craftsmen installing a precise finish. Following the opening of the Center, when a portion of the 'rough' ceiling was scraped and damaged, a specialist Italian plasterer was brought in to repaint a *faux*, 'rough', greenboard finish to conceal the damage.[46] While the drawn detail did not exert control over precision in the manner of Mies' detail practices, expectations of architectural quality in the cultural context of Chicago seemingly demanded this rough ceiling to be precisely detailed (Figure 11.5).

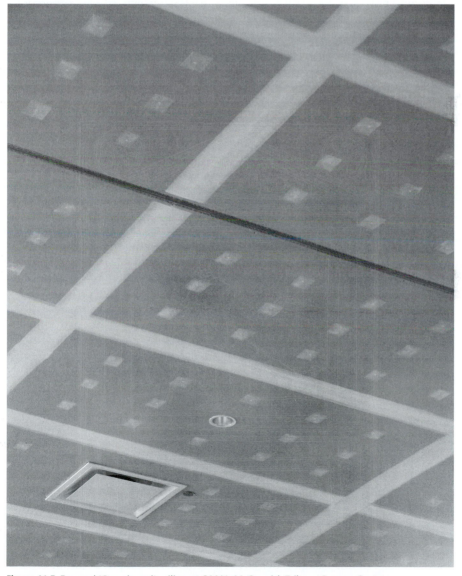

Figure 11.5 Exposed 'Greenboard' ceiling at OMA's McCormick Tribune Campus Center

Uncertainty and control

For the multi-layered, organisationally complex global ventures who now oversee the design and construction of architecture, the detail has become an instrument which seeks to convey every architectural intention to those who will construct the work amidst the uncertainties of site conditions. The degree to which the drawn detail is expected to control the final constructed work may vary; from uncompromised adherence to permitted adaptations. At both the Commons and McCormick Tribune Campus Center, specific but contrasting ideologies provided alternative responses to the challenges encountered by expanding architectural practices seeking to juggle numerous simultaneous projects, strict budget economies, large project teams of associate architects, consultants, builders and clients, and an overriding impetus to produce architectural work of significance and quality, despite the pressures placed upon the project. In each case, the architectural detail embodied a stance through which the pursuit of architecture was conceived and controlled.

The design and construction of the Commons was dictated by an attitude towards the pursuit of perfection which many have characterised as uncompromising. Here, the attempted control of craft required familiar, even conventional, materials and components tested through the iterative development of an edited palette in order to produce a precise answer to a rigidly defined question. The 'slow unfolding' of the corner detail of the Commons was 'refined' by its designers through years of work on the IIT campus, itself drawing from the experience of Mies' previous European work and informing other projects built elsewhere.[47] Having developed this system as a 'refined art', control of the Commons could be delegated to a team and yet require the near-perfect alignment of the ideal with the constructed result. Here, a particular concept of precision – familiar among architects with a modernist training – upheld expectations that the detail could control a perfect alignment between the architects' idea and the constructed result.

'Details mar the extraordinary', critic Blair Kamin concluded in relation to the completed McCormick Tribune Campus Center, testing the OMA project according to the expectations of perfect detailing more familiar to Mies. His Chicago expectations of the 'perfect' detail apparently collided with Koolhaas' ideology of 'rough' detailing. Drawing and specification could not control the actualities of multiple unconventional materials and applications meeting on-site. The 'slop joints' of the project stand in contrast to Miesian expectations of precision. Yet construction in the field demanded the regular presence of associate architects, conversing daily with builders who had been retrained to elevate a rough finish into one which, in actuality, demanded precise craftsmanship and care.

The ideologies of the two details contain shifting ideas of precision. At the Commons, architecture and detail are apparently constructed in service of both formal and cultural order – reduced, refined, supposedly perfected. At the McCormick Tribune Campus Center, conventional assumptions about control on the part of the associate architect and the greenboard subcontractor – derived from ideas of modern detailing which Mies did his part to reify – met the supposedly imprecise 'slop joint' of Koolhaas and OMA, where the curious contradiction-in-terms of the 'rough', unfinished finish is celebrated. Both ideologies contain their contradictions: that inhabitants of Mies buildings can ever live-up to the organisational perfection implied by precise grids and pared-down details; and that contemporary construction, even in Koolhaas projects, can somehow happen 'by chance', that building is ever other than deliberate, even if deliberate roughness is the aim. In each case, a particular ideology of the detail remained decisive in the process of elevating conventional materials to an unconventional quality.

Acknowledgements

I would like to thank the following for their help in writing this chapter: Paul Galloway, Architecture and Design Center, Museum of Modern Art, New York; The Collection of the Manuscript Division, Library of Congress, Washington, DC; Catherine Bruck, IIT Archives, Chicago; The Edward L. Duckett Collection, Art Institute of Chicago; Greg Grunloh, Holabird & Root, Chicago; Mark Schendel, Studio Gang, Chicago; Professor Kevin Harrington, Illinois Institute of Technology.

NOTES

1   [n.a], 'On Restraint in Design', *New York Herald Times*, 29 June (1959).
2   Rem Koolhaas, *S,M,L,XL* (New York: The Monacelli Press, Inc., 1995), p. 500.
3   John Vinci, 'IIT plans forget history', *Chicago Tribune* (March 20 2000), http://articles. chicagotribune.com/2000-03-20/news/0003200048_1_landmark-status-rem-koolhaas-architectural-historians [accessed 20 July 2011].
4   Rem Koolhaas, 'Miestakes', in *Mies in America*, ed. by Phyllis Lambert (Montreal: New York: Canadian Centre for Architecture and Whitney Museum of American Art, 2001), pp. 716–743 (p. 741).
5   Blair Kamin, 'IIT Center: Success will be in the details', *Chicago Tribune*, Sunday, February 15 (1998), Section 7, pp. 1, 8–9 (p. 1).
6   Kamin, 'IIT Center', p. 9.
7   Koolhaas, *S,M,L,XL*, p. 500.
8   Koolhaas, *S,M,L,XL*, pp. 513–514.
9   Nigel Hiscock, *The Wise Master Builder: Platonic Geometry in Plans of Medieval Abbeys and Cathedrals* (Aldershot: Ashgate, 2000), p. 198
10   Hiscock, *The Wise Master Builder*, p. 208
11   For a discussion of the separation between design from construction in the fifteenth century see Chapter 6 'The emergence of the architectural practitioner' in Colin Rowe and Leon Satkowski, *Italian Architecture of the 16th Century* (New York: Princeton Architectural Press, 2002).
12   David Leatherbarrow, *Uncommon Ground: Architecture, Technology, and Topography* (Cambridge, Mass: MIT Press, 2000).
13   Edward Ford, *The Details of Modern Architecture* (Cambridge MA: MIT Press, 1990), p. 7.
14   David Pye, *The Nature and Art of Workmanship* (Cambridge: Cambridge University Press, 1968), p. 14.

15   The paint specification used consistently throughout IIT for exposed steel is described in a
     letter from Joseph Fujikawa to Mr Minoru Yamasaki (08.04.57), Manuscript Division, Library
     of Congress.

16   Details from Frideman, Alschuler & Sincere's construction drawings (28.05.53) for the
     Commons and construction correspondence, Museum of Modern Art New York Archives.

17   Mies address at testimonial dinner, Palmer House (18.10.38), Manuscript Division, Library of
     Congress.

18   'Today our epoch is mothered by technology and economy', Mies wrote in a letter to Mr
     Henry Struts (05.02.60), Manuscript Division, Library of Congress.

19   Franz Schulze, *Mies Van Der Rohe: A Critical Biography* (Chicago; London: The University
     of Chicago Press, 1985), p. 14.

20   Interview by the author with Kevin Harrington, Professor, Art & Architectural History,
     Illinois Institute of Technology (06.06.10).

21   Koolhaas, 'Miestakes', p. 726.

22   'Within the week, 5,497 temporary structures had been erected and 200 permanent buildings
     were under way', Harold M. Mayer, and Richard C. Wade, *Chicago: Growth of a Metropolis*
     (Chicago and London: University of Chicago Press, 1969), p. 117.

23   Ibid., pp. 52, 53.

24   Ibid., pp. 428, 430.

25   Colin Rowe, 'Chicago Frame' in *The Mathematics of the Ideal Villa and Other Essays*
     (Cambridge MA: MIT Press, 1983), pp. 89–118 (pp. 99, 101).

26   Illinois Institute of Technology News Bureau (13.05.46), 'Alumni Memorial', IIT Archives.

27   Schulze, *Mies Van Der Rohe*, p. 223.

28   The Commons brief included: '1. Provide building in accordance with long range plan [...]
     Provide shopping facilities.' IIT Board of Trustees Building and Grounds Committee meeting
     (28.01.53), IIT Archives.

29   On 19.06.53. IIT Board of Trustees Building and Grounds Committee meeting (24.07.53),
     IIT Archives.

30   Edward L. Duckett Collection, Folders 1.10 and 1.11, Art Institute of Chicago.

31   Interview with Harrington (06.06.10).

32   Mies van der Rohe, letter to Mr Henry Struts (05.02.60), Manuscript Division, Library of
     Congress.

33   Letter from Mies to Mr Heald (10.12.37), Manuscript Division, Library of Congress.

34   Interview by the author with Greg Grunloh, Holabird & Root Architects (13.05.10).

35   *GA-214-96 Recommended Levels of Gypsum Board Finish* (Association of the Wall and Ceiling
     Industries-International (AWCI), Ceiling & Interior Systems Construction Association
     (CISCA), Gypsum Association (GA), and Painting and Decorating Contractors of America
     (PDCA), 1990).

36   Holabird & Root Report, 'Campus Center Programming' (21.11.96), IIT Archives.

37   Ibid.

38   'Renewing the Mies campus' undated report, IIT Archives.

39   Interview with Grunloh (13.05.10).

40   Ibid.

41   Kamin, 'IIT Center', p. 9.

42   McCormick Tribune Campus Center construction drawings: G1-1 Issued for Bid & Permit
     (04.06.01).

43   Kamin, 'IIT Center', p. 1, 9.

44   Interview by the author with Mark Schendel, Studio Gang (10.05.10).

45   Intereview with Schendel (10.05.10).

46   Interview with Grunloh (13.05.10).

47   Michael Cadwell refers to the steel detailing at Farnsworth House in *Strange Details*
     (Cambridge MA: MIT Press, 2007).

Chapter 12

Specifying transparency: from 'best seconds' to 'new glass performances'

Katie Lloyd Thomas

Today, window glass performs many functions additional to its fundamental daylighting role. The advent of new requirements for building such as the accommodation of information technology, and the development of new glass technologies to meet those requirements, for example the deposition of electroconducting coatings, are generating *new glass performances*.[1]

In architectural theory, there is already a growing interest in considering buildings in terms of what they do. David Leatherbarrow has argued, for example, in his essay in Branko Kolarevic's anthology *Performative Architecture*, that 'the actuality of building consists largely in its acts, its *performances*'.[2] The building, he suggests, should not be considered as a static object but as a constellation of actions. He extends this idea of action to materials themselves and to building elements – from columns to cladding – engaged in the 'performance' of maintaining an apparently static equilibrium in the finished building:

> There is another site of architectural action in which performance is less obvious but no less determining: those parts of the building that give it its apparently static equilibrium, its structural, thermal, material stability. When discussing these elements (columns and beams, retaining walls and foundations, but also cladding and roofing systems), it is common to talk of their 'behaviour' – not only talk of it but to anticipate it, even predict it.[3]

On the one hand, Leatherbarrow appears to be describing an approach that could be applied to any building. If, with the help of so-called 'new materialists' such as Manuel DeLanda or Brian Massumi or Gilles Deleuze and Felix Guattari, we are able to re-conceptualise it as such, the maintenance of the 'structural, thermal, material stability' of a building he identifies will always be a kind of 'architectural action'. It is up to us whether we consider it as a static object or in terms of behaviours. On the other hand, he writes that 'it is common to talk of [these elements'] behaviours' as if this is a peculiarly contemporary and widely accepted way of thinking about such elements that has some historical specificity. This suggestion is not developed in his essay. Like most architectural and cultural theorists (with the notable exceptions of Antoine Picon in *Digital Culture in Architecture* and Jon McKenzie in his brilliant *Perform or Else*),[4]

Leatherbarrow does not reflect on the shift towards performance that is also taking place in the industrial and contractual context. Moreover, he limits his understanding of the building's actions to its maintenance of structural equilibrium. In its descriptions, and in its design for new materials, industry already recognises more modes of material behaviour than Leatherbarrow remarks upon, and some of these are quantified directly in relation to inhabitants and environment. Behaviours are not just anticipated and predicted, they are designed and determined, and even sometimes embedded into the material itself. We need to go beyond the work of architectural theorists and philosophers to understand how this radical re-conceptualisation of materials in terms of effects and behaviours has already been established through the work of industry, and what its implications might be.

What glass *does*

Take two German parliament buildings of the twentieth century, both of which made use of glass screens between the visiting public and the debating chamber to manifest an ideological commitment to transparency in democracy in their political architecture. According to Peter Buchanan, equating an open political process with visual transparency and glass walls is a particularly German concern. It became explicit during the post-War reconstruction of Germany and can be traced further back to Hannes Meyer and Hans Wittwer's entry in the 1927 League of Nations competition where Meyer's design report apparently stated there would be 'no back corridors for backstairs diplomacy, but open glazed rooms for public negotiation by honest men'.[5]

Hans Schwippert's self-effacing modernist *Bundeshaus* opened on the banks of the river Rhine in Bonn in 1949. In her book on transparency in German political building, Deborah Ascher Barnstone includes a marvellous photograph of members of the public standing on tiered benches that were provided in the courtyard adjacent to the parliamentary chamber (Figure 12.1). They peer in through the glazed wall at the debate inside. One window is open and some members of the public appear to have climbed into the chamber to listen. But, Barnstone tells us, this possibility was limited only to two lengths of wall and, in any case, it was soon curtailed due to security concerns. Before long, there were drapes across the windows and access to the courtyard had been restricted to parliamentarians and their visitors.[6] In this building, the glass barrier gives visual access, drapes control light and sound transmission, and rules, fences and guards provide the security function.

Underneath the famous glass dome at Norman Foster's renovated *Reichstag* in Berlin, opened in 1999, there are two further domed glass screens between the public and the debating chamber with a press gallery in-between (Figure 12.2). From within the glass dome, it is almost possible to look down through the shallower glass domes on to the heads of MPs in the chamber below, and perhaps, with a pair of binoculars to decipher the comments they make in notebooks on their lap. But if we consider the glass screen at the *Reichstag* in

Figure 12.1 Members of the public peering into the parliamentary chamber at the *Bundeshaus*, Bonn. Architect: Hans Schwippert, 1949. Bundesarchiv B145, 00090889. Photograph: *Bundesbildstelle*

terms of what it *does* – its performances – a set of conflicting concerns that give it specific characteristics beyond its visual transparency are revealed; the glass has been engineered to withstand attack and to achieve the acoustic separation that prevents participation in the debates below. As Hisham Elkadi has observed, 'Visitors to the Reichstag [...] cannot listen or be listened to and are denied any real interaction [...] in contrast to [...] the public gallery in the House of Commons in London'.[7]

At the visual level, the glass suggests openness and accessibility but at the level of what the glass *does*, it hinders access and defends against it as a threat. Moreover, where at the Bonn *Bundeshaus*, the guards and drapes that performed these operations were highly visible and could be manipulated, at the *Reichstag* the operations are physically embedded in the glass itself and invisible. We might ask how these performances are inscribed and, following Madeline Akrich, what the effects of this translation to the material may be:

It makes sense to say that technical objects have political strength. They may change social relations, but they also stabilise, naturalise, depoliticise, and translate these into other media. After the event, the processes involved in building up technical objects are concealed. The causal links they established are naturalised. There was, or so it seems, never any possibility that it could have been otherwise.[8]

Figure 12.2 Looking down from the public area through the press gallery into the parliamentary chamber below at the *Reichstag*, Berlin. Architect: Norman Foster, 1999. Photograph by Linus Tan

To what extent are a set of intentions and ideas naturalised in these new glass performances about the relation of the social world outside to the politicians inside? What are the developments which have made it possible for glass to perform in these ways, and to what extent does this represent a significant change in the way we mobilise, and conceive of, materials? Here, I explore two different but related developments in how materials are engineered and in how they are described or specified. Each of these depends upon new regimes of quantification and testing that, I will argue, make it possible for new relationships to be made between human and non-human realms.

Meeting a 'specifically defined need': performance engineering and performance specification

In their *History of Chemistry*, Bernadette Bensaude-Vincent and Isabelle Stengers identify a change in the 1970s toward 'research on specific characteristics and specific materials' and, in particular, in making new types of plastics 'geared to specifically targeted performance'. 'Chemistry' they write, 'was put to work on a made-to-order civilisation.'[9] According to Michelle Addington and Daniel Schodek, the development and take-up of performance-engineered materials has been slower in the building industry than in other industries, but nevertheless it represents a significant shift away from traditional materials, in so far as they are selected or engineered 'to meet a specifically defined need':

> For many centuries one had to accept and work with the properties of a standard material such as wood or stone, designing to accommodate the materials' limitations, whereas during the twentieth century one could begin to select or engineer the properties of a high performance material to meet a specifically defined need.[10]

Moreover, those needs must themselves be defined as in terms of 'an array of physical behaviours' that already represent a move away from a conventional architectural understanding of materials.[11]

Glass is a particularly good example of a material that is increasingly designed toward specific performances. The online catalogue from glass manufacturers Pilkington is organised around the functions that their products perform, and shows the extent to which they have multiplied beyond the traditional daylighting role to include: solar control; thermal insulation; fire protection; noise control; safety/security; self-cleaning; decoration; and solar energy maximisation:

Pilkington Glass, by benefit

Solar control Reduces solar heat gain and offers high levels of natural light to provide comfortable and pleasant environments in which to live and work.	**Self-cleaning** Continuously cleans external glass such as windows and conservatories using the sun and rain to break down and wash away organic dirt.
Thermal insulation Helps to restrict the amount of heat loss from a building offering designers a choice of insulation levels and aesthetic options.	**Decoration** Offers an extensive choice of decorative options to provide style and privacy with maximum light.
Fire protection Provides passive protection from the effects of fire for up to 180 minutes allowing maximum use of natural light and enabling all areas of a building to be occupied.	**Glass systems** Provides the complete glazing installation through specialist techniques.
Noise control Reduces the noise inside a building to acceptable levels without sacrificing daylight.	**Special applications** Solutions to specific requirements for glass in buildings. **Solar energy** Glass for maximising solar energy conversion.
Safety/security Provides impact or impact penetration resistance to protect people from accidental injury. Defends people and property from deliberate attack and damage from criminal activity.	

If, in the *Bundeshaus* windows, most of these performances would have been achieved through a variety of more apparent means – windows kept clean with brushes, cloths and hard graft, for example, and rules, regulations, fences and guard patrols providing security – a variety of technologies now make it possible to embed these behaviours into the glass itself. Toughened glass provides additional strength and various kinds of laminated glasses, including those with high performance plastic interlayers (as near as possible to being transparent, of course), prevent glass from shattering into dangerous shards. Self-cleaning glass works by using a microscopic photocatalytic layer which makes use of light to break down organic matter and another 'hydrophilic' layer which prevents water from forming droplets so that it runs off in sheets taking the organic matter with it. A whole range of fine coatings are now applied to glass to reduce reflectivity, solar gain and reduce heat transmission and, as we see in the illustration below from a Pilkington publication, these films are defined not in terms of what they are but what they are *for* (Figure 12.3).

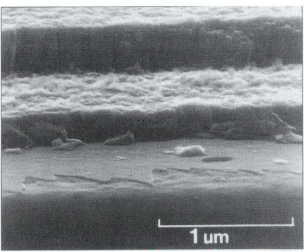

Three-layer coating on glass,
Pilkington Technology Centre,
Lathom, UK

The layers are
(1) thickness 200 Å, for adhesion;
(2) thickness 225 Å, for emissivity;
(3) thickness 2400 Å, for reflectivity

Figure 12.3 Glass coatings magnified and described by their behaviours

According to Hans Joachim Gläser, coatings like these did not come into use until the 1950s (when they were used in the panoramic windows of German sightseeing trains).[12] Schwippert's 1949 *Bundeshaus* predates their appearance and relied instead on drapes. Today the use of these almost invisible films in glass is widespread.

On the one hand, then, we can see that glass is now designed with its behaviours in mind, with new technologies supporting this and making it possible. It is not just a matter of thinking about the building through an alternative dynamic model, in terms of Leatherbarrow's 'idea of action' for example. The idea that materials are active is now central to the way they are designed and produced. Moreover, these are commonly the terms in which materials are described in sales literature (as in the Pilkington catalogue) and in the technical literature and specifications used by architects. These descriptions of materials in performance terms also influence the way we think about materials, and how we are able to use them in design.

In terms of the architectural specification – the contractual document which details the materials, workmanship and components of a building – it is widely recognised that performance specification, or the description of materials through their behaviours, is a relatively recent phenomenon. In 1989, technical author Ian Chandler could still refer to performance specifications as a 'newer range':

Those specifications written in terms which clearly point to one construction solution, with materials named, sizes given, and perhaps even suppliers named, are within the traditional category. The newer range of specifications are based on terms which describe what the material, construction detail or component is expected to do and how it must behave during and after placement; these are categorised as *performance specifications*.[13]

He contrasts them with 'traditional forms' which, in the typology I have developed from my own studies of specifications since the eighteenth century, would include amongst others 'naming' the material (whether by brand, species, petrological family etc.) and 'process-based' specification (which gives the details of how a material such as mortar or in-situ concrete is to be made up, or how a material such as timber is to be worked on-site). For Chandler, what differentiates the newer range of specifications is that they describe what the material or component 'is expected to do' and how it is to 'behave'. To see this distinction we can look at two contrasting specifications for glass. The first is an example that would fall into Chandler's 'traditional' category taken from the 'Glazier' section of a specification for the Bristol Asylum for the Blind and adjoining chapel published in 1835:

> The windows on basement floor, to the men's work-room, and basket-shop, to be glazed with good thirds. The chapel and vestry windows, and the whole of remaining windows of house, to be glazed with the best seconds, free from colour and air bubbles […] the whole of the windows throughout the buildings to be left perfectly clean and whole at the finish of the works.[14]

What is reflected here is the contemporaneous practice of grading and valuing glass according to its lack of discoloration and evenness, and a reminder to the contractor to leave the glass clean at completion. Although the evenness and cleanliness of the glass might contribute to its capacity for transparency and light transmission, the specification describes the glass as a particular material to standards common to the building industry, rather than by accounting for what it should achieve.

In sharp contrast is the contemporary performance specification for curtain walling in a new supermarket made by the architect Chetwoods® and shown in the extracts below.[15] The values have been taken out but what is immediately clear is that the whole description is configured around the specific functional criteria the glazed walling is to achieve:

H11 CURTAIN WALLING
To be read with Preliminaries/General conditions.

DESIGN/PERFORMANCE REQUIREMENTS
311 INTEGRITY: Determine the sizes and thicknesses of glass panes and panel/facings, the sizes, types and locations of framing, fixings and supports, to ensure that the curtain walling will resist all wind loads, dead loads and design live loads, and accommodate all deflections and movements without damage.

- Design wind pressure: _____ Pascals.
- Permanent imposed loads: _____
- Temporary imposed loads: _____

312 INTEGRITY: Determine the sizes and thicknesses of glass panes and panels/facings, the sizes, types and locations of framing, fixings and supports, to ensure that the curtain walling will resist all wind loads, dead loads and design live loads, and accommodate all deflections and movements without damage.

- Calculate design wind pressure in accordance with BS 6399-2, Standard Method:
    - Basic wind speed (V_b): _____
    - Altitude factor (S_a): _____
    - Direction factor (S_d): _____
    - Seasonal factor (S_s): 1.
    - Probability factor (S_p): 1.
    - Terrain and building factor (S_b): _____
    - Size effect factor (C_a): 1.
    - External pressure coefficients (C_{pe}): _____
    - Internal pressure coefficients (C_{pi}): _____
    - Permanent imposed loads: _____
    - Temporary imposed loads: _____

313 INTEGRITY: Determine the sizes and thicknesses of glass panes and panels/facings, the sizes, types and locations of framing, fixings and supports, to ensure that the curtain walling will resist all wind loads, dead loads and design live loads, and accommodate all deflections and movements without damage.

- Calculate design wind pressure in accordance with BS6399-2.
- Permanent imposed loads: _____
- Temporary imposed loads: _____

340 AIR PERMEABILITY: Permissible air leakage rates of $1.5 m^3/hr/m^2$ for fixed lights and $2.0 \ m^3/hr/lin.m$ for opening lights must not be exceeded when the curtain walling is subjected to a peak positive test pressure of _____ Pascals.

370 THERMAL PROPERTIES: The average thermal transmittance (U-value) of the curtain walling, calculated using the elemental area method, must be not more than _____ W/m^2K.

380 SOLAR AND LIGHT CONTROL: Glass panes or units in curtain walling must have:

- Total solar energy transmission of not more than _____ % of normal incident solar radiation.
- Total light transmission of not less than _____ %.

385 THERMAL STRESS IN GLAZING: Glass must have an adequate resistance to thermal stress generated by orientation, shading, solar control and construction.

410 ACOUSTIC PROPERTIES: The following minimum sound reduction indices to BS EN ISO 140-3 must be achieved:

- Between internal and external surfaces of curtain walling: _____
- Between adjoining floors abutting curtain walling: _____
- Between adjoining rooms on the same floor abutting curtain walling: _____

Moreover, the titles of each clause do not refer to a type of material or component and then give a brand name or method of fabricating it. Instead they list the functions that the glass or glazing system as a whole is required to achieve: 'integrity', 'air permeability', 'thermal properties', 'acoustic properties' and so on. Within the body of each clause, we see that, in most cases, these requirements are given in terms of the forces that the glazing is to withstand or as a property of the material or system itself. But, in clause 312, where the detailed design of the glazing is 'to ensure that the curtain walling will resist all wind loads, dead loads and design live loads, and accommodate all deflections and movements without damage', the ways in which the material is to perform are described explicitly and directly within the text.

The units used in performance specification and the techniques of quantification of material properties are derived from materials science, but their use in building and in the architectural specification is driven primarily by economic and legal imperatives. First, because it describes what a material or component is to achieve, the performance specification avoids being 'prescriptive' or specifying outright by name or supplier. The onus is on the contractor to select the material that fits the criteria and the architect need not run the risk of specifying a material that is not up to the task. Second, unlike the long process-based clauses that had been much in use since the nineteenth century, which gave details of how materials should be worked and made up, the performance specification concentrates on materials in their finished state. In stating 'requirements in terms of ends rather than means' (as Tony Allot put it, writing in 1971 about the principles on which the first UK standardised specification – the National Building Specification or NBS – would be based),[16] it is left to the contractor find ways of achieving the detail that are the most efficient and profitable for them. In the newest range of specifications, such as those offered to their clients by specification consultants Schumann Smith, the intention is to avoid any outright prescription and leave all clauses open to the contractor. Unlike the NBS, which uses a range of forms of specification in one document and may, indeed, allow the same material to be specified either in traditional terms (such as naming, process, reference and so on) or in performance terms, performance specification becomes the norm in the Schumann Smith specifications, albeit supplemented by other forms, such as the category of 'visual intent' which ties the specification to the drawings so that some control over visual appearance is retained. The increasing prevalence of performance specification is a result more of its contractual openness than some broader epistemological shift in the description of materials; and whether or not a material is described in performance terms may just as well depend on the contractual situation as on the kind of material being specified. What performance-specified materials and performance-engineered materials both depend upon is a regime of testing and quantification, where materials are manufactured in such a way that each sample is the same.

'Full testing procedures': the quantification of performance

In his 1972 article advocating the use of performance specification, George Atkinson made a number of recommendations for changes that would need to take place in the building industry for it to become more common. These included the encouragement of 'standardisation and variety reduction' and of 'scientific methods of building', as well as the necessity to:

> Strengthen, and where necessary, reform the institutional machinery for identifying needs for standardisation, agreeing and adopting standard codes of practice, design data, test methods, etc. for assessing and approving products and techniques and for quality control.[17]

Some sectors of the construction industry had already begun to use performance criteria; for example in the case of building standards discussed by Atkinson or in the production of materials for large-scale building projects or certain mass-produced products and components. But, as commentators such as Allot recognised, performance specification would not be possible for most building projects at the time, specifically those which were small scale building contracts and fully specified by the designer without access to materials science and testing facilities:

> The nearly pure performance specification can be appropriate, for example, where there is a large order, where design and development time can be allowed, where manufacturers or contractors have sufficient expertise, and where suitable tests exist: but the vast majority of designer specified building work is tendered for and built under conditions which make the pure performance approach difficult. Most projects are 'one off', not very large, needed quickly, built by small contractors, supervised by non-scientific staff, and do not always justify full testing procedures.[18]

A material or property can neither be performance specified nor engineered without 'full testing procedures'. Furthermore, it is not just the material's properties that must be quantified but also whatever force it is to withstand. The force of the wind acting on a sheet of glass must be described in terms of structural loads and pressure in order to evaluate the criteria that the glass is to meet. Other impacts that are referred to in specifications I have looked at in addition to climate include 'hard bodies' (stones), 'soft bodies' (footballs) and 'semi-hard bodies' (the human body). Figure 12.4 shows a testing rig which works with a head-shaped leather punch bag filled with lead shot to simulate the impact of a human body on a plane of glass.[19]

In the following table, we see that the capacities of different thicknesses composite and laminated glass are given in relation to bullets from specific named guns:

Composite structure required for different levels of attack

	Parabellum 9mm	Magnum revolver 44	Nato rifle 7.62mm	Shotgun 12 bore
Laminated glass (mm)	20-40	40-60	50-80	30-50
Glass/polycarbonate composite (mm)	15-25	25-30	30-50	-

Table from: David Sutton and Brian Pye, Glass in Building (London: Butterworth Architecture, 1993)

Here, testing and quantification make possible a direct relation between a given technical object and the material. But, at the same time, the specifier selecting the glass needs some idea of the likelihood of any one of these weapons being used in the local context of the building they are designing. Engineer Sergio de Gaetano points out that the 'threat assessment' is 'the starting point of any bomb blast evaluation' and will take into account a building's geographic location and use as well as 'the political stability and history of terrorism in the city and in the country'.[20] We can assume that this would have been necessary for calculating the forces – from rotten tomatoes to rifle bullets – that the glass screens at Foster's *Reichstag* were to withstand. According to the specifier of Richard Rogers Partnership's Welsh Assembly Building, which also uses a glass screen between its public space and parliamentary chamber to suggest 'transparency' and 'in Lord Callaghan's view represented the "open modern democracy" the Welsh Assembly ought to be', this was indeed the case.[21] The September 11th attacks took place during the writing of the specification and the resulting change in the perception of the building's security brought about a full re-design of the glazed areas. A set of assumptions arising out of the political and social context of the time, and the technological assemblages that might impact upon the building, determined the choice of glazing and were stabilised (invisibly) and naturalised in the physical make up of the transparent barrier.

We begin to see, then, that the performances that are already taken into account in the design and specification of a building extend well beyond the internal structural equilibrium recognised by Leatherbarrow to include social forces that only indirectly have physical implications. We can also see this

Figure 12.4 Glass-testing rig

operating at the smaller scale of the subject or inhabitant of the building. Where heat transmission is the criteria for the use of a piece of glass or a glazing system, something must also be known about the expected warmth of the space it is to contain. This involves precise quantifications of inhabitants' expected behaviours including, for example, the metabolic heat generated by various activities (unsurprisingly the guidance works with the bodily surface area of 'a typical man'):

Activities	W/m²
Reading	55
Typing	65
Walking	100
Lifting	120

Table from: David Sutton and Brian Pye, Glass in Building (London: Butterworth Architecture, 1993)

The specification of one of these quantities, then, assumes that the activities that will occur in any given space. Additionally, according to Pilkington, these figures need to be moderated by the degree of insulation of clothing that the reader or typist or walker is expected to be wearing, given in 'clo' – 'a relative value, with 1.00 being the measure for normal indoor clothing *for a man*'.

Clothing	Clo
Underwear, socks, shoes	0.70
Underwear, shirt, trousers, jacket, socks, shoes	1.00
Underwear, shirt, trousers, jacket, heavy quilted jacket and overalls, socks, shoes	1.85

Table from: David Sutton and Brian Pye, Glass in Building (London: Butterworth Architecture, 1993)

Here, once again, quantification enables direct relationships to be established between the clothing that someone is wearing and a material component of the space which will enclose them. These testing procedures construct equivalences between two previously heterogeneous modalities – the activities of the building's inhabitants and its material constitution. Without these chains of techniques, such a connection could not be made. Glass could be named, its properties could even be given, but it could not be described and mobilised in terms of a specifically defined need. With them it becomes possible for assumptions about the behaviours of a building's users to *directly* inform the selection or design of a material.

New material relations

In a famous speech in 1960, Adolf Arndt – a lawyer who had himself been a member of the 1949 *Bundestag* – asked: 'Shouldn't there be a connection between the public principles of democracy and inner and outer transparency and accessibility in our public buildings?'[22] This would become an explicit mandate for the architecture of the second *Bundeshaus* in Bonn designed by Günter Behnisch, opened in 1992, and for the restoration of the *Reichstag*. Norman Foster reiterates this ideology in his own equation between openness and the possibility of seeing at the *Reichstag*. 'All the building's processes are on view – it has no secrets,' he writes in a caption to a photograph of visitors looking down through the glass dome.[23] But there is a contradiction between what the glass symbolises and what it has been designed to do, which has rendered the transparency of the glass domes at the Reichstag radically different to the transparency of the glazed wall at the 1949 Bundeshaus in Bonn. This transformation, largely invisible in the physical appearance of the glass and in the cultural appraisals of the building, must be understood in terms of new technologies and forms of description which arise also out of the ways that industry, legal and contractual arrangements, and manufacturing processes, are organised. Nevertheless, it seems to challenge the kinds of stories we tell about materials and our understanding of what they do.[24]

So, a discussion of performativity in architecture needs to recognise that the current tendency to consider a building through 'its acts, its performances' is also constituted in industry and production. This is not only a conceptual shift but also a material and physical one with specific effects that demand investigation. Although Jon McKenzie may be overstating it when he suggests (following Jean François Lyotard)[25] that if, with Michel Foucault, we understand discipline as the key formation of power in the eighteenth and nineteenth centuries, we must now in the twentieth and twenty-first centuries understand performance as the emergent 'onto-historical formation of power and knowledge';[26] the performance matrix is deeply entrenched in the conditions and logics of production. But what may be most significant about an exploration of these 'new performances' for the question of architectural culture is that the constellation of processes required for their production and specification are enabling new relations to be made at the level of the material.

While many of the performances that are currently specified and designed relate to the internal integrity of the building or its parts, we have seen that others involve more socially determined and socially determining forces. Self-cleaning glass embeds a cultural imperative to appear clean and always new into the material. The Turkish company BCE Glass can promote their glass on their website in direct terms of protection against specific attacks:

We offer protection against from a plain street assault with a 9mm hand gun, to an all out attack up to 12.7mm machine gun. Whatever the threat level, we can produce the optimum composition to insure maximum security.[27]

And Pilkington make a business case for using their glass to improve the comfort of office buildings and to attract a good workforce.[28] Might we suggest that the possibility that social forces, intentions and expectations can be directly related to, or even 'inscribed' in, the material in these ways is in fact a radically new development?

In their brilliant and incisive discussion of 'materials *à la carte*' Bensaude-Vincent and Stengers make an extraordinary and unexplained claim. 'Whether functional or structural,' they write, 'new materials are no longer intended to replace traditional materials. They are made to solve specific problems, *and for this reason they embody a different notion of matter*'.[29] The traditional notion of matter they refer to is hylomorphism, the idea that form imposes itself on passive indeterminate matter. These new materials, they suggest, might be considered instead as 'informed', 'in the sense that the material structure becomes *richer and richer in information*.[30] Andrew Barry's work on new pharmaceuticals also picks up on their notion of informed materials:

> Pharmaceutical companies do not produce bare molecules – structures of carbon, hydrogen, oxygen and other elements – isolated from their environments. Rather they produce a multitude of informed molecules [...] The molecules produced by a pharmaceutical company are already part of a rich informational material environment, even before they are consumed. This environment includes, for example, data about potency, metabolism and toxicity and information regarding the intellectual property rights associated with different molecules.[31]

Barry extends the notion of the molecule's informational environment to include 'extra-physical' factors such as property rights in a similar way that we have seen here in relation to performance-led glass. What he doesn't ask, however, is whether it is just a change in the degree of information that characterises these new molecules. The point, it seems to me, is that these may also be new modes of information. It is the possibility that they can come into an interactional relation with material that might be understood as radically new.

The historian of engineering, Cyril Stanley Smith, has observed that the work with the combination of properties of materials 'that is needed for a given service' can involve the materials engineer in projects that are '*social* in nature'.[32] He goes on to explain, moreover, that it will involve the bringing together 'of fields that because of their special complexities have been unrelated: it would minimise the difference between the scientist and those who try to understand the human experience'.[33] In his view, it appears that the performance engineering of materials make new connections between the previously unrelated realms of social and human experience and physical materials. What is engineered in performance engineering, performance specification and their related techniques, is not so much new materials or even new performances, as the possibility of new relations between the material and the social. This may well be a shift that could be considered in terms of a 'new notion of matter' (and indeed I have developed this idea elsewhere in relation to Gilbert Simondon's philosophy of individuation).[34] It is because these developments are constituted, and operate, at a technical and industrial level that they remain largely invisible within architectural discourse. But they need to be part of discussions about architectural culture precisely because it is through the naturalised technological and material register that they generate a set of often-insidious cultural and social implications and effects.

NOTES

1   David Button and Brian Pye (eds) *Glass in Building* (Oxford: Butterworth Architecture, 1993), p. vii. My emphasis.

2   David Leatherbarrow, 'Architecture's Unscripted Performance' in Branko Kolarevic (ed.) *Performative Architecture* (London: Routledge, 2005), p. 7.

3   Leatherbarrow, 'Architecture's Unscripted Performance', p. 13.

4   Picon looks at performativity in relation to the digital but he is unusual in that he recognises a broad range of developments, both industrial and practical – from new forms of specification to ecological concerns – that contribute to what can be easily understood as a more general shift. For example: 'The new attention to activity can be traced at various levels. On a technological standpoint, recent evolution points towards the substitution of dynamic performance criteria to static indicators. The ecological character of a building can be apprehended only in dynamic terms. To be green is not a passive attribute; it is the result of a continued action. Similarly, architectural affect is not given once and for all but produced through continuous interaction between subjects and objects.' Antoine Picon, *Digital Culture in Architecture* (Basel: Birkhäuser, 2010), p. 109.

5   Peter Buchanan, 'When Democracy Builds' in Norman Foster (ed.) *Rebuilding the Reichstag* (London: Weidenfield & Nicholson, 2000), p. 169.

6   Deborah Ascher Barnstone, *The Transparent State: Architecture and Politics in Postwar Germany* (London: Routledge, 2005), pp. 125–126.

7   Hisham Elkadi, *Cultures of Glass Architecture* (Aldershot: Ashgate, 2006), p. 48. He notes that it applies to many other buildings including office blocks which open their ground floors to the gaze but 'exclude people'.

8   Madeleine Akrich, 'The De-scription of Technical Objects' in Wiebe Bjiker and John Law (eds) *Shaping Technology/Building Society: Studies in Sociotechnical Change* (Cambridge MA: MIT Press), p. 222.

9   Bernadette Bensaude-Vincent and Isabelle Stengers, *A History of Chemistry* (Cambridge MA: Harvard University Press, 1996), p. 206.

10 Michelle Addington and Daniel Schodek (eds) *Smart Materials and Technologies for the Architecture and Design Professions* (Oxford: Architectural Press, 2005), p. 3.

11 See Ibid., p. 29: 'In the traditional engineering approach the material is understood as an array of physical behaviours. Then in the traditional architectural and general design approach the materials is still conceived as a singular static thing, an artefact.'

12 Hans Joachim Gläser, 'The European History of Coatings on Architectural Glazing', http://www.glassfiles.com/library/article.php?id=1051&search=coatings+history&page=1 [accessed: 27.07.09].

13 Ian Chandler, *Building Technology 2: Performance* (London: Mitchell, 1989), p. 183.

14 Rickman and Hussey Architects, 'Specification of the work, and particulars of the materials to be used in the erection of an asylum for the blind, Bristol', (1835), in a bound collection entitled *Specifications*, RIBA library, EW 2772.

15 Chetwoods®, Specification for Sainsbury's, Maidenhead, (2005), Clause H10.

16 Tony Allot, 'NBS: A Progress Report' in *RIBA Journal*, February (1971): 82–83.

17 George Atkinson, 'Performance Specification' in *Building*, 17 March (1972): 116.

18   Allot, 'NBS: A Progress Report', 82.

19   See Figure 16.3, Test rig, Pilkington Glass Ltd., St Helens, UK, in Button and Pye (eds) *Glass in Building*, p. 258.

20   Sergio de Gaetano, 'Design for Glazing Protection against Terrorist Attacks', http://www.glassfiles.com/library/article.php?id=958&search=Gaetano&page=1 [accessed: 27.07.09].

21   Deyan Sudjic with Helen Jones, *Architecture and Democracy* (London: Lawrence King Publishers, 2001), p. 118.

22   Adolf Arndt, '*Bauen für die Demokratie*' in Ingeborg Flagge and Wolfgang Jean Stock (eds) *Architektur und Demokratie: Bauen für die Politik von der amerikanischen Revolution bis zur Gegenwart* (Stuttgart: Hatje, 1996), p. 59. Cited and translated in Barnstone, *The Transparent State*, p. 5.

23   Foster, *Rebuilding the Reichstag*, p. 137. Caption to picture of visitors looking down from the press lobby on to the debating chamber.

24   For a very incisive development of the argument in relation to two uses of different types of mirrored glass, that it may be at the technological level and not at the 'stylistic' that significant architectural changes occur, see Reinhold Martin, 'Mirror Glass (A Fragment)' in Michael Bell and Jeannie Kim (eds) *Engineered Transparency: The Technical, Visual, and Spatial Effects of Glass* (New York: Princeton Architectural Press, 2009). See also Edward Wainwright's summary of the contradiction between security demands on glass façades and their persistence 'as symbols of open societies' that glass engineering endeavours to resolve in his conference review: 'Engineered Transparency' in *arq: Architectural Research Quarterly*, 12, 1 (2008): 10–11.

25   Jean-François Lyotard, *The Postmodern Condition: A Report on Knowledge* (Minneapolis: University of Minnesota Press, 1984).

26   Jon McKenzie, *Perform or Else* (London: Routledge, 2001), p. 18.

27   Online promotional material for BCE glass: http://www.bceglass.com/armouredglass.asp, [accessed: 07.05.11].

28   See Button and Pye, *Glass in Building*, p. 121: 'Demands for improved comfort by the building occupants will increase in industrialised countries during the 1990s for several reasons. First, the older working population will have higher comfort expectations. Second, competition for employees will generate incentives by employers; a healthy comfortable working environment will be just such an incentive in the United States where the number of young adults will fall by 40% creating a shortage of entry level employees.'

29   Bensaude-Vincent and Stengers, *A History of Chemistry*, p. 206.

30   Ibid., my emphasis.

31   Andrew Barry, 'Pharmaceutical Matters: The Invention of Informed Materials' in Mariam Fraser, Sarah Kember, Celia Lury (eds) *Inventive Life: Approaches to New Vitalism* (London: Sage, 2006), p. 59.

32   Cyril Stanley Smith, *A Search for Structure: Selected Essays on Science, Art and History* (Cambridge MA: MIT Press, 1981), p. 124.

33   Ibid., p. 125.

34   Katie Lloyd Thomas, *Building Materials: Concepts of Materials via the Architectural Specification*, unpublished PhD thesis, submitted to CRMEP, Middlesex University, May 2010.

Chapter 13

Making plans: Alberti's ichnography as cultural artefact

Paul Emmons and Jonathan Foote

The assertion of architecture's liberal, humanistic status – comparing architects to the 'greatest exponents of other disciplines', by Leon Battista Alberti in the fifteenth century[1] – coincides with what is usually considered the beginning of modern architectural practice when, following the increasing availability of paper in the West, architects left construction sites to work remote from building activities.[2] As medieval representations of architects directing work on building sites gave way to Renaissance portraits of architects at desks with books, instruments and paper, they took up drawing at a table in a scholarly study.[3]

What follows will examine a drawing attributed to Alberti, demonstrating intimate interconnections between drawing and building, theory and practice. Despite often being misunderstood as merely providing technical information, architectural drawings are edifying because they simultaneously convey and construct culture. With design newly distanced from construction, early modern drawing practices originated as indexes of construction. As the horizon of the site corresponds to the horizontal drawing board with its paper attached, so the pulling of knotted ropes to measure out a building on site became the pen's drawing of lines across the site of the paper.

Plan drawings are probably the most ancient and enduring form of architectural representation, imparting both practical and ritual significance.[4] Today, plans are conceived as horizontal sections through abstract Cartesian space. Before the modern era, however, they were called *ichnographia*; literally footprints impressing a vestige or marking of the building's weight delving into the virgin earth. Vitruvius identified *ichnographia* as the first idea of the architect and specified that they are to be constructed 'with skillful use of the compass and rule'.[5] In Cesare Cesariano's 1521 commentary on Vitruvius, he explains *ichnographia* as both plans inscribed on white paper on a drawing board and architects walking snowy sites to mark out the future walls with footprints along with stakes and ropes.[6] Alberti already referenced the ancient divinatory practice of marking plans with white chalk or flour on the earth.[7] This unity between plan drawing and earth marking explains why architect's drawing boards are primarily horizontal, as Alberti contrasted the vertical easel of the painter with the horizontal plan of the architect. Cesariano's poetic example of projecting the architect's imaginal body onto the site through the drawing shows that the site of the drawing is an analog to the construction site.[8] In drawing the scale plan, the architect imaginatively projects him or herself into the miniature world of the drawing in order to conceive of inhabiting the possible future world of the building.

The close reading of drawing practices offers a window into the discovery of the architectural conception through the non-arbitrary use of marks, traces, and tools in the making of a drawing. This examination of the physical making of a drawing instigates a wider discussion as to how the act of construction is deeply embedded in the workings of Alberti's architectural imagination. Considering the process of its facture helps us to understand the particularities of the architect's embodied imagination in the projection of the future work onto the building site. Of this process, Alberti himself wrote of drawing, to: 'describe it as though we were ourselves about to construct the building with our own hands.'[9]

Re-constructing Alberti's thermal bath drawing

The sole plan drawing ascribed to Alberti describes an un-built project for a thermal bath, probably for an existing structure (Figure 13.1).[10] Made with a straightedge, ink, drypoint and black chalk on paper, it was apparently trimmed at the edges when incorporated into a volume of drawings in the seventeenth century.[11] The attribution of the drawing to Alberti, based in part upon the handwriting, was debated after Howard Burns published his ground-breaking analysis in 1979 but recent scholarship seems to have quelled the early disagreements.[12] Our own analysis of Alberti's line work in his annotated copy

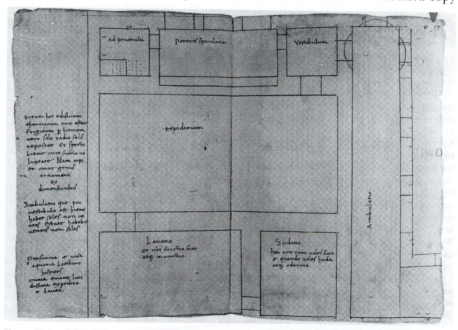

Figure 13.1 *edificium thermarum*, attributed to L.B. Alberti, *Biblioteca Medicea Laurenziana*, Ash. 1828, fol. 56v, XIV century

of Euclid's *Elementa* further supports Alberti's authorship.[13] Burns' very thorough analysis of the dimensions, transcriptions, and proportions suggest a clear link between Alberti's drawing practice and his larger theory of architecture.[14] Robert Tavernor's more recent study of the thermal bath drawing identifies it as an unrealised project for the Palazzo Ducale in Urbino.[15] The textual annotations, describing how rooms would be used and experienced as if made for a patron, provide essential information as to how Alberti inhabited the plan with his bodily imagination.

The plan has been described as drawn to a carefully determined scale so as to reflect harmonic musical proportions.[16] Burns' speculations on the scale of the drawing place is somewhere in the range of 1:100, a proposition which Tavernor accepts and is confirmed in his placing of the bath complex within the context of the Palazzo Ducale.[17] As Tavernor confirms, however, such an open matter cannot be determined by the formal properties of the drawing alone. Whatever the exact ratio, Alberti would have constructed the drawing dimensionally, using a local bodily measure such as the *Urbino braccia* (a common measure of length from elbow to finger tip).[18] It was a widespread practice to refer to the measure in scale as 'little' ('*braccia picchole*').[19]

Practices embedded in making drawings can reveal the architect's theoretical approach to the conception of architecture. When compared to other planimetric drawings of the same period, such as Francesco di Giorgio's drawings in the *Opusculum de architectura*, the starkness and simplicity of Alberti's draftsmanship is even more evident.[20] In this case, it seems likely that Alberti was following his own advice, underlining the importance of a simple and unadorned drawing to best judge a design's lineaments. In contrast to the painter, who works with perspective and shadows, the architect:

> rejects shading, [and] takes his projections from the ground plan and, without altering the lines and by maintaining the true angles, reveals the extent and shape of each elevation and side – he [the architect] is one who desires his work to be judged not by deceptive appearances but according to certain calculated standards.[21]

Such nakedness allows for a more proper assessment of the lines and angles, without the seduction of unnecessary distractions. The economy of lines corresponds with the simplicity of his drawing tools, and Alberti appears to have constructed the drawing using only a straight edge. While it was common practice to open dividers to a measure on a scale away from the drawing and then 'walk' the compass legs across the paper to create a dimension, there is no evidence of pricks in the drawing paper (as some scholars have assumed), which usually indicate their use.[22] It may be that the divider was used very lightly, or perhaps a strip of paper was marked with the scale to transfer measures directly with dots as an early forerunner of the modern fiduciary rule.[23] In Alberti's annotations in his copy of the *Elementa*, the line work is strikingly similar to the bath drawing; and likewise, there is no evidence of the use of a compass. The apparent lack of use of tools used in geometric constructions is noteworthy, as there appears to be no use of a square either (dots can be found on both ends of the lines). What does seem certain is that Alberti was relying on the guidance of nascent *punta secca*, or black chalk lines, as well as inscribed lines, laid down as a kind of scaffolding of occult lines which supported the construction of the drawing before it was rendered in ink.[24] These lines, along with the irregular crossing or missing of ink lines at intersections, suggests the use of a straight edge ruler only, with the perpendicular being found through the pacing off of dimensions rather than the use of a construction tool, such as a compass or square. Alberti's clear emphasis was on harmonic measured lines, rather than geometric shape, consistent with his architectural theory.

The bath drawing's apparent austerity at first invites close attention to its large variety of marks of lines and dots, which can be read to begin to reconstruct its sequence of construction. The accompanying graphic analysis helps to re-imagine the drawing's narrative, as a process of both drawing and building. In Alberti's first imaginary walk across the paper (Figure 13.2),[25] it appears likely that he began by placing four large dots, with circles around them, at the four corners of the drawing (the lower left corner cannot be confirmed due to the trimming of the sheet). From here, Alberti traced two horizontal occult or incised lines between the four corners. He then paced out a series of inked dots along these primary occult lines in order to set up the network of vertical occult lines, as shown in Alberti's second walk (Figure 13.3). It can be seen in the drawing analysis that a whole series of vertical occult lines may be interpolated between the dots along the primary horizontal occult lines. Once these were set, Alberti thirdly embarked on a series of secondary horizontal occult lines, all of which were located through the making of inked double dots. Nearly all of the horizontal occult lines may be connected through these double sets of dots, made parallel with the line. It would make sense, then, that these double dots do not signify a measure but rather a perpendicular directionality as clarification from other earlier dots. Nearly all of the double tick marks are located at intersections of the occult lines, meaning that, once set, these lines could act as a confident support to begin inking.

The subsequent category of dots appears as a kind of 'walking' across the building site. These single tick marks were the residue of a dimensioning process, whereby a room is so many dots or paces across. This is particularly evident in the *vestibulum*'s evenly spaced series of dots. After setting overall dimensions, smaller proportional relationships are seemingly developed. This is why multiple sets of dots are used to distinguish between the first overall set and the later more detailed groups of relations to avoid confusion after the single dots were laid down.

At this point, the inking of the drawing probably began, with a sufficient network of marks and occult lines to begin denoting the remaining walls (Figure 13.4). Still, dot marks come into play in a final type of mark that would have entered into the drawing after the primary walls were inked. These are mostly indicated by single ticks, which would have been made using previously inked lines as a guide, rather than the denoting lines. They signify the measures of the lines made for the openings between rooms, and set the stage for what appears

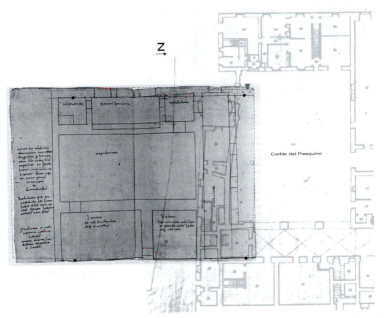

Figure 13.2 Alberti's Walk, First Pass. Alberti would have started in the southeastern portion of the Cortile del Pasqino, setting a stake for the northeast corner of the bath complex. He then makes a path setting the three other stakes, designating the four corners. With these four stakes, Alberti stretches the first two string lines, between them, along the east and west extends of the project. With these lines he sets the first round of single tick marks, and the first east/west strings are ready to be pulled

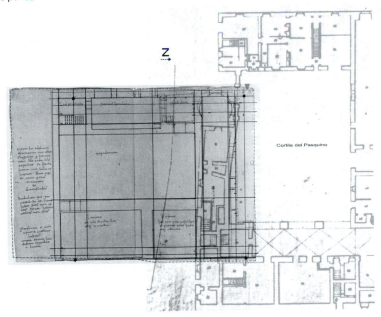

Figure 13.3 Alberti's Walk, Second Pass. Once the primary strings have been established, Alberti pulls the subsequent network of strings across the building site, adding tick marks along the way to designate corners of rooms, and openings

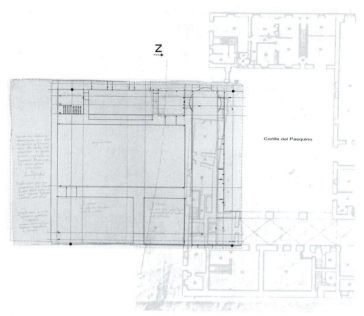

Figure 13.4 Alberti's Walk, Third Pass. Following the string lines, Alberti may ink the lines of the main walls and establish the locations for openings and the stair

to be the final lines made on the drawing. They include: the bench set into the wall of the *porticus specularis*, the wall openings made between rooms, and the mark for the floor penetration in the *ad penetralia*. The series of several dotted lines of marks, located in the *ad penetralia*, has been understood by scholars to indicate a stair, probably downward.[26] The making of Alberti's drawn lines, thus proceeds with a sort of pacing back and forth around the site.

Ichnographic drawing practice as embodied theory

With a description of the drawing's possible construction, we may begin to speculate on how a process such as this would relate to how a building was constructed. That Alberti conceived of the construction of a drawing in an analogous way to the construction of the building is well supported through various passages in his treatise.

The embodiment of the plan as an *ichnographia* shows that the bath is almost certainly an addition to an existing building. As the drawing was evidently later cut to fit into a collection book, one could easily imagine that the project originally extended further up and to the right.[27] The cut at the end of the page in the lower right suggests a connection to another part of the building, and the arcade along the *ambulatio* suggests a possible courtyard enclosure since the arcade appears to continue around the corner.

Perhaps the most striking connection between drawing and building may be found in Alberti's discussion for the laying out of foundations on the building site where the derivation of the guiding string lines is discussed as if one were marking and making a drawing on paper:

> Our usual method of defining the foundations is to trace out [*dirigere*] several lines, known as baselines [*lineas radices*], in the following manner. From a midpoint at the front, we extend a line right to the back of the work; halfway along it we fix a stake into the ground, and through this, following the rules of geometry, we extend the perpendicular. We then relate all the measurements to these two lines. This works wonderfully in every way: the parallel lines are easily drawn [*demetiendum*], the angles can be defined accurately, and the parts conform and correspond exactly to one another.[28]

This passage is striking for several reasons. First is the clear analogy between drawing on the drafting board and the drawing-out (*dirigere*) of lines on the construction site. The first act of transference between the two would be the stretching of string lines, and the architect's imagination would find great advantage to working between them. Second, in the laying out of foundations, the first act, also associated with divinatory rites, is the making of a *templum*, or a cross of string lines, from which all other angles and lines are derived.[29] In this way, the lineaments of both the drawing and building are initiated through making a *templum*. However, the thermal bath drawing contains no evidence of such a construction. Instead, just after describing the crossing of strings in the *templum*, Alberti offers an alternative method in his treatise whenever existing buildings or walls would otherwise obstruct an open site. In this case, he states that the laying out of the building is best derived from the existing structure:

> you must trace out the parallel lines wherever there is some unobstructed space. Then mark out the point of intersection, and by setting the gnomon and projecting a transverse line, and tracing out further parallel lines at right angles, you will easily overcome the problem [of working around existing walls].[30]

In the thermal bath drawing, Alberti appears to have taken this approach by deriving the originating lines from the existing building, bolstering Tavernor's argument that the project is attached to an existing edifice. If the drawing was initiated by placing two marks with circles around them at the bottom and top right of the drawing (Figure 13.2), then this corresponds to where the proposed bath would intersect with the existing portico of the Cortile del Pasquino of the Palazzo Ducale. From these two dots, parallel lines were extended southward through the marks in circles to pull the two outside strings between an approximation of the four corners, with the northeastern corner corresponding to the existing portico (Figure 13.3). This would work well with Alberti's advice that, before beginning any excavation, 'it is advisable to mark out all the corners and sides of the area to the correct size and in the right place several times, and with great care'.[31] With this point, it seems likely that Alberti's making of the bath drawing is clearly imagined as a kind of walking across the building site in preparation for the excavation of the foundations. The use of simple drawing tools seems to support this point, as the setting of the perpendiculars in the drawing relies on pacing (dimensioning) rather than geometric construction.[32] Having approximated the four corners, as suggested in his treatise, he could then begin to locate the subsequent perpendicular occult lines by setting the gnomon (or by sighting with his body). With these in place, he could derive the corners of the rest of the rooms and their openings through the use of a straight edge (Figure 13.4).

The orientation of the drawing to an existing building can also be understood through Alberti's posture while constructing the drawing as recorded in the alignment of the text. The architect is oriented to the drafting board from a primary side and it is this relationship that sets the orientation of the drawing with the primary entry closest to the architect. In this way, the architect moves from the physical relationship to the drawing into an imaginative inhabitation of the plan as if stepping into it. Where the belly of the architect is in close contact with the drawing, the project is conceived and birthed. It provides orientation to a plan more important than aligning north as 'up' (since the magnetic compass).[33] This suggests that the primary entry in Alberti's plan is in the lower right hand corner, confirming Tavernor's supposition that it is an addition to an existing arcade. Furthermore, the only occasion in the drawing where an inked line crosses an open space occurs at what would be a joint between existing and proposed construction. The arcade at the top of the sheet is thus much less likely to be an entry, given the slope of the land on the proposed site, explaining why it is a 'speculum' just like the existing palace loggia on the same side with spectacular views in front of the bath by Francesco di Giorgio. Upon completing his walks, Alberti proceeded to construct the interior lines and angles, including openings and furnishings. Just as Alberti defined colonnades, doors, windows and stairways as 'openings' within walls, so he first inked the extent of the walls and only afterwards 'cut' the openings with cross lines through them.

In the relationship between paces and contemplative lines, there were several places for pause which led to changes and additions. Pacing back and forth in his drawn walks across the site, Alberti's drawing underwent revisions and corrections as it was constructed – an important aspect of Alberti's design process:

> But I can say this of myself: I have often conceived of projects in the mind that seemed quite commendable at the time; but when I translated them into drawings, I found several errors in the very parts that delighted me most, and quite serious ones; again, when I return to drawings, and measure the dimensions, I recognize and lament my carelessness [...][34]

In observing the diagrams of Alberti's only other surviving line work, in the *Elementa*, the role of erasure and revision is quite evident, and it appears as an integral technique in his realization of an idea.[35] Such a process is confirmed quite clearly in the thermal bath drawing in two places (Figure 13.1). First, an occult line within the wall between the *ambulatio* and the *tepidarium* may still be observed, about two millimeters offset from the actual inked line of the *ambulatio* wall. This would appear to be a revision, as the offset corresponds nearly exactly to the offset observed in two sets of double ticks, located at the lower right corner of the drawing. It is very conceivable that these lines record a modification made by Alberti to the original location of the walls of the *ambulatio*.

Second, and more convincingly, we find several re-inked lines in the drawing at the doorway from the Cortile del Pasquino and the *ambulatio*, in the northwest corner of the bath complex. Alberti appears to have had difficulty working out the relationship between the portico facing the courtyard and the resolution with the entrance at the west end of the *vestibulum*. At this point, it may be observed that Alberti inked several lines very close to one another and it is a matter of interpretation as to which one holds the greatest certainty. It seems there are some conflicts between having the two façades (existing and new) of the courtyards work together as well as making an agreeable entrance into the *vestibulum*. This shows up both in the multiple tick lines along the façade of the *ambulatio* as well as in the multiple arcs present in the niche between the *ambulatio* and the *vestibulum*. There can be little doubt that Alberti was using the drawing itself to help work through some of the design difficulties between new and existing.

Alberti's visual language of dots and lines demonstrates the immediacy of his theoretical language. The small dots on the drawing indicating places to draw lines are probably more appropriately called 'points'. In *Elements of Painting*, creating a practical geometry from Euclid, Alberti defines a painter's point as 'that small inscription than which nothing can be smaller' while a line is 'that very fine inscription that goes from one point to another' and 'a line is said to be almost like a point stretched out in length'.[36] An alternate translation gives Alberti's line as 'a point moving' – which is of course the pen point drawing across the paper's surface.[37] These definitions differ from Euclid and instead describe the actions of Alberti's construction of drawings, from marking points as stakes in the earth and then joining two points across the sheet as lines to represent walls. Thus, connecting two points to make a line is Alberti's drawing technique as well as his geometrical definition.

Alberti explains harmony through sounds and the length of strings that emit them. Since harmony is the relationship between the strings, the architectural plan reveals harmony in its lines. Thus, the primary element of the drawing is not geometric shape, but rather lines with particular dimensions and how they relate to one another that result in figures: 'For us, the outline is a certain correspondence between the lines that define the dimensions; one dimension being length, another breadth, and the third height.'[38] In the thermal bath drawing, Alberti similarly emphasises line over shape because of the way the lines are primary elements and the shapes they make are secondary as can be seen in the inconsistent intersections of lines at corners.

Inhabiting the building site through ichnographic drawing

Far from mere marks on paper, the many dots and lines of the thermal bath *ichnographia* reveal a deep significance for Alberti's architecture. It seems clear, upon this analysis of the bath drawing, that Alberti constructed the drawing as if he were actually laying out the foundations for the future walls on the addition to an existing building. The originating dots with circles around them are drawn manifestations of stakes driven into the earth with ropes tied around them. In the final analysis, this investigation into drawing practices adds credence to Tavernor's speculations on the connection of the bath complex to the Palazzo Ducale. In addition, such an inquiry yields insight into the tight relationship between drawing and building. Alberti's drawing practice is an embodiment of the act of construction itself, a prudent endeavour which both recalls the memory of past experience as well as projects the future design onto a building site.

Alberti described the practical geometry of the painter as '*la più grassa Minerva*' or literally, 'a fatter wisdom'; explaining that while mathematicians examine forms separate from matter, artists use a more sensate wisdom.[39] Alberti understood that, although in geometry a series of points cannot form a line, according to the applied geometry of design, a line is derived from an 'extended point'.[40] He thus uses '*la più grassa Minerva*' in a precise sense, distinguishing the breadthless line of the geometer that only exists in the mind from the physical, yet slender line of the painter. In the first three books of his edifying treatise on architecture, Alberti moves from the first book on lineaments of the geometer's line in the mind to the second book on materials with the subtle matter of a drawn line on paper and a rope line pulled on site to the third book on construction with the thick line of a masonry wall. As Alberti well knew, Minerva, goddess of wisdom, presides over two kinds of knowledge: both of intellect and of craft.

The much embraced idea of *festina lente* – hurrying slowly – was represented in the Renaissance as a dolphin intertwined in an anchor and in the fifteenth-century *Hypnerotomachia Poliphili* as a woman partly sitting and partly walking while holding a turtle in one hand and wings in the other (Figure 13.5).[41] The saying 'make haste slowly' was attributed to Augustus in the ancient world (to whom Vitruvius dedicated his ten books on architecture) to mean prudently combining resolute action with restraint.[42] Alberti's bath drawing demonstrates *festina lente* in the slow and careful touch to locate points with well-tuned harmonic dimensions and then followed with the fast gesture of pulling the line in order to realise the intention. This performative action is remembered in the marks of the drawing and evokes visceral responses in the observer.

That plans can be cultural constructs rather than merely technical descriptions is clear when one looks beyond the bias of isolating theory from practice. The unspoken desire or dread to maintain a schism between theory and practice, the high and the low, obscures their intimate interconnections. This linkage was certainly true for Alberti whose writing on architecture was directed to the educated ruling class as a demonstration of humanist principles, but who also integrated a significant range of very practical experience, addressing materials, weathering, and water drainage, for example. Alberti wrote in a text known as *On The Tranquillity of the Soul*, that when he seeks 'relief from bitter worries and sad thoughts', he 'composes in his mind and constructs some well-designed building, arranging various orders and numbers of columns with diverse capitals and unusual bases, and linking these with cornices and marble plaques which give the whole convenience and a new grace'. Christine Smith concludes from this that Alberti's 'activity of architecture bridges the gap between the active and contemplative lives, and the architect himself may be raised to the status of moral exemplar'.[43] Practical philosophy – the origin of why architects 'practice' – considers localised instances within the prudent judgement of ethics and is in-between the universal vision of theory and the pragmatic concerns of production.[44] The performance of the making of an architectural drawing already provides its meaning and demonstrates its theory. Architectural drawing, at least in the case of Alberti's thermal bath ichnographia, is culture-evoking and culture-building.

Figure 13.5 *Festina lente* from Hypnerotomachia Poliphil; (Venice, 1499)

NOTES

1   Leon Battista Alberti, *On the Art of Building in Ten Books*, trans. Joseph Rykwert, Neil Leach and Robert Tavernor, (Cambridge: MIT Press, 1988) p. 3. 'quem tu summis caeterau disciplinarum uiris compares'.

2   Marco Frascari, 'A Reflection on Paper and its virtues within the material and invisible factures of architecture', in Marco Frascari, Jonathan Hale and Bradley Starkey (eds) *From Models to Drawings, Imagination and Representation in Architecture* (London: Routledge, 2007), pp. 23–33.

3   Dora Thornton, *The Scholar in His Study: Ownership and Experience in Renaissance Italy* (New Haven: Yale University Press, 1997).

4   Paul Emmons, 'Site Drawing :: Drawing Site' in Suzanne Ewing, Jérémie McGowan, Chris Speed and Victoria Clare Bernie (eds) *Architecture and Field/Work* (London: Routledge, 2011), pp. 119–128.

5   'Ichnographia est circini regulaeque modice continens usus, e qua capinuntur formarum in solis arearum descriptions.' Vitruvius, I. II. 1.

6   Cesare Cesariano, commentary in Vitruvius, *De Architectura*, trans. Cesare Cesariano (Como, 1521) XIII.v. See also: Carol Krinsky, 'Introduction' in Vitruvius, Cesare Cesariano (trans.), *De Architectura* (München: Wilhelm Fink, 1969), p. 13.

7   Alberti, *On the Art of Building*, p. 101.

8   Antonio Averlino, *Filarete's Treatise on Architecture*, John Spencer (trans.), (New Haven: Yale University Press, 1965), p. 311; David Leatherbarrow, 'Leveling the Land' in *Topographical Stories: Studies in Landscape and Architecture* (Philadelphia: University of Pennsylvania Press, 2004), pp. 114–130.

9   Alberti, *On the Art of Building*, p. 61. Alberti is here explaining the process of building, an analogous procedure to the making of a drawing.

10 The drawing is preserved in the Biblioteca Medicea Laurenziana, Codex Ashburnham 1828, fol. 56v–57r. This drawing was studied in person in July 2009. The only other known architectural drawing by Alberti exists in his letter to Matteo de' Pasti, November 1454, where Alberti resorted to a small sketch in order to illustrate the roof condition on the Tempio Malatestiano. Robert Tavernor, *On Alberti and the Art of Building* (Yale University Press, 1998), pp. 194–200.

11 Cod. Ash. 1828. An Urbino architect, Muzio Oddi, included this in his collection of drawings. Howard Burns, 'Un disegno architettonico de Alberti e la questione del rapporto fra Brunelleschi ed Alberti', *Filippo Brunelleschi: il suo opera e il suo tempo* (1980), p. 105.

12 Howard Burns, 'A Drawing by LB Alberti', *Architectural Design* (1979): 45–56. Tavernor reviews recent scholarship and re-affirms the authenticity of the drawing as from the hand of Alberti in Tavernor, *On Alberti*, p. 194. Christine Smith states that the authorship is unsupported on the evidence of Alberti's *De re aedificatoria*, although she does not deny its authenticity. Christine Smith, 'Attribiuto a Leon Battista Alberti: Pianta di un complesso termale', in *Rinaschimento da Brunelleschi a Michelangelo: La rappresentazione dell'architettura* (Milan, 1994), p. 458. Lucia Bertolini recently confirmed the drawing as autograph in Bertonli, 'Firenze, Biblioteca Medicea Laurenziana: Ashburnham 1828 Appendice', in *Leon Battista Alberti: La Biblioteca di un Umanista* (Mandragora, 2005), pp. 367–368.

13 Alberti's copy of Euclid's *Elementa* is in the Biblioteca Nazionale Marciano, Lat. VIII, 39 (3271). See especially Alberti's diagrams on 90v, where the corner intersections of the lines do not meet in a very similar manner to the thermal bath drawing. See also n. 37 below.

14 Burns, 'Drawing by LB Alberti', p. 47.

15 Tavernor, *On Alberti*, pp. 189–202.

16 Burns contends that the unit of the drawing is based on the width of one pier of the *porticus specularis*. With this unit, a whole host of proportional measures emerge from an analysis of the other room dimensions, many of which are discussed in Alberti's treatise. In this way, for example, the proportion of the *lavatio* is 3:5 and the *sudatio* is 8:9; all proportions which have been found in Alberti's built work or are discussed in his treatise. In order to establish this,

however, Burns must finally argue that, 'wall thicknesses are negatively determined by the need to give the correct proportions to the rooms, while containing the whole design within a square of fixed dimensions [34 x 34 units]'.

17 Tavernor, *On Alberti*, p. 197.

18 Robert Tavernor, *Smoot's Ear: The Measure of Humanity* (New Haven: Yale University Press, 2007).

19 Antonio di Tuccio Manetti, *The Life of Brunelleschi*, Catherine Enggass (trans.), (University Park: Pennsylvania State University Press, 1970), p. 103, line 1063. See also Filarete, p. 82.

20 See Francesco di Giorgio's autographed planimetric drawings of military forts in: *Opusculum de architectura*, British Museum, London. The line work of the planimetric drawing of the dome of Santa Maria del Fiore by Gherardo da Prato (1426) is rendered in red ink wash and sepia line using a wider variety of tools including a compass, and is preserved in the Archivio di Stato, Firenze, which also stands in relative contrast to Alberti's drawing.

21 Alberti, *On the Art of Building*, II. 1, p. 34.

22 Paul Emmons, 'Drawn to Scale' in Marco Frascari, Jonathan Hale and Bradley Starkey (eds) *From Models to Drawings, Imagination and Representation in Architecture* (London: Routledge, 2007), pp. 64–78. Tavernor (1998) and Bertolini (2005) both presume Alberti's use of dividers to make the drawing. Furthermore, the *Vestibulum's* circular arcs show no evidence of a compass pricks although it would be very unusual to construct a circle with a template at that time.

23 Scamozzi, though later, advises against perforating the paper with the compass tip and mentions the use of paper for temporary drawing tools. Vincenzo Scamozzi, *l'Idea della architettura universal* (Venice, 1615), Part 1, I. 15 translated in Marco Frascari, *Eleven Exercises in the art of architectural drawing* (London: Routledge, 2011), p.184. Measuring scales become established *c.*1450 in Italy and a century later in northern Europe, often on the arms of other equipment such as squares, sectors or rules. Of course, rules with measures existed, but because the length of any measure was so variable, the measure was usually recorded on the drawing itself and the practice was to take a measure from a rule or scale with a pair of dividers and then transfer it to the drawing, rather than using a scale on the drawing to mark a length as became common in the nineteenth century and remains common practice today. Maya Hambly, *Drawing Instruments 1580–1980* (London: Sotheby's, 1988), p. 115.

24 Burns also notes these lines, identifying them as 'black chalk' lines, Burns, 'Drawing by LB Alberti', p. 49. In our analysis of the drawing, some 30 years after Burns, these faint lines have become nearly imperceptible. Marco Frascari has suggested that the lines were probably made using a dry point or *ematita*, a fifteenth-century leadless version of the Italian *matita*. For examples of other fifteenth-century drawings exhibiting such faint 'construction' lines, see Henry Millon, *Rinascimento: da Brunelleschi a Michelangelo, la rappresentazione dell'architettura* (Milan: Bompiani, 1994), pp. 109–110. Occult lines (*linee occulte*) are from Serlio, who used these lines to denote hidden, invisible relationships between the apparent, visible lines of a drawing. Sebastiano Serlio, *On Architecture, Volume One*, Vaughan Hart and Peter Hicks (trans.), (New Haven: Yale University Press, 1996), p. 48.

25 Alberti used the word '*podismata*' or pacing out. Alberti, *On the Art of Building*, IX. 10, p. 317.

26 Burns, 'Drawing by LB Alberti', p. 48. Alberti indicates in the margin that the 'furnaces and cauldrons of water shall be hidden from the guests'. There is a remarkable consistency with the dashed lines (6 dots each, aligned throughout) and they appear to go from lighter to heavier, possibly suggesting descent. Although steep, such a service stair would fit the Urbino site's topography.

27 Burns, 'Drawing by LB Alberti', p. 46.

28 Alberti, *On the Art of Building*, III. 2, pp. 62–63.

29 Joseph Rykwert, *The Idea of a Town: The Anthropology of Urban Form in Rome, Italy and the Ancient World* (Princeton: Princeton University Press, 1976).

30 Alberti, *On the Art of Building*, III. 2, p. 63. Alberti also censures the inexperienced, who 'do not know how to set out these angles without first removing everything within the area, leaving the ground clear and absolutely level' (p. 62).

31   Alberti, *On the Art of Building*, III. 1, p. 62.
32   This is consistent with Carpo's claims, but suggests it preceded the printed book. Mario Carpo, 'Drawing with Numbers: Geometry and Numeracy in Early Modern Architectural Design' *Journal of the Society of Architectural Historians*, 62, 4 (December, 2003): 448–469.
33   This can be seen in Scamozzi's plan where the north arrow gives way to the principal entrance ('*entrata princip.*') at the bottom of the sheet to orient the plan on the paper. Vincenzo Scamozzi, *l'Idea della Architettura Universale* (Venice, 1615) First Part, II. 8, pp. 126–127.
34   Alberti, *On the Art of Building*, IX. 10, p. 317.
35   *Elementa*, see esp. fol. 79v and 81v for evidence of erasure through the scraping and scratching on the surface of the parchment. See note 13.
36   Leon Battista Alberti, *The Elements of Painting*, Kim Williams and Richard Schofield (trans.) in *The Mathematical Works of Leon Battista Alberti*, Kim Williams, Lionel March and Stephen Wassell (eds) (Basel: Birkhäuser, 2010), pp.144–145. See also the commentary by Stephen Wassell, ibid., pp. 156–157.
37   'Lineam dicunt puncto in oblongum deduct'. Paola Massalin and Branko Mitrovic, 'Alberti and Euclid', *Albertiana* XI-XII (2008–2009), p. 168.
38   Alberti, *On the Art of Building*, IX. 5, p. 305.
39   This also applies to the architect as Alberti advised architects require training in both painting and geometry. Alberti, *On the Art of Building*, IX. 10, p. 317.
40   John R. Spencer, notes and introduction in Leon Battista Alberti, *On Painting* (New Haven: Yale University Press, 1970), p. 43. Alberti, *On Painting*, Cecil Grayson (trans.), (London: Penguin, 1991), I. 1. See also: Carolyn Wilde, 'Painting, Alberti and the Wisdom of Minerva', *British Journal of Aesthetics* 34 (January, 1994): 48–59.
41   Francesco Colonna, *Hypnerotomachia Poliphili, The Strife of Love in a Dream*, Joscelyn Godwin (trans.), (New York: Thames & Hudson, 1999). For the claim that Alberti was the book's author, see: Liane Lefaivre, *Leon Battista Alberti's Hypnerotomachia Poliphili* (Cambridge: MIT Press, 1997).
42   Suetonius, *Lives of Caesar*, II. 25. 4.
43   Leon Battista Alberti, *Profugiorum ab aerumna* (1441 or 42) translated in Christine Smith, *Architecture in the Culture of Early Humanism: Ethics, Aesthetics, and Eloquence 1400–1470* (Oxford: Oxford University Press, 1992), pp. 13, 18.
44   Hans-Georg Gadamer, 'What is Practice? The Conditions of Social Reason' in *Reason in the Age of Science: Studies in Contemporary German Social Thought*, Frederick Lawrence (trans.), (Cambridge: MIT Press, 1982), pp. 69–87.

Chapter 14

How the mind meets architecture: what photography reveals

Hugh Campbell

In this chapter, I will read closely two photographs.[1] The first is one of a series made by the German photographer Candida Höfer of the *Neues Museum* in Berlin, made between the completion of its reconstruction by David Chipperfield and Julian Harrap and the installation of its permanent exhibition in 2009 (Figure 14.1).[2] Like many in the series, this photograph is made with a large-format camera. Symmetrically balanced, it centres on an octagonal space, its lofty coffered ceiling extending out of shot, with rooms extending *enfilade* beyond the facing opening to a distant vanishing point. The red and green hues of the room's wall panels are vividly present, as are the decorative scenes on its recessed apses. The room is not pristine: the photograph shows evidence of extensive gaps and discontinuities in its tiled floor, and of staining and repair on its plaster coffers. The crisp, even light which pervades the image renders all these details clear and palpable. Notably, the space depicted is empty – empty not only of humans but of the usual signs of human occupation; of furniture and equipment. It reads like a space held in suspension.

In a second image – also a recent photograph of a recent architectural project – there is a similar feeling of suspended animation, although the space here is occupied. This diptych is one of a continuing series made by Walter Niedermayr of buildings by the Japanese firm SANAA, the collaborative office of Kazuyo Sejima and Ryue Nishisawa.[3] Dating from 2006, it shows the Glass Pavilion at the Toledo Museum: a building completed that year and one of the practice's first projects outside Japan (Figure 14.2). The pair of images offers discontinuous but comparable views of the pavilion's interior of sinuously curved glass screens loosely delineating areas of circulation and display. The views seem informal despite being organised around a strong central horizon line. Blurred figures are seen moving in front of, and behind, glass. Colours are subdued. Forms seem to float in the evanescent atmosphere.

Reading these images, in the context of the series of which they form part, it is immediately clear that each emerges from an established and distinguished artistic practice. And, in each case, the architecture portrayed exemplifies a particular philosophy and sensibility. Already, a kind of dialogue has opened up between photographic intentions and architectural ambitions. At the same time, both pictures also clearly pay attention to the phenomenological qualities of the places they depict: they are interested in conveying what it is like to be in them. One might go a little further and suggest that they are also interested in

Figure 14.1 *Neues Museum*, Berlin. Photographed by Candida Höfer, 2009. Architects: David Chipperfield and Julian Harrap

conveying what it is like to *be* these places. These photographs might best be considered as portraits of architecture.

This denomination brings with it the implicit requirement that they not only depict what the subject is like, but also depict what it is like to be the subject. We look at portraits of people – like those by Rembrandt and Bonnard – with the expectation that the pictorial rendering of external aspects of appearance can reveal inner states of being. We want to be able to inhabit the subject from the inside out. Can we really have the same expectations for depictions of architecture? Can we suppose that architecture might be as ripe for portraiture as the self?

Space in architecture and in consciousness

Imbuing space with form, purpose and cultural significance is central to the activity of architecture. Discerning those same properties is, in turn, critical to the meaningful experience of architecture. These properties might be regarded as integral to the very fabric of the built space, but they may also be seen as aspects of a quite separate and distinct unifying conceptual, or 'ideational', force. The space of the Pantheon, for instance, can be explained as a circular domed enclosure of certain dimensions and certain materials, lit centrally through an open oculus. But something more than that is communicated by the space itself: a higher organisational idea; a proposition about a spatial order which is simultaneously abstract and embodied. The physical facts of the building are the only phenomena verifiably present so the quality must derive from them, and yet it seems of a different order and type. Architecture is born of, but is ultimately distinct from, building. When Walt Whitman wrote that 'All of architecture is what you do to it when you look upon it', it seems he that meant something like this.[4] His elaboration of this statement through musical analogy makes the meaning clearer. It is not in the mere facts of the notes, the singers and the instruments that the music resides, 'it is something nearer and farther than they'. But he also makes clear that this quality emerges through the encounter, through the 'look upon it'. This 'look upon it' can extend to encompass all forms of representation, including photography. For instance, in his well-known photograph of the Pantheon's interior, the German photographer Thomas Struth is interested precisely in the overlapping spatial realms of the architecture, of the viewing subject, of the camera itself – in this case, another chamber lit by a single circular aperture – and of the resulting image. Built space, and the spaces of conception, of perception and of appearance form a single continuous realm.

Conscious experience is what binds this realm together. Indeed, it might be considered that, in its capacity to confer coherence and continuity upon the 'raw data' of experience and sensation, consciousness is entirely analogous with architecture for the way in which it gives conceptual, functional, sensory and symbolic coherence to 'mere matter'. And just as architecture must ultimately be seen as something 'over and above' the physical facts of its existence, so

Figure 14.2 Walter Niedermayr, Bildraum S 152 | 2006 – diptych, color. Courtesy Galerie Nordenhake Berlin/Stockholm; Galleria Suzy Shammah, Milano; Robert Miller Gallery, New York. Glass Pavilion at the Toledo Museum. SANAA Architects.

consciousness is usually understood as something quite separate and distinct from the mass of neural activity which ultimately produces it.

'All good thinking, then, can be said to aspire to the condition of architecture', wrote Rudolph Arnheim in 1977, elaborating that 'since all human thoughts must be worked out in the medium of perceptual space, architecture, wittingly or not, presents embodiments of thought when it invents and builds shapes.'[5] The passage comes from his idiosyncratic book *The Dynamics of Architectural Form* published in 1977. In fact, psychological states feature only briefly in a publication whose main purpose is to establish an equivalence between bodily dispositions and built form. In doing so, Arnheim draws on his early study of Gestalt theory with Max Wertheimer and also on the methods and insights of empathy theory. Emerging in nineteenth-century Germany, this philosophy of aesthetic reception laid emphasis on what Mitchell Schwarzer has termed 'the consolidating perception between object and subject'. [6] In empathy theory, the ideas constantly forming and reforming in the active mind are explained as attempts to conceptualise the perceived world in the human image. As Heinrich Wölfflin saw it:

Forms become meaningful to us only because we recognize in them the expression of a sentient soul. Instinctively we animate each object [...] We read our own image into all phenomena. We expect everything to possess what we know to be the conditions of our own wellbeing. Not that we expect to find the appearance of a human being in the forms of inorganic nature: we interpret the physical world through the categories that we share with it. We also define the expressive capability of these other forms accordingly. *They can communicate to us only what we ourselves use their qualities to express.[7]*

More recently, the term empathy has enjoyed a new lease of life in the study of consciousness. Research on so-called mirror neurons, with their capacity to echo sensations and emotions being felt by others, suggests that the potential for empathy is central to the construction of the self. For Nicholas Humphrey, the existence of mirror neurons reinforces his view that consciousness evolves from the outside in rather than, as might more usually be thought, from the inside outwards. As the processing of perception begins to happen at a remove from the site of its generation (i.e. as central brains begin to evolve in organisms), there is a concomitant development away from immediate, responsive action towards reflexive perception. A gap opens between action and reaction. It is in this gap that sensation, and hence self-awareness, emerges. Where once there was only the bare capacity to react to external stimuli, there is now an added ability to be aware of and control that action. Sensation, in other words, is reaction reacted to.[8] As immediate reactions evolve into internal states of reflection, consciousness perpetuates the feeling of there being a slight distance between the organism and what happens to it. Thus, even when we are examining our own actions and mental activity, we replicate the manner in which we examine the world beyond. For Humphrey, consciousness, with its self-reflexive capacities, may be an illusion – a by-product of the perceptual process – but is a 'deliberate trick' rather than 'an honest error', a trick which, because it allows us to survive and flourish, becomes increasingly part of our genetic make-up.

Humphrey's is but one of many 'materialist' explanations of consciousness which have emerged over the past two decades, all building on the central insights of Gilbert Ryle's *The Concept of Mind*, in which he insisted that it was the very conditions which produce conscious experience also create the compelling illusion of it emerging from somewhere else: the famous 'Ghost in the Machine'.[9] In his magisterial book *Consciousness Explained*, Daniel Dennett, one of the most dedicated of the materialists, chips away methodically and relentlessly at the intuitions and 'folk psychology' which keep the Ghost alive and principally at our overriding sense of being aware of our own conscious experience as it unfolds. We do not think of consciousness simply as the sum total of the activities of thinking – acting, sensing and remembering and so on – but as our ongoing awareness of this activity. Our sense of self and our conscious experience seem to be fundamentally premised on this capacity always to be aware of our own being.

But in explaining this kind of awareness, Dennett wants to dismantle the 'Cartesian Theatre' in the mind, the place where all sensation and thought is relayed before entering consciousness. (In his short prose piece, *Company*, Samuel Beckett refers to this as the 'devised deviser devising it all for company'.) In its place, Dennett proposes what he calls the Multiple Drafts theory in which, as he writes, 'there is no single, definitive "stream of consciousness" [...] Instead [...] there are multiple channels in which specialist circuits try, in parallel pandemoniums, to do their various things, creating Multiple Drafts as they go'.[10] Unity of consciousness is an illusion, albeit a powerful one. Consciousness, for Dennett, is 'gappy and discontinous', given stability only by an evolving 'Centre of Narrative Gravity', which allows our mental activity to coalesce around certain patterns and thus produce a coherent and continuous sense of self. Rather than having any originary status, the self is something continuously enacted through perception and experience. The sensation of consciousness – the 'what it is like' to be a sentient human – is a kind of by-product of the processes of perception; a fiction we construct to lend coherence and continuity to our life experience.[11] Consciousness is the result of mental activity rather than the originator of it.

The neurologist Antonio Damasio shares this idea of consciousness as a product of mental activity. However he sees conscious experience as something more consistent and uninterrupted. Mental activity is a kind of continuous mapping which eventually produces conscious experience:

> A spectacular consequence of the brain's incessant and dynamic mapping is the mind. The mapped patterns constitute what we, conscious creatures, have come to know as sights, sounds, touches, smells, tastes, pains, pleasures and the like – in brief, images.[12]

Damasio's notion that everything that populates consciousness might be considered as images resonates with Barbara Maria Stafford's assertion that the content of consciousness is largely non-verbal and cannot be understood through the application of linguistic models. ('We lack a deeper, richer understanding of the nonverbal 'inner life' of the self'.)[13] The corollary is to suggest that images can convey the feeling of consciousness more fully and immediately than language.

Armed with this understanding of the shared capacity of consciousness and of architecture to bring order and coherence (sometimes fleeting, sometimes sustained) to experience, and of the potential of the image to register that coherence, let us return to the photographs with which this essay began.

Clarity and lucidity: Höfer

Since the mid-1980s, Candida Höfer has, almost exclusively, photographed public and institutional interiors. She is interested in the sober, scrupulous depiction of interior space. While her chosen spaces vary significantly in type, size and age – from Venetian *palazzi* and *scuoli* to research laboratories and municipal libraries – they are usually depicted absent of people but full of the signs and equipment of occupation.

Höfer is the most senior of the so-called 'Dusseldorf School' of photographers. Along with Thomas Ruff, Thomas Struth and Andreas Gursky, she was part of the first generation of students to be taught at the Dusseldorf Academy by Bernd and Hille Becher. From the Bechers, she inherited a commitment to the extensive documentation of specific architectural types and to a 'straight', objective, mode of picture-making. Many commentators on Höfer's pictures have drawn attention to their qualities of stillness and quietude and to a slight feeling of distance or of absence which they convey. In one of Höfer's major exhibition publications, *The Architecture of Absence*, Mary-Kay Lombino describes the work as 'achieving complete clarity and evoking detached tranquility'.[14] Through her developing technique, Höfer seems to have perfected this aesthetic effect. Working initially with a 35mm camera, she introduced a 6x6cm Hasselblad to her practice in 1994, and has more recently used a large-format camera making digital prints. At each stage, the change in equipment has enabled an increase in the scale of her exhibition prints (her most recent images extending to 150cm square and larger). Her viewpoints have also changed, from the diagonal viewpoints which had allowed her accommodate the full dimensions of the space within the frame of the smaller camera to the elevated, centralised, single-point perspective permitted by the larger apparatus. It is as if the frame of the camera, the pictorial space of the photograph and the space of the architecture have, finally, achieved absolute alignment. Höfer has referred to her most recent images as 'more static, more in themselves […] sitting in themselves', as if, in achieving this perfect alignment, they no longer need the involvement of the viewer. Michael Fried has recently diagnosed the 'absorptive' quality of Höfer's images.[15] However, this is not to lose sight of what Lombino calls their ability to give 'blankness an emotional plentitude'.[16]

So these are pictures which, in depicting empty spaces, can seem paradoxically full of presence. In the specific case of the *Neues Museum*, the quiet attentiveness of Höfer's photography means that the building's layers of history resonate strongly through the images. Chipperfield's design strategy for the project was clearly to distinguish between existing fabric and new additions. But it is where the clarity of this distinction breaks down that the architecture is at its most powerful. At a recent lecture, responding to a question about making decisions on 'value and hierarchy' on site, Chipperfield abandoned his usual position of detached conceptual clarity and spoke of his many close-up encounters with the fabric of the building and of being faced ultimately with trying to find the point at which all the inert material, new and old, from which each of these spaces is ultimately composed, comes to life.[17] It is at this point that the revived space assumes a more thoroughgoing conceptual clarity – as if it had been fully inhabited by a new animating idea. This is what illuminates Höfer's images of the building. As with Struth's photograph of the Pantheon, she depicts a realm which encompasses not just the physical space and all the layers of history embedded within it, but also the space as envisaged by the architect and the space as experienced by the visitor. Höfer's photograph distills these layers to a pure lucidity. It clarifies.

Always on the edge of becoming: Niedermayr

While Walter Niedermayr's photographs might be seen as sharing some of the absorptive qualities of those of Höfer, they seem more overtly concerned with atmosphere and feeling. He has spoken recently about how his practice has 'moved from a documentary approach to one concerned with forming and representing an impression of space'.[18] Niedermayr had initially become well known for his large-scale images of skiers and climbers traversing Alpine landscapes. His interest was in depicting the figures in relative scale to the landscape so that the feeling of the setting's vastness would be accurately conveyed. He assembled multiple-panel images from large prints, allowing the eye to follow figures from one panel to the next as they traversed the terrain.

Niedermayr subsequently began exploring interiors with the same photographic language so that they too became rendered as large, floating spatial fields. As he explains, 'nothing in the image should dominate, so that all the elements have the same valence and visibility, from people to objects and architectural structures'.[19] The use of multiple panels helped in eliminating formal hierarchies, but Niedermayr makes multiple technical adjustments at every stage of the photographic process – prolonging exposure times, using strong filters, lightening the print during development, reducing colour densities while enlarging the images – all in the service of trying to get closer to an essential spatial and mental experience. 'The most exciting moment', Niedermayr explains in a 2003 interview, 'is always when you are perceiving the space with all of your senses and the image, or the idea of the image, takes shape in your mind'. 'Then', he suggests, 'comes the making of the picture [...]'. 'This experience of space has nothing to do with architecture' he goes on to assert, rather surprisingly. 'An architect would probably have no interest in my images as documents of his or her work.'[20] However, in SANAA, Niedermayr acknowledges that he has found an architectural practice with distinct echoes of his own sensibility and aesthetic. He refers approvingly to what he calls the 'densified simplicity' of their work. They are interested less in the moment of a building's completion, more in its original inception and in its subsequent reception. SANAA have acknowledged the capacity of Niedermayr's pictures to get back, somehow, to the underlying 'idea' of the architecture, to the initial dream of what the spaces might be like. Nishizawa suggests that 'because we share a sensibility, the photograph always has some strong connection to the "purest" intentions of the work'.[21] And for Sejima, architecture often corresponds more closely to what she sees in the mind's eye than to the finished building. It is as if she wants the building to remain always on the edge of becoming. One finds echoes of this attitude in the work of their contemporary Sou Fujimito, who, in his text *Primitive Future*, spoke of making an 'in-between architecture':

> In Le Thoronet, it is difficult to understand if the light came first or the stone came first. That is because it may be a state prior to division into light and object. To make architecture is perhaps to produce a primal unified condition, just before the division into light and object, space and object, natural and artificial, inside and outside, city and house, large and small.[22]

'People meet architecture in photography'[23]

Antonio Damasio has described the stream of images, real and recalled, from which our conscious experience is constituted:

> Sometimes the sequences are concurrent, running in parallel; sometimes they intersect and become superposed. When the conscious mind is at its sharpest, the sequence of images are streamlined, barely letting us glimpse the surrounding fringes.[24]

Consciousness effortlessly incorporates episodes of alertness and of drifting inattention and all points between.

If these two photographs are to be interpreted equally as reports on conscious experience and spatial conditions, then Walter Niedermayr's *Bildraum* series might be seen as the embodiment of Nicholas Humphrey's 'thick moment' of consciousness. Both the architecture and the images are trying to inhabit a realm on the edge of consciousness, a daydream. Höfer's *Neues Museum* images on the other hand – single rather than paired, symmetrically organised around a centre rather than dispersed towards the edges – seem born of a wide-awake world in which everything is lucid, deliberate, knowable. One set of images reveals an immanent sense, the other, an animating idea.

Visitors to the *Neues Museum* today will find displayed in that octagonal space photographed by Höfer one of the great treasures of the collection – a small bust of Queen Nefertiti dating from the fourteenth century. The painted sculpture is remarkably intact, its forms sure and clear, its colours vivid. And somehow this material artefact exudes a powerful feeling of inner life; she seems for all the world a living, conscious presence. The best portraiture in sculpture and painting has this capacity: to imbue inert material with life and communicate conscious experience.

This essay has argued that the architectural photograph has the potential to produce equally rich and vivid portraits, which allow a very direct access to building as designed and as experienced. The photograph involves the photographer in a close, extended dialogue with the built environment. Over the course of this dialogue, the focus shifts periodically from a close attention to the given situation to the question of how to make a picture of it, to achieving the best technical realisation of the picture, and then back to the situation depicted. Stephen Shore has described how, through this kind of extended dialogue, photography discovers an 'inherent architecture' in every scene it depicts.[25] As sources of information about architecture, photographs are often dismissed as being inevitably partial, deliberately misleading, hopelessly subjective or simply second-hand. But, as is clear from the two photographs discussed here, sometimes it is the very strategies of viewpoint, distance, framing and manipulation that allow the photographer get closer to architecture's complex presence.

Taken simply as a transparent window, a photograph can offer very direct access into the place it portrays. But – considered as a complex realm which not only contains the traces of its own making but also speaks of how people relate to space, and of how architecture rhymes with consciousness – the photograph can prove endlessly revealing.

NOTES

1   This essay has benefited from extensive discussion with, and input from, Alice Clancy, an architect and photographer with whom I teach a graduate seminar on photography and architecture entitled 'Space Framed'. See www.spaceframed.blogspot.com [accessed:

17.07.11]. An earlier version was presented as a paper at the Society of Architectural Historians 64th Annual Meeting, New Orleans, 13–17 April 2011.

2   Although they have not yet been exhibited, an extensive selection of the photographs is published in David Chipperfield Architects in collaboration with Julian Harrap, *Neues Museum Berlin* (Cologne: Verlag der Buchhandlung Walter Köning, 2009).

3   A catalogue of the images was produced in conjunction with an exhibition at deSingel arts centre, Antwerp, 15 February – 6 June 2007: *Walter Niedermayr/Kazuyo Sejima + Ryue Nishizawa/SANAA* (Ostfildern: Hatje Cantz, 2007).

4   Walt Whitman, 'Carol of Occupations', in *Leaves of Grass* (1855) (Oxford: Wilder Press, 2008), p. 71. The complete passage is as follows: 'All architecture is what you do to it when you look upon it / Did you think it was in the white or gray stone? / or the lines of the arches and cornices? / All music is what awakes from you when you are reminded by the instruments; / It is not the violins and the cornets / it is not the oboe nor the beating drums / nor the score of the baritone singer singing his sweet romanza / nor that of the men's chorus / nor that of the women's chorus / It is nearer and farther than they'.

5   Rudolf Arnheim, *The Dynamics of Architectural Form* (London: University of California Press, 1977), p. 274. Arnheim refers to Freud's drawing of the mind: 'a translation of a system of forces into a perceptually tangible medium'.

6   Mitchell Schwarzer, *The Emergence of Architectural Space: August Schmarzow's Theory of Raumgestaltung (spatial forming)*, Assemblage, 15, August (1991), pp. 48–61.

7   Heinrich Wölfflin, *Prolegomena to a Psychology of Architecture*, translated and published in Harry Francis Mallgrave and Eleftherios Ikonomou (eds) *Empathy, Form and Space, Problems in German Aesthetics, 1873–1983* (Santa Monica: Getty Center Publications, 1994), pp. 149–192, p. 152. The italics are in the original.

8   Nicholas Humphrey, *Seeing Red: A Study in Consciousness* (Cambridge MA: The Belknapp Press of Harvard University Press, 2006), p. 127. In evolutionary terms, the capacity of humans to receive a continuously updated report on our own condition confers clear advantages.

9   Gilbert Ryle, *The Concept of Mind* (Chicago: University of Chicago Press, 1949).

10 Daniel Dennett, *Consciousness Explained* (London: Penguin, 1993), pp. 253–254. Dennett continues: 'The basic specialists are part of our animal heritage. They were not developed to perform peculiarly human actions, such as reading and writing, but ducking, predator-avoiding, face-recognising, grasping, throwing, berry-picking, and other essential tasks. They are often opportunistically enlisted in new roles, for which their native talents more or less suit them. The result is not bedlam only because the trends that are imposed on all this activity are themselves the product of design. Some of this design in innate, and is shared with other animals. But it is augmented, and sometimes even overwhelmed in importance, by micro-habits of thought that are developed in the individual, partly idiosyncratic results of self-exploration and partly pre-designed gifts of culture. Thousands of memes, mostly borne by language, but also by wordless "images" and other data structures, take up residence in an individual brain, shaping its tendencies and thereby turning it into a mind.'

11 Ibid., p. 412. Dennett quotes David Hume's *Treatise on Human Nature* (1739): 'For my part, when I enter most intimately into what I call *myself*, I always stumble on some particular perception or other of heat and cold, light or shade, love or hatred, pain or pleasure. I never can catch *myself* at any time without a perception, and never can observe anything but the perception.' But while for Hume this incapacity to separate self from perception might have been frustration, for Dennett it is simply an accurate reflection of the self's inchoate, endlessly evolving nature.

12 Antonio Damasio, *Self Comes to Mind: Constructing the Conscious Brain* (London: Heinemann, 2010), p. 70. His thinking is elaborated later: 'In brief, while plunging into the depths of the conscious mind, I discover that it is a composite of different images. One set of those images describes the objects in consciousness. Other images describe me, and the me includes: (1) the perspective in which the objects are being mapped (the fact that my mind has a standpoint of viewing, touching, hearing, and so on, and that the standpoint is my body); (2) the feeling that the objects are being represented in a mind belonging to me and to no one else

(ownership) (3) the feeling that I have agency relative to the objects and that the actions being carried out by my body are commanded by my mind and (4) primordial feelings which signify the existence of my living body independently of how objects engage it or not' (p. 140).

13   Barbara Maria Stafford, *Visual Analogy: Consciousness as the Art of Connecting* (Cambridge MA: MIT Press, 1999).

14   Mary-Kay Lombino, 'Inner Order', in Candida Höfer, *The Architecture of Absence*, (New York: Aperture, 2004), p. 26.

15   Interivew with Höfer, 'Through the Lens of Candida Höfer': http://www.youtube.com/watch?v=gfAmjCyPcZw&feature=related [accessed: 30.06.11]. Michael Fried's treatment of Hofer's work is in *Why Photography Matters as Art as Never Before* (New Haven: Yale University Press, 2008), pp. 281–294. Fried introduces the terms 'theatricality' and 'absorption' in his seminal publication *Art and Objecthood* (Chicago: University of Chicago Press, 1998) and his later elaboration of those themes in relation to the work of Gustave Courbet and others.

16   Höfer, *The Architecture of Absence*.

17   The response was made at a lecture in National Gallery, Dublin, 11 November 2010. In the course of the lecture, Chipperfield showed several composite photographic survey images of room elevations which make an interesting counterpoint to Höfer's images.

18   Walter Niedermayr lecture, Copenhagen (25.01.11). Notes from Alice Clancy.

19   Marion Piffer Damiani in conversation with Walter Niedermayr in: Walter Niedermayr, *Civil Operations* (Ostfildern: Hatje Cantz, 2003), pp. 160–162.

20   Ibid., p. 161.

21   Transcribed from a conversation with Ryue Nishisawa as part of a roundtable discussion chaired by the author on 'Empathy and Imagination' at Venice Biennale (26.07.10).

22   Sou Fujimoto, 'Primitive Future' in *2G*, 50 (2009): 136.

23   This was the title of another roundtable discussion at the 2010 Venice Biennale. Ironically, although Niedermayr featured prominently in Sejima's exhibition, he was not involved.

24   Damasio, *Self Comes to Mind*, p. 71.

25   'Let's say I'm photographing this intersection and I see it as almost a three-dimensional problem that I have to resolve in some way. Where am I going to stand in this? Where am I going to cut it off? How much am I going to show? Am I going to wait for a person to stand in or for a car to stop? I was also interested in the fact that as I walk down the street, really paying attention to what I'm seeing, I see a constant change in relationships and space. It's seeing things in the background relating to things in the foreground. As I move, a telephone pole bears an ever-changing relationship to a building next to it or behind it, this mailbox changes its relationship to the telephone pole. These changes occur all the time as one simply takes a walk and looks with conscious attention at what's there while one is walking. I wanted somehow to record that experience in a still photograph'. Stephen Shore in interview with Lynne Tillman in Shore, *Uncommon Places* (New York: Aperture, 2004), pp. 182–183.

Epilogue

The concluding chapter – by Marco Frascari – is not a reading of a building or a document, but instead reviews what close reading is for.

This book began with a quotation from Carlo Ginzburg. He speculated that the first stories were told by hunters who pieced together a sequence of events from the animal tracks, broken branches and tufts of hair that they encountered. Storytelling, he claimed, began with the reading of clues. And, he implied, close readings ever since have necessarily been acts of storytelling.

Frascari develops this argument. He argues that architectural design, and architectural well-being, are rooted in storytelling. He finds poignancy in architecture and architectural details that are, in themselves, capable of storytelling. He argues that buildings are not experienced as data 'fed to passive spectators' but, instead, are experienced culturally through the stories found embodied in buildings and retold by architects. Design, he claims, remains dependent on storytelling: on the stories we tell ourselves as architects to help concretise ideas; and on the stories we tell others to persuade them to build our designs. Architectural practice, he suggests, fuelled by digital technologies whose implications are often semi-understood, is forgetting to harness the resonant potential of storytelling which allows architects to 'serve the deeper needs of human communities'. Where other professionals often trade in quantitative data, he implies, architects frequently trade in persuasive stories. And data remains more-or-less meaningless without the stories that help people to anchor it in their culture and experience.

The chapters in this book have read buildings and documents for their cultural insights. They have told stories. The fabric of the artefacts remains the same following those stories, but it is also made differently. While Hopwood Park Services, 67 *rue des Menieres*, the CaixaForum, three house extensions in Cardiff, specifications for glass and Candida Höfer's photographs stand as they did before, the readings collected here can help other readers approach their stories differently, and tell new stories about their cultures, in words and through architecture. Compelling stories open up new readings, new opportunities and new ways to make architecture.

Chapter 15

An architectural good-life can be built, explained and taught only through storytelling

Marco Frascari

Humans are storytelling organisms who individually and socially lead storied lives.[1]

The need to tell a story, and the fascination compelling us to listen to anyone that has a good story to tell, is at the origin of all human communications. Storytelling involves the process of developing connections between one's past experiences and those of others. By facilitating both humanistic and scientific thinking, storytelling also nurtures an integrative, systems-oriented view of conceiving architecture; a system that, by focusing on the connections between people, processes, and materials, creates the setting for a 'cultural making'. Storytelling, by using a more broadly conceived world of making – *cosmopoiesis* – encompasses both the natural and cultural realms.

According to Antonio Damasio, Dornsife Professor of Neuroscience and Director of the Brain and Creativity Institute at the University of Southern California, storytelling is vital for the functioning of the human brain. In his book *The Feeling of What Happens*, Damasio dwells on the relevance to the human organism of telling stories. He affirms that storytelling is at the core of human consciousness in its non-verbal origin.[2] Knowing springs to life in the stories that are told in the brain; they inhere in the constructed neural patterns that constitute the non-verbal accounts. Furthermore, Damasio points out that we hardly notice this kind of storytelling-making that is taking place in our brains because the images that dominate the mental display are those of things of which we are conscious – the objects we see or hear – rather than those that summarily constitute the feeling of us in the act of knowing. Sometimes, all we notice is the whisper of a subsequent verbal translation of a related inference of the account: yes, it is in seeing or hearing or touching, in life images playing out in the theatre of the mind. Instead of a cameraman or a sound editor, nature has provided us with eyes and ears and muscles to pan our internal cameras from scene to scene. Instead of a nicely packaged DVD, we end up with memories.

In a very real way, the telling of stories is how human brains register events occurring throughout the course of a lifetime. Damasio hypothesises that those stories happen in the form of brain maps, which we use to judge things and events, based on the emotions stirred by a story. Emotions are also vital to the higher reaches of distinctively human intelligence. Damasio demonstrates that contrary to some popular notions, emotions do not 'get in the way of' rational thinking; 'emotions are essential to rationality'. Storytelling is an essential and emotional ability, the tool by which our brains interpret life minute-by-minute. Human brains are wired for it. We respond to storytelling automatically as we store memories and use storytelling commonly in life interactions. Human skills with stories make them comfortable tools to use in any kind of human endeavour and venture.

The appeal of storytelling is understandable since it is natural and easy and entertaining and enlivening. Stories facilitate the understanding of complex situations. They can help to enhance or to change perceptions. Stories are easy to remember and inherently non-adversarial and non-hierarchical. They bypass the normal defence mechanisms of our thinking and engage our feelings. Nevertheless storytelling has little recognition. We are in an epoch where storytelling is seen as suspect if applied outside of the field of entertainment. Most scientists tend to find it disdainful; most philosophers and logicians ignore it. Even before our time, storytelling did not have a respectable standing among people of high culture: Plato, in the *Republic*, identified poets and storytellers as deceitful fellows who put defective knowledge into the heads of children, suggesting that storytelling has to be subject to strict censorship. The antagonism toward storytelling may have reached a peak with Cartesian thinking and the determined effort to reduce all knowledge to analytic thinking.

The most important rule framing architectural thinking is the recognition that the buildings we erect both reflect and transform our own human consciousness. The intent of this essay, however, is not to deliver causal or structural explanations or to seek to account for the union of architectural creativity and communication, either by reducing it to a different order of reality (whether by hermeneutics or market psychology) or by explicating the shift in meanings across successive social and historical contexts. Instead, this essay aspires to suggest and embody possible ways of understanding for practising the tangled duality of storytelling and creativity. It does so by juxtaposing contrasting yet interlinked scenarios or entailing multiple stories and tellers. In other words, the essay is in itself a storytelling.

Making stories

In architecture, storytelling can be accepted as a procedure that can be used both for teaching and for conceiving of, developing and erecting proper buildings. Architectural stories, told face-to-face, possess a remarkable ability to convey architectural ideas and concepts so that people can readily understand them. Just as important, stories can be extremely inspirational if architects tell them the right way. Powerful narrative techniques help architects to introduce new designs, strategies for conceiving buildings and changes in plans. They can also comprise a very useful tool to present and achieve details for a future building, to motivate the builders and to communicate with customers and other key external audiences.

Architecture does not exist in isolation from culture and society; rather, it forms an interrelated connection of people, processes, and material worlds. This multi-faceted world of making articulates architectural stories with cosmogonies that detail the coming-to-being of the physical universe of architecture. Over the past century, the processes of building have transitioned from being a cosmogony of product-based architectural foci to being a procedure-based architectural commencing out of information modelling. There is a distinction between informative cases, which are determined by a built environment, and stories, which are *determinative of an architectural environment*. Behaviour is the name for activities determined by a built environment, while action is the name for activities determinative of an architectural environment. Storytelling declares architecture and articulates it by showing the actions necessary for determining it.

The architectural *cosmopoietic* concepts of today are developed in part from the artful thinking of the Ancients, in the same manner as the beginning of modern algebraic geometry were worked out by Arabs, Hindus, Chinese and Greeks sometime around 1100 AD. Cosmospoiesis is as much concerned with understanding the dynamics of imagination as it is with cross-pollinating the products of creativity. *Cosmopoiesis* is world-making since it is a process that 'always start[s] from the world already at hand; the making is a remaking'.[3] Architectural cosmospoiesis is based on architectural tales since 'storytelling is a form of what Nelson Goodman calls world-making'.[4]

Perhaps the best way to conjure up buildings for clients and builders in our architectural era is still through a storytelling that will arrange, amend, change and animate reality only because storytelling embraces multiple viewpoints and extends perception. However, to achieve this return of storytelling in the facture[5] of architecture is to exclude in its entirety the empty fast-talking used by too many architects to unfold building proposals presented with new media. The required change is chiastic: it is necessary to adjust storytelling to the contemporary media and this media to an innovative understanding of the manner for performing an effectual storytelling.

The crafty process of storytelling

The making of storytelling is effectively an amalgam of oral narrative with visual expressions ruled by well-determined cultural rituals. A story is told using a blend of oral narrative, music, painted or drawn images, proxemic face expressions and body movements. Drawings and petroglyphs scratched onto the walls of caves or on rocks have been part of the deep history of storytelling. Within the history of storytelling, ephemeral media such as coloured sands, leaves and carvings on the trunks of living trees have also been used to make the images for storytelling. The images traditionally used by storytellers can be figurative, abstract or both. Architectural storytelling has been, until recently, based on the same principles of amalgamation. However, as contemporary architectural presentations are changing, the images are no longer static and displayed at the sides of the storytellers; the images have become dynamic and are set off against the other components of the amalgam making them fade away, if not causing them to cease to exist.

Vitruvius writes of an exemplary event of architectural storytelling in a paradigmatic practice of promotion for professional services that is found within the preface of the second book of his *De Architectura libri decem*; a book devoted to sensible definitions of construction procedures, descriptions of the qualities of different materials and methods of practice. It is the story of a fourth century BC Macedonian architect looking for a very specific job: Dinocrates, an architect of tall stature, pleasing countenance, and altogether dignified appearance, used the ruse of dressing-up as Hercules – his body anointed with oil, wearing a lion skin and a wreath of leaves on his head, holding a knobby club – in order to get the attention of Alexander the Great and get the commission he badly wanted. Having captured the attention of the king through his marketing trick, Dinocrates narrated to Alexander the story of how he planned to re-shape Mount Athos into the form of a man whose left arm would embrace the walls of a mighty city, and whose right hand would hold a bowl which was supposed to receive the water yielding from the mountain and from there flowing into the sea. Alexander, delighted by the brilliant presentation, asked Dinocrates if the fields in the vicinity of the mountain would produce grain. At the architect's negative reply, Alexander declared that, for that reason, Mount Athos was not the right location on which to found a city. But he was so impressed by Dinocrates' storytelling capabilities that he appointed the Macedonian architect as chief designer of the future city of Alexandria.[6]

Dinocrates' tale demonstrates that the role of the architect is to be a storyteller. At the same time, the story told by Vitruvius epitomises the conception of architecture as an open work of world-making or *cosmospoiesis*. Bridging between the known and the unknown, architectural storytelling lies at the foundation of a cognitive knowledge that, by being focused on things, turns them into thoughts. The real architectural craftsmanship is the crafting of a good story; which depends on previous stories about certain kinds of craftsmanship, that is, certain ways of assembling building materials, and to show and tell about their factures. Building a homology between the acting of the builder and the architect, we can say that the precision of a building detail is the precision of a point in an argument of design.[7] The work of the craftsmen tells tales like the work of the architects does.

This crafty process defines the proper making of thoughtful and thought-making architecture by grounding the future built world on the experience conveyed by stories that embody abstract moral values and speak for human institutions. This expanding, mirror-like role of the process of architectural conceiving, and the connection of material artefacts to emotive process, heralds a call for more human-centred methods that thoughtfully assimilate people, processes, products, and environments into an environment of meaning, i.e. a *cosmospoiesis*, a contextualised world making. Architectural storytelling is the most powerful expression of such methods. Architects tell stories to give order and share their *cosmospoietic* experiences. Architectural storytelling induces the listeners to dwell on architectural artefacts by allowing them to establish ways of living in common, in intellectual and spiritual communities in which there is confirmation for the story that constitutes one's life. Stories not only help us make sense of the actions of others, they serve to shape our own identities.[8] The fundamental implication is that architectural sense-making and the construction of identity are powerful narrative constructions.

The proper making of thoughtful and thought-making *architectura beata* is simply based on the experience conveyed by storytelling, not by the briefing given through photo-renderings. Experience, passing from mouth to ear to mouth, is the oral lineage from which architectural storytelling has been generated. This condition is based within the lore-notion of a storyteller as an individual who has travelled far and wide or someone who has learned the admirable stories of the region, the epics of different trades or the heroic materiality of objects. The medieval architects were incredible itinerant storytellers, moving from building-lodge to building-lodge, from one region to another region. All medieval architectural knowledge – practical and theoretical – was passed this way from architectural masters to master craftsmen and apprentices through storytelling.[9]

Storytelling experiences

The storyteller takes his stories from lived experience; either his or others, and with perspicacity changes them into experience for the listener. In an essay entitled 'The Storyteller: Reflections on the Works of Nikolai Leskov', Walter Benjamin demonstrates that storytelling is entranced in the cadence of the craftsmanship's labour that most naturally assimilates the act of storytelling.[10] Storytellers draw from their experiences or, indirectly, from those of others for what they are telling. In turn, those listening to their tales make those experiences their own. Storytelling is a crucial condition for making sense of both individual experience of architecture and social interactions that take place in it.

As Benjamin points out, the art of storytelling is vanishing and with it is fading the human potential for bartering experiences (he uses the German word *Erfahrungen*), the essence of storytelling. Storytelling is disappearing because the lore of faraway places, pooled with the lore of the past, the epic side of truth, is lost. This lore is nullified by information. Information is antithetical to the essentially useful deformations generated by storytelling. Information conveys dry, isolated facts and figures; it explicates impersonal objects and events. However, storytelling explains nothing and implicates those who are present and those who are absent. Fundamentally, this is the reason why it does not matter how many times a story is told as it always offers food for thought.

The education of architects has always followed a curriculum based on storytelling. 'What we do in schools of architecture is to teach people how to stand beside a bunch of representations of a project and tell a sincere story.'[11] However, this element of architectural training is changing. Students holding a remote control present their designs in a temporal sequence of slides and movies (PowerPoint, Keynote, etc.), where every image annuls the previous one. The same phenomenon is happening with professional presentation. This mono-sequential procedure prevents any possibility of a rich multi-dimensional understanding of the story told. The storyline is only one. The presenter, who has the command of the duration and sequence of the images displayed, controls the visual path of the story telling. This digitally engaged setting is prejudicial for a clear critical participation and discussion of design ideas developed in the story, and the viewers of the presentation are not challenged to think within architecture, instead steered merely to think about architecture.

The tradition of architectural storytelling is vanishing drastically. Even if architects wear Armani suits to replace the Lion skin and hold a red rose or a laser pointer instead of a club, they are mostly swapping storytelling with a lengthy synopsis of factual notions relaying on a new authority developed through digital presentations (3D CAD Models, photo renderings, 3D walk-throughs). These presentations are thought and staged as the ideal solutions for professional works that must appears as 'factual projections' of future buildings. The resulting request is that, at the end of construction, a building must look precisely as shown in the architect's presentation. Alternatively, the photographic images of the buildings taken at the end of construction must appear identical to the images previously shown in the photo-renderings.

Overwhelmed and dazzled by the use of these 'powerful' means, architects are rarely telling stories any more, but merely briefing the clients. Information is unhelpful to the essentially constructive formations and deformations generated by the facture of architectural artefacts. These projected 'architectural briefings' have become relentless hoards of pseudo-photographic executive summaries conveying dry, isolated facts and figures, explicating impersonal objects, circumstances and events and missing completely the ineffable nature of architecture which can only be expressed in drawings that narrate telltale construction details rather than showing a 'look'. Buildings, as architectural objects, are not data, bits and pieces to be fed to passive spectators; rather they are factures that must be revealed to active subjects as a direct consequence of some local control exerted by that subject through the intermediary of some functioning object:

> Objects, indeed, become significant objects only through activity and exploration. One does not have them apart from the activity that defines them. They are a dynamic concept. Their being is their being found or made.[12]

Storytelling is not a simple form of entertainment: it is a mirror for processing and reconstituting experiences. Architects tell stories to give order to their experiences. Stories are about characters whose actions are sequentially organised and causally related. Characters have roles and the roles are motivated. What are architectural artefacts, what do they do, why do they do it, and what difference does it make? These questions could and should be answered and explained by stories. Stories are, thus, explanatory devices that help us make sense of the random and inexplicable happenings of everyday life. People aren't characters until stories make them so. Events aren't grouped in logical chains until a storyteller groups and imposes logic on them. In *Sylvie and Bruno,*

Lewis Carol explains to us with a surprising allegory how this kind of objective telling of circumstances and events is unconstructive and cannot become a storytelling:

> 'Don't ask so many questions!' Sylvie interposed, anxious to save the poor old man from further bewilderment. 'Suppose we get the Professor to tell us a story.'

> 'Bruno adopted the idea with enthusiasm. Please do. He cried eagerly. Sumfin about tigers—and bumble-bees—and robin-redbreasts, oo knows!'

> 'Why should you always have live things in stories?' said the Professor. 'Why don't you have events, or circumstances?'

> 'Oh, please invent a story like that!' cried Bruno.

> The Professor began fluently enough. 'Once a coincidence was taking a walk with a little accident, and they met an explanation – a very old explanation – so old that it was quite doubled up, and looked more like a conundrum–' he broke off suddenly.

> '*Please* go on!' both children exclaimed.

> The Professor made a candid confession. "It's a very difficult sort to invent, I find. Suppose Bruno tells one first.'

> Bruno was only too happy to adopt the suggestion.

> 'Once there were a Pig, and a Accordion, and two jars of Orange-marmalade—'

> 'The *dramatis personae*,' murmured the Professor. 'Well, what then?'[13]

In the *dramatis personae* of his storytelling, Louis I. Kahn, a Philadelphia architect and storyteller, included walls, columns, bricks and arches. He told us about them by using a dialogue between materials building element and the individual builder.

> The wall did well for man. In its thickness and its strength, it protected man against destruction. But soon, the will to look out made man make a hole in the wall, and the wall was pained, and said, 'What are you doing to me? I protected you; I made you feel secure – and now you put a hole through me!' And man said, 'But I see wonderful things, and I want to look out.' And the wall felt very sad. Later man didn't just hack a hole through the wall, but made a discerning opening, one trimmed with fine stone, and he put a lintel over the opening. And soon the wall felt pretty

well. Consider also the momentous event in architecture when the wall parted and the column [...] became the giver of light.[14]

In another storytelling dialogue, Kahn demonstrates how storytelling can be a powerful tool for delivering the value of craftsmanship engaged in tectonic reasoning. Kahn's story reveals a happy cosmopoietic architectural facture by setting a proper questioning of the building materiality.

'What do you want Brick?'

And Brick says to you

'I like an Arch.'

And if you say to Brick

'Look, arches are expensive, and I can use a concrete lintel over you. What do you think of that?'

'Brick?'

Brick says:

'... I like an Arch.'[15]

No super-photo-rendering of brick walls, columns, openings and arches will ever have the guiding and convincing power with which Kahn, as a modern Dinocrates, or as the epitome of the oral communication of architectural theory, is saturating his tectonically built narrative by setting stories that can lead to powerful architectural factures.

Stories not only help us make sense of the actions of others, but in the making of an architectural world they serve to shape architects' identities.[16] Storytelling is not just a useful tool but also a driving force for both thinking and decision-making design processes. The recognition of storytelling as a procedure can be used both for teaching and for conceiving proper architecture.

Articulate conditions

The primeval task of architectural storytelling is to guide our mind to the realisation that its main role is to make our life pleasant and happy – an invaluable *vita beata* or blessed life, the good life. The fundamental implication is that architectural sense-making and the construction of identity are storyline constructions. Architectural storytelling involves the process of developing connections between one's past experiences and those of others.

As I have mentioned before, the amalgam of architectural storytelling is drastically changing. The use of projections of photo renderings, dynamic drawings and 3D models has replaced the displays of drawings and models used until recently by architects to tell their architectural stories. The problem is that, to achieve good projections, the rooms where the presentations take place need to be darkened, and the viewers can't see the facial and the body expressions of the storyteller. Worse yet, those viewers also lose the capacity to move freely between the different images while the storytelling is unfolded. This manner of presentation is not an effective and real conjuring up of future edifices for a good life.

The reviving of architectural storytelling, in its original conjuring authority but with the use of the new powerful digital means, is not – and cannot be – a unitary project but rather a plurality of understandings that are probably contradictory, a free-for-all for contesting interpretations. It is cosmogony that will lead to a cosmopoiesis; a world making where there is no neutral space between interpretations, in which a confrontation between them can be conducted. There are no impartial criteria to arbitrate between interpretations. Storytelling does not aim to rationalise explanations of the past or to cast unchangeable representations. There are no inherent trends, underlying meanings or background structures on which to work to get things right. Descriptions, small narratives and local conversations bring about an effective architectural conception that is stripped of any claim to universality and inter-subjectivity. Consequently, architectural conception does not make any claims of truth and has no privileged status, since it is evanescent, 'local' and *ad persona*.

A keen mind must make architecture by the telling of an architectural story, in new digital terms. It is a commonly held belief that narrative and interactivity are diametrically opposed, meaning that one can have a story or one can have interactivity but not both simultaneously. Nevertheless, Carolyn Handler Miller, in her discussion of digital storytelling, indicates that one of the conditions that distinguish digital storytelling from a traditional one is interactivity: members of the audience can be active players and have a direct impact on it.[17] In digital storytelling the members of the audience should have a direct impact in the projections of the multiple images. In this digital process of projection, the architect controls the sequence of images but the audience also controls a few of those images interactively. In this manner it is possible to create active and cognitive processes that are similar to those the audience lived when it could move freely to gaze across the assembly of the drawings and pictures pinned up beyond the narrator during the traditional storytelling of an architectural presentation; processes that are now denied to the audience by the sequentially informative staging typical of the current technique of digital presentations. A new approach to architectural presentation is indeed necessary to make clear that conceiving and communicating architectural factures and artefacts is based on a dialectic relationship between perceiving the world in terms of cases (information) and perceiving it in terms of histories (storytelling).

The entire nature of architecture can be crystallised in the allegory of storytelling both in its facture and its artefacts, and therefore it follows that the return to the well-being embedded in the built environment (*architecture beata*) and its local actualities requires a new understanding of architectural thinking. It is as if architecture must progress under its own tradition and immerse itself in an articulate condition based on five major components: design generation, authoring, presenting, interacting, and static and dynamic design management. In this process 'under tradition' the voice of the architect would become evident again and serve the internal logic of a local monitor. In a sense, architecture should be placed under the demands of praxis whereby its storytelling powers and potencies would be empowered to serve the deeper needs of human communities.

The cognitive imagination embodied in architecture is an expression of the power of human beings to make and to think, to achieve architectural factures. Architects should again begin to face the challenge of providing for cognitive imagination. The effective presence of tectonic condensation, and the poignancy of building details and constructs, results from tectonic pathos, from built storytelling. The energy embodied in artefacts and their factures can be reactivated beyond the threshold of rational understanding to the point that the work of architecture is the interplay of the sum of sensual perception and thought. The individuality of a particular existence and the generality of types are united in one image. In architecture, percept and concept are revealed as two aspects of one and the same experience and can be only delivered in architectural storytelling.

Notes

1   C. Lauritzen and M. Jaeger, *Integrating Learning through Story: The Narrative Curriculum* (Albany NY: Delmar Publishers, 1997), p. 35.

2   Antonio Damasio, *The Feeling of What Happens: Body, Emotion and the Making of Consciousness* (London: Heinemann, 1999).

3   Nelson Goodman, *Ways of Worldmaking* (Indianapolis: Hacket Publishing Company, 1978), p. 6.

4   James Alasdair McGilvray, *Tense, Reference, and Worldmaking* (Montreal: McGill-Queen's Press, 1991), p. 180

5   [Editor's Footnote]. This rich word, laden with meaning, is important to Frascari's writing. He outlines it in his book *Eleven Exercises*: 'The word "facture" derives from the past participle of the Latin verb "facio", "facere", meaning both to make and to do; it this has the same derivation as "fact", which might be defined as something evidently done. Understood in this way, "fact" and "facture" are closely related; to consider an artefact the same way as its facture is to consider it as a record of its having been made. Architectural drawings don't just represent something – they are something in their own right [...] In Italian, "facture" is *fattura* and [it is] also the casting of the spell of the evil eye, a process based on the power of the insidious gaze'. Marco Frascari, *Eleven Exercises in the Art of Architectural Drawing: Slow Food for the Architect's Imagination* (London: Routledge, 2011), p. 11.

6   Vitruvius, *De architectura*, translated by B. Thayer, 2004. See http://penelope.uchicago. edu/Thayer/E/Roman/Texts/Vitruvius/home/ [accessed: 14.07.11].

7   Mark Wigley, 'Network Fever', *Grey Room*, 4, Summer (2001): 82–122 (82).

8   Paul Ricoeur, *Interpretation Theory: Discourse and the Surplus of Meaning* (Fort Worth: Texas Christian University Press, 1976).

9   Joseph Rykwert, 'On the Oral Transmission of Architectural Theory' in Jean Guillame, André Chasstel (eds) *Les traités d'Architecture de la Renaissance* (Paris: Piccard, 1988), pp. 31–48.

10   Walter Benjamin, 'The Storyteller, Reflections on the Works of Nikolai Leskov' in *Walter Benjamin: Selected Writings*, Volume 1, 1913–1926 (Harvard: Harvard University Press, 2002), pp. 143–146.

11   Wigley, 'Network Fever', p. 82.

12   John William Miller, *In Defense of the Psychological* (New York: W.W. Norton Co., 1983), p. 171

13   Lewis Carroll, 'Sylvie and Bruno Concluded' in *Complete Illustrated Lewis Carroll* (London: Wordsworth Editions, 1998), p. 658.

14   John Lobell, *Between Silence and Light: Spirit in the Architecture of Louis I. Kahn.* (Boulder: Shambhala Publications, 1979), p. 42.

15   Louis Kahn, *Louis Kahn: Essential Texts*, ed. by Robert C. Twombly (New York: W. W. Norton & Company, 2003), p. 270.

16   Ricoeur, *Interpretation Theory.*

17   Carolyn Handler Miller, *Digital Storytelling: A Creator's Guide to Interactive Entertainment* (Waltham: Focal Press, 2008).

Select bibliography

Andrew Ballantyne, 'Architecture as Evidence' in D. Arnold, E. A. Ergut and B. T. Özkaya (eds), *Rethinking Architectural Historiography* (London: Routledge, 2006), pp. 36–49.

George Baird, 'Criticality and Its Discontents', *Harvard Design Magazine*, 21, Fall/Winter (2004/2005): 16–21.

Roland Barthes, 'The Death of the Author' in *Image, Music, Text* (London: Fontana, 1993), pp. 142–148.

Catherine Belsey, *Critical Practice* (London: Routledge, 2002).

—*A Future for Criticism* (Oxford: Blackwell, 2011).

Walter Benjamin, 'The Storyteller, Reflections on the Works of Nikolai Leskov', in *Walter Benjamin: Selected Writings*, Volume 1, 1913–1926 (Harvard: Harvard University Press, 2002), pp. 143–146.

Michael Bentley, *Modern Historiography* (London: Routledge, 1999).

Pierre Bourdieu, *Distinction: A Social Critique of the Judgement of Taste*, trans. by Richard Nice (London: Routledge, 1984).

—*The Rules of Art: Genesis and Structure of the Literary Field*, trans. by Susan Emanuel (Cambridge: Polity, 1996).

Peter Burke (ed.), *The French Historical Revolution: Annales School, 1929–1989* (London: Polity, 1990).

Carol Burns and Andrea Kahn (eds), *Site Matters* (Routledge: London, 2005).

Michael Cadwell, *Strange Details* (Cambridge MA: MIT Press, 2007).

Antonio Damasio, *The Feeling of What Happens: Body, Emotion and the Making of Consciousness* (London: Heinemann, 1999).

Lorraine Daston (ed.), *Things That Talk: Object Lessons from Art and Science* (New York: Zone Books, 2008).

Vittorio di Palma, Diana Periton and Marina Lathouri (eds), *Intimate Metropolis* (London: Routledge, 2008).

George Dodds, *Building Desire: Photography, Modernity and the Barcelona Pavilion* (London: Taylor and Francis, 2007).

Allison Dutoit, Juliet Odgers and Adam Sharr (eds), *Quality Out of Control: Standards for Measuring Architecture* (London: Routledge, 2010).

Paul Emmons, 'Size Matters: Virtual Scale and Bodily Imagination in Architectural Drawing', *arq: Architectural Research Quarterly*, 9, 3/4 (2006): 227–235.

—'The Lead Pencil: Lever of the Architect's Imagination' in Susan Piedmont-Palladino, *Tools of the Imagination: Drawing Tools and Technologies from the Eighteenth Century to the Present* (New York: Princeton Architectural Press, 2006), pp. 31–40.

Edward Ford, *The Details of Modern Architecture* (Cambridge MA: MIT Press, 1990).

Michel Foucault, 'Panopticism', in *Discipline and Punish: The Birth of the Prison*, trans. by Alan Sheridan (New York: Random House, 1995), pp. 195–228.

Marco Frascari, 'Tell-the-tale Detail', in Kate Nesbitt (ed.), *Theorizing a New Agenda for Architecture: An Anthology of Architecture Theory 1965–1995* (New York: Princeton Architectural Press, 1996), pp. 498–515.

—*Eleven Exercises in the Art of Architectural Drawing: Slow Food for the Architect's Imagination* (London: Routledge, 2011).

Marco Frascari, Jonathan Hale and Bradley Starkey (eds), *From Models to Drawings, Imagination and Representation in Architecture* (London: Routledge, 2007).

Murray Fraser, 'The Cultural Context of Critical Architecture', *Journal of Architecture*, 10, 3 (2005): 317–322.

Hans-Georg Gadamer, 'What is Practice? The Conditions of Social Reason', in *Reason in the Age of Science*, trans. Frederick G. Lawrence (Cambridge MA: MIT Press, 1981), pp. 69–87.

Carlo Ginzburg, 'Clues: Roots of an Evidential Paradigm', in *Myths, Emblems, Clues*, trans. by John and Anne C. Tedeschi (London: Hutchinson, 1990), pp. 96–125.

Stuart Hall, 'Cultural Studies: Two Paradigms', *Media, Culture and Society*, 2 (1980): 57–72.

—*Representation: Cultural Representations and Signifying Practices* (London: Sage, 1997).

Jonathan Hill, 'Criticism by Design: Drawing, Wearing, Weathering', *Journal of Architecture*, 10, 3 (2005): 285–293.

—*Weather Architecture* (London: Routledge, 2012).

K. Michael Hays, 'Critical Architecture: Between Culture and Form', *Perspecta*, 21 (1981).

—*Oppositions Reader: Selected Essays 1973–1984* (New York: Princeton Architectural Press, 1998).

Dean Hawkes, 'The Centre and the Periphery: Reflections on the Nature and Conduct of Architectural Research', *arq: Architectural Research Quarterly*, 1, 1 (1995): 8–11.

Glenn Jordan and Chris Weedon, *Cultural Politics* (Oxford: Wiley-Blackwell, 1994).

Andrew Leach and John Macarthur (eds), *Architecture, Disciplinarity, and the Arts* (Ghent: A&S Books, 2009).

Andrew Leach, *What is Architectural History?* (Cambridge: Polity, 2010).

David Leatherbarrow, *Uncommon Ground: Architecture, Technology and Topography* (Cambridge MA: MIT Press, 2000).

—*Topographical Stories: Studies in Landscape and Architecture* (Philadelphia: University of Pennsylvania Press, 2004).

—*Surface Architecture* (Cambridge MA: MIT Press, 2005).

—'Architecture's Unscripted Performance', in Branko Kolarevic (ed.), *Performative Architecture* (London: Routledge, 2005).

—*Architecture Oriented Otherwise* (New York: Princeton Architectural Press, 2010).

Henri Lefebvre, *The Production of Space*, trans. by Donald Nicholson-Smith (Oxford: Blackwell, 1991).

Harry Levin, 'Semantics of Culture', *Daedalus*, 94, 1 (1965): 1–13.

Katie Lloyd Thomas, 'Specifications: Writing Materials in Architecture and Philosophy', *arq: Architectural Research Quarterly*, 8, 3/4 (2004): 277–283.

—(ed.), *Material Matters: Architecture and Material Practice* (London: Routledge, 2006).

Reinhold Martin, 'On Theory: Critical of What? Toward a Utopian Realism', *Harvard Design Magazine*, 22, Spring/Summer (2005).

Angela McRobbie, *The Uses of Cultural Studies* (London: Sage, 2005).

J. Mordaunt Crook, 'Architecture and History' in *Architectural History*, Design and Practice in British Architecture: Studies in Architectural History Presented to Howard Colvin, 27 (1984): 571.

Daniel Miller (ed.), *Material Cultures: Why Some Things Matter* (London: Routledge, 1997).

Doina Petrescu, Florrian Kossak, Tatjana Schnieder, Renata Tyszczuk and Stephen Walker, *Agency: Working with Uncertain Architectures* (London: Routledge, 2009).

Antoine Picon, *Digital Culture in Architecture* (Basel: Birkhäuser, 2010).

Jules David Prown, 'Mind in Matter: An Introduction to Material Culture Theory and Method', *Winterthur Portfolio*, 17, 1, Spring (1982): 1–19.

Jane Rendell, *The Pursuit of Pleasure: Gender, Space and Architecture in Regency London*, (London: Continuum, 2002).

—'Architectural Research and Disciplinarity', *arq: Architectural Research Quarterly*, 8, 4 (2004): 141–147.

—'Architecture-Writing', *Journal of Architecture*, 10, 3 (2005): 255–264.

Jane Rendell, Jonathan Hill, Murray Fraser and Mark Dorrian (eds), *Critical Architecture* (London: Routledge, 2007).

Paul Ricœur, *Interpretation Theory: Discourse and the Surplus of Meaning* (Fort Worth: Texas Christian University Press, 1976).

—'The Function of Fiction in Shaping Reality', in *A Ricœur Reader* (Toronto: University of Toronto Press, 1991), p. 130.

Colin Rowe, 'Chicago Frame', in *The Mathematics of the Ideal Villa and Other Essays* (Cambridge MA: MIT Press, 1983).

Joseph Rykwert, *The Idea of a Town: The Anthropology of Urban Form in Rome, Italy and the Ancient World* (Princeton: Princeton University Press, 1976).

—'On the Oral Transmission of Architectural Theory' in Jean Guillame, André Chasstel (eds), *Les traités d'Architecture de la Renaissance* (Paris: Piccard, 1988), pp. 31–48.

Flora Samuel, *Le Corbusier in Detail* (London: Architectural Press, 2007).

Robert Somol and Sarah Whiting, 'Notes around the Doppler Effect and other Moods of Modernism', *Perspecta*, 33 (2002): 7.

Robert Tavernor, *Smoot's Ear: The Measure of Humanity* (New Haven: Yale University Press, 2007).

Barbara Tversky, 'Remembering Spaces', in Endel Tulving and Fergus I. M. Craik (eds), *Handbook of Memory* (Oxford: Oxford University Press, 2000), pp. 363–378.

Robert Venturi, Denise Scott Brown and Steven Izenour, *Learning from Las Vegas: The Forgotten Symbolism of Architectural* (Cambridge MA: MIT Press, 1977).

Dalibor Vesely, *Architecture in the Age of Divided Representation: The Question of Creativity in the Shadow of Production* (Cambridge MA: MIT Press, 2004).

Antony Vidler, *Histories of the Immediate Present: Inventing Architectural Modernism* (Cambridge MA: MIT Press, 2008).

Hayden White, *Metahistory: The Historical Imagination in Nineteenth Century Europe* (Baltimore: Johns Hopkins University Press, 1973).

Raymond Williams, *Culture and Society 1780–1950* (London: Penguin, 1971).

—*Culture* (London: Fontana, 1981).

Index

Note: page references in *italics* indicate illustrations; *n* = note.

NA
2560
.R38
2012

Diane M. Halle Library
ENDICOTT COLLEGE
Beverly, MA 01915